The Emergence of Grid and Service-Oriented IT

AN INDUSTRY VISION FOR BUSINESS SUCCESS

The Emergence of Grid and Service-Oriented IT

AN INDUSTRY VISION FOR BUSINESS SUCCESS

PUBLISHED BY

Tabor Communications, Inc.

This book made possible in part by a grant from Intel Corporation

Copyright ©2006 Tabor Communications, Inc.

All rights reserved. No part of this book may be reproduced or transmitted in any form or by any means, electronic, or mechanical, including photocopying, recording, or by any information duplication system, without written permission from the copyright holder. Excerpts (not to exceed 500 words) may be quoted for reviews, provided "The Emergence of Grid and Service-Oriented IT, published by Tabor Communications, Inc., 2006" is attributed.

The views expressed in this book are those of the contributors and should not be regarded as representing the views of the publisher. While every effort is made to ensure that all material in "The Emergence of Grid and Service-Oriented IT" is accurate and correct, the publisher cannot accept any responsibility for any errors or omissions. Correspondence concerning this book should be addressed to Tabor Communications, Inc., 8445 Camino Santa Fe, San Diego, CA, 92121.

Designations used to identify company products are usually claimed as trademarks or registered trademarks. In all instances in which Tabor Communications, Inc. is aware of a claim, the product names appear in initial capital or all capital letters. Readers should contact the relevant companies for additional information regarding trademarks, registration, and products. Trademarks used throughout this publication are the registered trademarks of their respective owners.

Printed in the United States of America.

ISBN 1-4276-0025-2

The Emergence of Grid and Service-Oriented IT

AN INDUSTRY VISION FOR BUSINESS SUCCESS

Sponsors

"The Emergence of Grid and Service-Oriented IT: An Industry Vision for Business Success" represents a collaborative perspective assembled to help the global community of IT decision makers evaluate the potential benefit, progress, and lessons learned from both the suppliers and implementers of leading-edge technical and business computing solutions.

The publisher wishes to thank the following organizations for their support and contributions:

Premier Sponsor

Intel Corporation

Premier Analyst Sponsor

The 451 Group

Platinum Sponsors

BEA Systems, Inc.

Capgemini

Dell Inc.

IBM

SAP

Sun Microsystems

Gold Sponsors

DataSynapse

HP

Platform Computing

Silver Sponsors

GemStone Systems

Penguin Computing

Table of Contents

13   Letter from the Publisher

15   Letter from the Premier Sponsor

17   Editorial Review Advisory Board

19   CHAPTER 1: A COLLABORATIVE INDUSTRY VISION

20   Introduction: A Vertical Perspective on Enterprise Adoption
William Fellows and Steve Wallage, The 451 Group

23   The Innovator's Opportunity:
Capitalizing on the Convergence of Business and IT
Robert Fogel, Intel Corporation

29   From Big to Small: Moving from Monolithic Applications
to Granular Services
Andy Mulholland, Capgemini

38   Adaptive Computing: Thinking Beyond the Box
Amit Sinha, SAP

42   The Evolution of IT Infrastructure into a Service-Oriented
Model: Grid Computing and a Moore's Law for Services
*Robert B. Cohen, Cohen Communications Group and
the Economic Strategy Institute*

44   On the Edge of the Grid: Using the Grid to Digitally Enable
the Point of Action
Tom Gibbs, Intel Corporation

48   Virtual Application Infrastructure (Grid) and the Migration to SOA
Kelly Vizzini, DataSynapse

52   The Global Grid Forum:
Leading the Journey to Pervasive Grid Adoption
Mark Linesch, Global Grid Forum and HP

contents

55   CHAPTER 2: UNDERSTANDING THE BUSINESS BENEFITS OF GRIDS AND SERVICE-ORIENTED IT

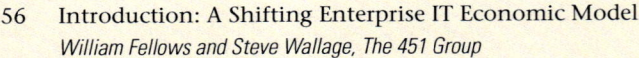

56   Introduction: A Shifting Enterprise IT Economic Model
William Fellows and Steve Wallage, The 451 Group

59   How SOA is Changing IT
William Mougayar, Aberdeen/Group/

63   Critical Technology Factors for the Successful Future of 'Services': How and Where to Create Business Benefit with the SOA Revolution
Andy Mulholland, Capgemini

67   Grid and SOA in Business Solutions
Ellen J. Stokes and Matthew P. Haynos, IBM

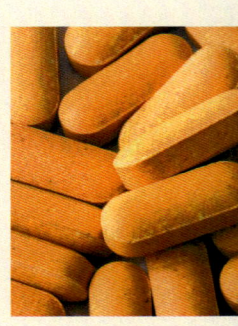

71 CHAPTER 3: CONNECTING THE DOTS

72 Introduction: Tackling Data in an Enterprise IT Environment
William Fellows and Steve Wallage, The 451 Group

75 The Future of HPC: Second-generation Clusters, Grid Management Software, and Greater Commercial Adoption
Donald Becker, Penguin Computing

80 Standards Landscape in Service-Oriented Grids
Ravi Subramaniam, Intel Corporation

84 The Scalable Enterprise Architecture: A Practical Underpinning for Grid Computing
Jimmy Pike and Tim Abels, Dell Inc.

88 Get Started with Grid for a Competitive Advantage
Sherry Brewer and Rob Vrablik, IBM

92 SOAs and Grid Computing—A New Generation of Middleware for Grid-enabled Data Centers
Heinz J. Schwarz, Sun Microsystems, Inc.

98 Implementing Computing Grids Using Blade Servers
Narayan Devireddy and Michael Brundridge, Dell Inc.

102 Rewriting the Rules for Enterprise IT: Using Grid to Orchestrate Enterprise IT Resources
Songnian Zhou, Platform Computing

106 Preparing Grid for the Mainstream: An Interview with HP's Mark Linesch
Contributed by HP

109 Understanding the Impact of Grid and Service-Oriented IT: An Interview with Microsoft's Tony Hey
Contributed by Microsoft

114 Leveraging City Planning and other Social Metaphors to Guide SOA—Why Meta Matters
Annie Shum, BEA Systems

contents

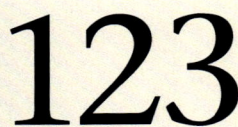
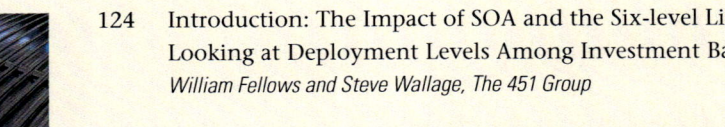
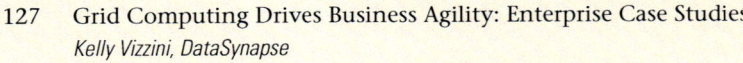

123   CHAPTER 4: GRIDS AND SOA IN ACTION: LESSONS LEARNED

124   Introduction: The Impact of SOA and the Six-level Lifecycle Model: Looking at Deployment Levels Among Investment Banks
William Fellows and Steve Wallage, The 451 Group

127   Grid Computing Drives Business Agility: Enterprise Case Studies
Kelly Vizzini, DataSynapse

132   Stripped-down Grid: A Lightweight Grid for Developing Countries
Contributed by HP

135   A Broad New Role for Grid in Commercial Applications: A Financial Services Case Study
Victoria Livschitz, Sun Microsystems, Inc.

139   Delivering Results with Grid: An Industry Perspective
Patricia Chavez, IBM

142   Reconstructing the Big Bang! What the Business of Particle Physics Has in Common with Business IT
Robert Shecterle, Platform Computing

145   Building and Scaling Out a Database Grid Using Industry-standard Grid Components
Zafar Mahmood and Anthony Fernandez, Dell Inc.

151 CHAPTER 5: FROM INDUSTRY VISION TO BUSINESS SUCCESS

152 Introduction: Enterprise Grid Adoption to Accelerate, Driven by 'Agility'
William Fellows and Steve Wallage, The 451 Group

155 Where is Enterprise Grid Computing Going, and How Do we Get There?
William Fellows and Steve Wallage, The 451 Group

159 Taking a Fresh Look at Grid Computing
Dan Kusnetzky, IDC

162 Grid Solutions for the Enterprise
Parviz Peiravi and Enrique Castro-Leon, Intel Corporation

168 Accelerating Analytics in the SOA
Lothar Schubert, SAP

171 Enterprise Data Fabric: Weaving an Information-centric Grid Strategy
Bharath Rangarajan, GemStone Systems

175 RFID and SOA: A Marriage Made in Heaven
Dan Stimson, SAP

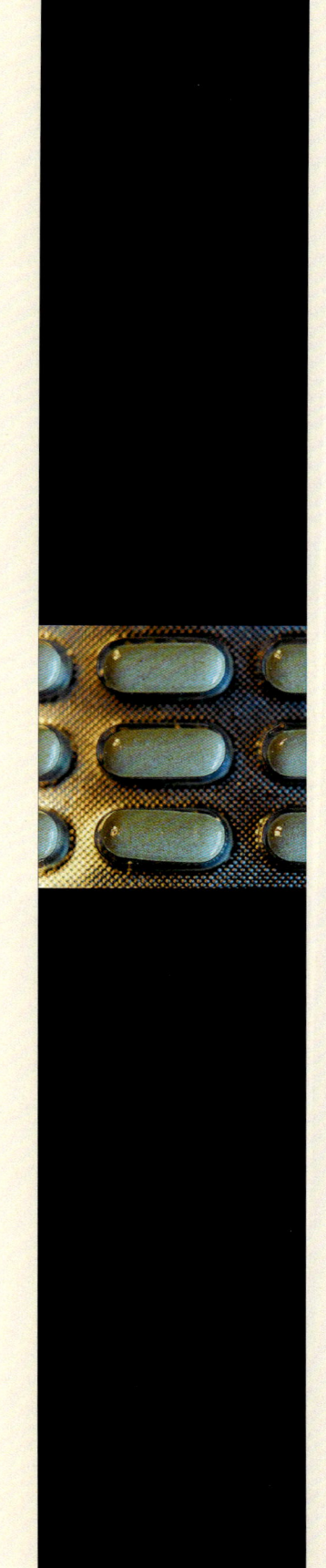

179 CONTRIBUTORS, CONTACTS, AND GLOSSARY

181 Contributors and Contacts

187 Glossary
Contributed by the Open Grid Services Architecture Working Group, Global Grid Forum

Letter from the Publisher

Thomas B. Tabor

Publisher

President and
CEO, Tabor
Communications, Inc.

Looking back over three decades of information technology (IT), and the monumental progress that's been made in computing, communications, and networking, it's quite amazing to think that we can barely keep up with an insatiable global IT appetite. Worldwide, those responsible for global IT infrastructures are still on a quest for efficient resource utilization and finding new and better ways to do business.

Back in the 1970s, the high end of mainstream computing was represented by very large and very expensive mainframes—mainframes that today would barely keep up with the processing power of a PC. The IT challenge of the mainframe era was learning how to operate those goliaths with as few wasted CPU cycles as possible. More than three decades have passed, and efficient resource utilization is still a primary concern for those planning enterprise IT infrastructures.

Has nothing really changed? Or has some cloud of confusion and an overabundance of market hype masked the reality of our current situation?

As you read this book and share in the journey of many of the early adopters of Grid and Service-Oriented IT, I believe it will become obvious.

Everything has changed. We are entering a new era of information technology.

And, considering how far we've already come, the journey of computational achievements—including the significant progress made in data-intensive, high-end computing—is only beginning.

Today, in a number of industries, 'Grids' of computing resources are assembled as 'virtual' environments in which the compute, data, and network resources can be dynamically and automatically allocated. But Grid is about much more than just saving money or better utilization of resources. Grid, as part of a new computing and data infrastructure, has the potential to improve the quality of life.

The emphasis on Grid continues to grow. What has changed is the realization that Grids are not the stand-alone solution—but rather a key building block of an exciting new approach to redesigning the enterprise IT infrastructure. Grids are the enabling component of Service-Oriented IT.

Yes, everything has changed. We are in fact entering the dawn of the next-generation data center.

As a pioneer in launching the industry's first Grid-focused publication, *GRIDtoday*, we have been very close to the excitement, anticipation, and in some cases, disappointment surrounding this industry. We've worked hand-in-hand with many industry thought leaders to collaborate on education and information distribution.

The marriage of Service-Oriented IT and Grid, and the onset of a powerful new environment based on Grid and Web Services, brings a new level of versatility to traditional applications. More important, this gives us an architectural framework that enables new usage models that span the computing spectrum from Voice-over-the-Internet to on-demand computing.

The realization of these new usage models will start to gain traction as we get our hands on the next generation of application development and system management tools.

The need for education based on real-world experience is paramount. We are proud to have played a small part in helping bring together this collaborative effort—the articles in this book represent a wide array of companies and a number of different perspectives on technology solutions, yet they all have a common theme and common interest.

This book will take you on a journey. We hope the contributions in this publication will help you explore the different paths that are possible—over various types of terrain—all leading toward the same destination: a new level of business efficiency and success.

Join us now on a journey to discover "The Emergence of Grid and Service-Oriented IT."

Thomas B. Tabor, Publisher
President and CEO, Tabor Communications, Inc.

Robert Fogel

Vice-Chairman, Global Grid Forum

Worldwide Director of Grid and Service-Oriented IT, Intel Corporation

Letter from the Premier Sponsor

Intel is very pleased to have the opportunity to be a part of this collaborative industry vision focused on the future of information technology (IT) and the role that IT can play to enable business success and competitiveness through globalization, agility, efficiency, and the delivery of new business value to end customers.

We are facing what seems to be another very critical crossroad between IT and business. The client-server and PC in the '80s, and more recently the Internet in the '90s, were two critical crossroads proving that new disruptive technologies and usage models have the power to turn long-established business practices and IT structures completely upside-down and inside-out. The McKinsey Quarterly, "Ten trends to watch in 2006," makes a keen observation about how "new global industry structures are emerging." And, "in response to changing market regulation and the advent of new technologies, nontraditional business models are flourishing... Similarly, corporate borders are becoming blurrier as interlinked 'ecosystems' of suppliers, producers, and customers emerge. Even basic structural assumptions are being upended... Winning companies, using efficiencies gained by new structural possibilities, will capitalize on these transformations."

With the emergence of Grid, along with other key enabling technologies such as SOA (Service-Oriented Architecture), utility computing, virtualization, Web Services, and XML, as well as new transformational technology such as RFID and sensor nets, mobile devices and handhelds, VoIP and IPTV, WiFi and WiMax, and multi-core processors, we are probably facing the most significant disruption yet.

Service-Oriented IT is about using standards-based Web Services protocols to deliver IT as a service. In combination with Grid, a new way of thinking about IT emerges and creates an essential, interlocking partnership with the business itself, which can empower your enterprise to take control of its own destiny to be profitable and competitive while simultaneously taking advantage of every applicable technology innovation that will help your business maximize its long-term success.

As corporate borders become blurred into an integrated global ecosystem, an enterprise requires IT infrastructure to mirror the naturally distributed nature of the business itself in order to deliver truly scalable, business-driven, on-demand processes and services that:

1. Increase agility through better alignment of business and IT.

2. Deliver new business value to your customers.

3. Improve operational efficiency via lower total cost of ownership and increase utilization of the infrastructure, as well as outsourcing non-core business functions.

4. Share resources to gain access to more compute, storage, and network power.

5. Collaborate with business partners and third-party service providers.

Whether you are exploring, prototyping, or actually deploying Grid and service-oriented technology in a production environment, our hope is that this publication will help you by providing some guidance and insight on an important trend that could have very profound implications on the way that you do business, and the way that you build the information technology infrastructure that runs your business.

Robert Fogel
Vice-Chairman, Global Grid Forum
Worldwide Director of Grid and
Service-Oriented IT, Intel Corporation

The Emergence of Grid and Service-Oriented IT

AN INDUSTRY VISION FOR BUSINESS SUCCESS

Thomas B. Tabor
Publisher

Mike Bernhardt
Managing Editor

Ann Redelfs
Editorial Director

Mo Viele
Designer

TABOR COMMUNICATIONS, INC.

Thomas B. Tabor
President and CEO

Anthony May
Director of Advertising

Brianna Johnson
Director of Business Operations

Tony Fogel
Director of Information Technology

Ana Vasquez
Manager of Circulation

John Shandor
Webmaster

Tabor Communications, Inc. is the publisher of HPCwire and GRIDtoday, the leading publications in their respective fields. Both online publications provide timely news, authoritative commentary and feature interviews with leaders in the fields of high-end, data-intensive computing.

HPCwire: The Leading Source for Global News, Information, and Events on High Performance Computing
http://www.hpcwire.com/

GRIDtoday: The Leading Source for Global News, Information, and Events on Grid and Service-Oriented IT
http://www.gridtoday.com

TABOR COMMUNICATIONS, INC.
8445 Camino Santa Fe
San Diego, CA 92121 USA
858.625.0070
http://www.taborcommunications.com

Editorial Review Advisory Board

Al Bunshaft
Vice President, Infrastructure Solution Sales, IBM

Robert Fogel
Vice-Chairman, Global Grid Forum
Worldwide Director of Grid and Service-Oriented IT, Intel Corporation

Wolfgang Gentzsch
Coordinator, D-Grid

J.S. Hurley, Ph.D.
Senior Manager, Distributed Software and Systems Integration, Mathematics and Computing Technology, The Boeing Company

Adam B. Needles
Vice President, Client Service Operations, Development and Marketing, The 451 Group

John O'Callaghan
Executive Director, Australian Partnership for Advanced Computing

Satoshi Sekiguchi
Director, Grid Technology Research Center, National Institute of Advanced Industrial Science and Technology, Japan

Annie Shum, Ph.D.
Vice President, SOA Strategy, BEA Systems, Inc.

Amit Sinha
Director, Solution Marketing, SAP NetWeaver, SAP Labs USA

Steve Yatko
Global Head of Research and Development IT, Credit Suisse First Boston

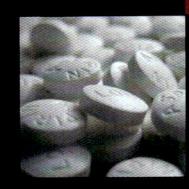

A Collaborative Industry Vision

introduction

A Vertical Perspective on Enterprise Adoption

The 451 Grid Adoption Research Service (GARS) focuses on understanding the needs of early adopters of Grid computing within enterprise organizations. The service's agenda also looks at the broader enterprise role Grids are playing as the underpinning for activities such as Service-Oriented Architecture (SOA), utility models, and data center automation. Through this service, over the past two years, analysts at The 451 Group have interviewed more than 200 early adopters and have since tracked their adoption using an extensive database. As a result, 451 analysts have been able to tap into this community and have been able to analyze early adopter implementation track records, identify barriers to increased adoption, and examine the effectiveness of vendors' strategies, products, and positioning.

Ongoing research by The 451 Group is looking at challenges and opportunities related to specific business functions, i.e., how to measure value, the implications of software licensing, and managing data on Grids. The 451 Group has learned that many of the same key challenges and concerns are shared by early adopters across different vertical markets, as well. There are, however, differences between them in the evolution and levels of enterprise adoption, and some of the challenges and issues they are facing are more important than others. For this reason, before diving into the broader

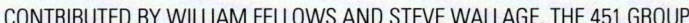

CONTRIBUTED BY WILLIAM FELLOWS AND STEVE WALLAGE, THE 451 GROUP

industry vision, it is important to identify the status of enterprise adoption within these vertical communities.

Telecommunications

There has been a lot of work going on under the covers within the telecommunications sector. Telecom providers are keen to understand how they can use Grid technology both internally and in developing customer offerings. The European incumbent telcos have been at the front line, with the public affirmation of Grids, by BT in particular, pushing other carriers to move from testing to evaluation. Deutsche Telekom, France Telecom, Telefonica, and Telecom Italia have also led the charge to further introduce Grids into the enterprise. However, AT&T has pushed its way ahead of European rivals with a long-term strategy to move business customers onto Grids, via server consolidation and virtualization. AT&T's strategy is seen by other vendors in this sector as a first-mover play and has already elevated the role of Grids within BT's 21st Century Network to the core of its plan. Other telcos are poised to follow suit.

While telcos have many ideas about how they can use Grids, they are still lacking provable business models. The ideas vary from using Grids internally for data analytics to the notion of the 'virtual private Grid.' Although some telcos have been guilty of applying the term 'Grid' liberally to new infrastructure, 451 analysts expect them to quickly ramp up adoption as the first telco Grid projects are revealed.

A key issue is the future relationship between telcos and IT vendors in Grid computing. Some major IT vendors have traditionally relied on the telco sector as a key revenue source. Now some of the telcos believe that Grids play to their strengths in areas such as network management, scalability and billing. However, The 451 Group believes that the telcos will still need to rely on the IT vendors, since customers simply will not trust telcos to unilaterally provide Grid-based services.

Financial Services

The 451 Group estimates that at least 75% of major investment banks are already using Grid computing within their organizations. Most of these initial applications have been driven by individual lines of business-to meet specific needs such as complex Monte Carlo simulations. Early adopters in this sector, for the most part, are anticipating a larger role for Grids within and across their organizations after having proved the benefits in these limited deployments.

Leading adopters are typically at the point of moving the use of Grid technology out beyond these initial applications or lines of business and into wider use, with leading banks such as JPMorgan already beyond this stage. The greatest challenge to accelerated adoption is organizational, rather than technological: trust, control, sharing, and executive and cross-organizational commitment. For example, lines of business typically have not trusted other groups' applications enough to want to share computing facilities (except mainframes). Going forward, IT requirements include policy management and prioritization, support for front-office/general-purpose computing, chargeback and accounting, and supporting Excel on Grids.

Grid computing is not the endgame for financial services companies. Most investment banks see establishing a Service-Oriented Architecture (SOA) as the strategic goal, and Grid technology is one way—though not the only way—to underpin this. Banks will consider Grid vendors that can participate in SOA stacks as more valuable than those that cannot.

A recent trend within financial services has been for wider adoption of Grid computing in retail banks, stock exchanges, and insurers. Drivers include the publicity around the investment banks' successes and regulatory challenges such as C3 Phase II for insurers.

Pharmaceuticals

Pharmaceutical firms have a clear need for greater enterprise computing power. The major companies are examining up to 10,000 diseases and are searching through databases containing millions of compounds and proteins. Re-

> Many of the same key challenges and concerns are shared by early adopters of Grid computing across different vertical markets.

searchers are often scattered across various countries, particularly as many pharmaceutical firms have grown through acquisition, and improving communication and interaction among these groups is a major challenge.

Most pharmaceutical firms have at least assessed Grid computing, but for the majority of them, the jury is still out on Grid technology. They hear the hype around some of the early adopters but have yet to identify a compelling reason to adopt Grid technology. Early adopters such as Johnson & Johnson and Novartis are well ahead of other companies, and they are likely to remain so as they seek to adopt Grid technology across all parts of their businesses.

Some other pharmaceutical firms will be happy to stick to clusters or small Grid deployments running one or two applications. This approach circumvents what is often the biggest pain point for pharmaceutical companies—software licensing. Others will look at Grids again in a couple of years as part of a move toward SOA.

Digital Content Creation and Distribution

What is called Grid computing in most industries is simply a 'render farm' to entertainment industry users who are using Grids to produce and distribute digital content. Render farms are critical to movie studios and production houses. Their importance will only increase as the need for ever-more sophisticated animation and special effects drives greater demand.

Render farms vary in type from permanent installations at large studios to the 'per movie' investments of smaller players. Utility services, as used by DreamWorks, are attractive because the peak workloads come at the end of the movie production process, when time to market is key. It is a specific opportunity for IT vendors that are keen to show mileage for their utility models. As for other verticals, two key challenges for IT vendors are to offer users a way around the software licensing problem, and to support a wide range of industry-specific applications. The entertainment industry, however, also appears more paranoid than many others, with concerns about cost, location, data movement, security, and performance.

Grid technology attributes—including virtualization, collaboration and heterogeneity—will be important as studios seek to better manage their digital assets and reduce the number of masters or scans required to create the burgeoning range of products spawned by a movie.

Two key challenges for IT vendors are to offer users a way around the software licensing problem, and to support a wide range of industry-specific applications.

Utility service models also offer significant advantages to online and massively multiplayer game concerns, despite some disappointments from early adopters. Their requirements for scalability, fault tolerance, load balancing and providing an always-on, complex world are exactly what utility service providers should be able to offer.

Manufacturing

Numerous research and product groups within the manufacturing sector have used clusters and Grid middleware to improve the performance of design and simulation models. But only a few manufacturers have so far moved beyond this stage to broader enterprise adoption downstream from initial high-performance computing applications, or have embraced a strategic goal such as building SOAs using a Grid underpinning. Those that have done so are able to better address changing conditions (both internal and at a customer-level) and do more new things more quickly.

While there is no killer application or unique use for Grids in the manufacturing sector versus other segments we have examined, what's immediately striking is the effectiveness of Grids in doing what they're good at—the grunt work.

Manufacturing users that want more flexible licensing terms from software suppliers in order to run their applications on Grids are actively seeking utility suppliers and models that can provide not only bare-metal capacity but application rental, too. Manufacturers are keen to use Grids to improve collaboration between locations, often in different countries. But this brings in new challenges in terms of bandwidth costs, security, and data management.

The Innovator's Opportunity:
Capitalizing on the Convergence of Business and IT

Robert Fogel

INTEL CORPORATION

Our global appetite for new technology and mobile devices is fueling business transformation at an ever-increasing pace. New, rich usage models are emerging across many industries, including finance, healthcare, education, science, government, manufacturing, energy, and others, enabling new users at every reach of the world to have more timely access to higher quality information so that they can make better decisions and conduct more complex business transactions. Competitive forces today not only demand that businesses be extremely efficient and agile, they must also deliver new and better value to their customers in the face of extraordinarily complex social, technological and geopolitical circumstances. The way that we have been building IT infrastructure for the last 50 years is not designed to easily and efficiently handle globalization or massive volumes of data from RFID devices and streaming video; nor handle a seamless flow of business processes across firewall boundaries that integrate more effectively with outsourcers, supply and delivery chains, mergers and acquisitions, and customers, as well as the Internet at large. In addition, the rapid integration of new technology and distributed devices, government compliance, 24x7 operations, and employee mobility are pushing current IT information architectures past their limits—and as a result these architectures are imposing significant complexity and operational costs.

Key Usage Models Supported by Grid and Service-Oriented IT

Simulation—shared resources are aggregated to support a single compute-intensive application such as modeling economic or physical systems like the stock market, automobiles, drug discovery or the universe.

Consolidation—multiple applications share a pool of resources to compensate for highly variable workloads, and often involve business transactions with rapid response requirements.

> A company's information infrastructure is not just a supporting tool for the business—it must reflect the very nature of the business and its processes and workflows.

Communication—services ranging from voice, text, and streaming media share a pool of resources with stringent real-time constraints to avoid artifacts easily detected by the human ear and eye.

Collaboration—multiple users communicate interactively while sharing multiple applications; this requires both high-performance communication and very responsive processing power.

We have discovered over that past decade that a business' IT infrastructure is indeed the business itself; the two must be very closely aligned, and this alignment often must to be done with flat or even declining IT budgets. Business transformation, IT challenges, business demands, and the convergence of technology are reaching a critical intersection point that mandates new IT infrastructure solutions. The "innovator's opportunity" is to capitalize on this critical intersection by quickly embracing the convergence of key enabling technologies such as Service-Oriented Architectures (SOA), Grid, and utility computing, which are proving to be powerful approaches and ultimately the means for

realizing the vision of delivering IT as a service to the business processes and workflows that actually define and run a global business enterprise.

Globalization Drives New Business Demands

Many factors have converged to accelerate the globalization of business: instant communication via cell phone, satellite video, the Internet, and the World Wide Web; the emergence of China as an economic powerhouse; free trade agreements that open and normalize markets; and the need to establish manufacturing in many places around the world. Along with new opportunities, globalization brings intense competition. This forces an enterprise to look closely at their business processes to ensure that they are focusing precious resources where they have a distinct advantage, and operating their critical processes at the highest possible efficiency. Enterprises are experimenting with new business models, new value chains, and new information technologies to help maintain their edge in the global business environment and create global business processes that dissolve the constraints of distance, time zone, language, corporate structure, as well as rigid marketing, delivery, and support channels. In these global business scenarios, a company's information infrastructure is not just a supporting tool for the business—it must reflect the very nature of the business and its processes and workflows. Companies such as Amazon.com and Google's Googleplex take this to the literal extreme, but more conventional firms also need global IT processes that are closely aligned with global business processes. This presents an opportunity for IT to elevate itself from being an overhead to actually being an integral term in the business value equation.

Business Transformation

The realities of operating in a global business environment are driving leading companies to work harder to create a competitive advantage by using information in new ways. For example, traditional vertical integration within a single company is giving way to global value chains that bring together many suppliers to provide products and services. Major commercial aircraft and automobile companies have become literal or *de facto* consortiums of suppliers that are tightly linked by common designs, standards, processes, and information systems. These companies are now tracking products in real time every inch of the way from their genesis as a scattering of parts in the factory, through assembly, transport, and delivery to the customer's doorstep. The U.S. Armed Forces are using similar technology to redefine "mobilization" in the 21st Century with electronic logistics systems that can track equipment and personnel with speed and accuracy never before possible.

The R&D process is also changing. Aircraft companies now "fly" their new airframes on computers before the first part is fabricated. Automakers now do significant crash testing via computer models and simulations in order to make cars safer and at a lower cost to build. Pharmaceutical companies identify promising new drugs through computer models and simulations, some of which run as applications distributed across the PC desktops in the company.

In another sector, the financial services industry has evolved into a global network operating 24x7. This network moves vast sums of currency and clears transactions at the speed of light, provides ATM services to individuals throughout the world, and is seamlessly integrated with Web-based retailing operations like Amazon.com and eBay. At the same time, Amazon, Google, Yahoo and other "dot.com" companies are opening up their technology platforms to allow partners to build new businesses using their huge databases, software components, and even their data center computing hardware.

As cities compete for business by "getting wired" with fiber or wireless connectivity in their business parks and campuses, the volume of consumer-generated digital data continues to explode. Digital cameras, video players, PDAs, and MP3 players are being built into millions and millions of cell phones. We're seeing only the tip of the iceberg with Web-based sharing and archiving of photos and video clips, blogging, iTunes and other Internet music services, digital mapping services, and movies-on-demand.

Increasingly, human-generated information is being joined by data coming from autonomous data sources such as RFID tags, "smart dust" and sensor networks embedded in all kinds of mechanical, chemical, and biological processes in consumer, industrial, and natural settings. RFID tags are being used to track everything from goods in transit, to newborn babies in large hospitals, to Alzheimer's patients that would otherwise be isolated in special wards. An undeniable trend is underway especially with Walmart, the DoD, and now Target joining the ranks of issuing an RFID compliance mandate to its suppliers. Wireless sensor networks are being used to track the outbreak of fires in cities, monitor rainfall in grape vineyards, validate the integrity of buildings after an earthquake, and support preventative maintenance on oil tankers. These new data sources provide continuous, real-time feedback at critical measurement points, allowing humans and computers to cooperate on the monitoring and management of all kinds of business and physical processes.

Business Process Orchestration

At the heart of the new usage models we've discussed so far is the notion of *global business process orchestration*, i.e., using globally connected information systems to integrate, accelerate, monitor, and automate business activities without limitations due to geographical, temporal, or artificial technical and physical boundaries. Global business process orchestration creates innovative new sources of competitive advantage. For example, companies can:

- Quickly model new business processes and workflows, especially ones that interact with customers, mobile workers, partners, and other external entities. New business process modeling and development tools based on Web standards can now turn a business process model directly into a functional operational system supporting a virtually unlimited number of users.

- Rapidly construct applications from a portfolio of pre-existing services, and instantly deploy them on a flexible, scalable infrastructure. Variations in workload are handled automatically by provisioning services that allocate additional compute, storage, and network resources as needed.

- Orchestrate business activities using "closed loop" applications, i.e., applications that employ feedback at critical points so adjustments can be

> **Grid and SOA are powerful, standards-based technologies that are clearly the future direction of IT.**

made continuously, in real-time, as needed to stabilize and optimize the process. These adjustments can be made automatically based on pre-determined policies, or by human decision makers who are alerted only when exceptional conditions are encountered.

- Support event-driven business processes, i.e., a process that responds to external events as they happen, rather than assuming a fixed order of activity. This makes applications more responsive to user needs and less error prone. It also makes them easier to develop since they are inherently more robust and flexible.
- Creating business systems that provide secure interactions with external entities. Traditional fixed "perimeter defenses," (i.e., firewalls), which are largely ineffective in a global business process environment, are replaced by integrated and federated security services based on known trust relationships among the interacting parties. It's like the trust that you assign to sellers on eBay who have done a lot of business there and have a high rating from a large number of prior customers. You feel safe to buy from that seller because they have earned a degree of trust, even though you don't know them personally.

> Utility computing and consolidation introduce no competitive advantage—these actions will only keep companies at parity *if their competitors do nothing innovative.*

IT Challenges

Current IT infrastructures are already strained to the breaking point with the conventional demands of back office information processing, on-line databases, document management, business intelligence, email, Web sites and so on. They are simply not up to the task of efficiently and effectively supporting the business transformation and demands, technology convergence. Increasingly, IT must be able to support:

- 24x7 operations across an entire business worldwide.
- Secure, seamless interactions across firewalls with outsourcers, suppliers and customers.

- Massive data explosion from integrated voice, streaming video, and RFID and other autonomous data sources.
- New traceability and security requirements for government regulation and compliance.
- Expanded employee productivity via mobile computing platforms and wireless connectivity.
- Real-time business process orchestration (closed-loop processes that react to real-time data).
- Rapidly changing business processes to respond to market changes, competition, and user needs.

Even in the face of all these new requirements, there will be no blank check for IT. To maintain competitiveness, companies will be looking to implement these capabilities within existing, or even reduced, IT budgets. While the inherent complexity of the IT infrastructure will grow tremendously, management will need to maintain or reduce IT staffing.

Technology Convergence

The key to meeting these new demands lies in the convergence of three new IT technologies: Service-Oriented Architectures (SOA), Grid infrastructure, and Utility Computing. The combination of these approaches enables a fundamentally new IT infrastructure called the "Service-Oriented IT," essentially a fourth wave in the evolution of computing, following the first three waves of mainframe, client-server, and 3-tier architectures. The goal of Service-Oriented IT is to create a distributed IT infrastructure that operates without boundaries, directly paralleling the goal of business to operate on a global basis without boundaries.

Clearly, the Internet and World Wide Web are enablers of this shift since they allow information to be shared more broadly, at a speed never before possible. But simple connectivity is only a first step. With the potential to eventually connect virtually every computer and storage device on the planet, the traditional lines between communications (networking), computing (processing) and content (data storage and management) are blurring. With processing and storage embedded at every level of the Internet, and linked by ubiquitous high-bandwidth connections, we can start thinking of the Web not just as a way to access static pages, but also as a way to access application services, processing power and data storage resources. This notion is commonly referred to as the Grid computing paradigm. Ian Foster of Argonne National Laboratory and the University of Chicago, a leading computer scientist in the Grid developer community observes, "The Internet virtualizes communications, permitting any person or device to connect with any other person or device, regardless of location or the means used to do so. The result has been an explosion of innovative functions...The goal of those of us now developing the Grid is to virtualize computing and information so that any person or device can furnish software services to any other and—equally significant—so that access to disparate collections of such services will be secure and reliable."[1]

The technology to first take advantage of this new paradigm has been developing behind the scenes, in university computer labs, industry standards bodies, R&D labs of major vendors and innovative start-ups, and pilot projects of forward-thinking IT departments. A key element of this technology is called Service-Oriented Architecture (SOA), a set of open standards that defines a "loosely-coupled" architecture for constructing Web-based applications based on XML and SOAP protocols. SOA enables disparate software modules to interact at the business logic layer without limitations on their origin, programming language, or execution environment. Using SOA standards, applications can be constructed as an aggregation of small, independent software units that interact asynchronously over the Internet, through well-defined service interfaces. It doesn't matter where the services execute or where the data resides, because all components can interact via the Internet through common service interfaces. SOA is a critical enabler of business process orchestration because it allows supporting applications to be assembled quickly and made available to users who need to interact with each other in complex business transactions anywhere in the world.

Grid extends the virtualization paradigm by allowing us to share physical processing and data resources without worrying about the platform manufacturer, model number, or physical location. Foster has compared this view of computing to the electrical utility grid: "Digital networks are getting faster and faster, so why not assemble "computers" dynamically from distributed pieces so that users can call on resources—processing, storage, data and software—regardless of location and from any suitable supplier? That is, why not virtualize general computational services? Such a computing "Grid" could be as ubiquitous as the electric grid—and just as useful."[2]

Based on this notion of computing as a standardized service, so-called "Utility Computing" is changing how we deploy our application services. Traditionally, applications are vertically integrated with specific physical platforms sized to meet the highest peak loads. Unfortunately, this approach results in very low efficiency—typically a mere 10–20% utilization. Excess capacity cannot be easily used because applications are locked into vertical "silos" due to proprietary interfaces between software modules and the hardware platforms on which they run. To provide greater flexibility, Grid provides a horizontal integration layer between services (software programs) and physical computing resources (processors and storage), just like the virtual execution environment provided by mainframe operating systems (see Figure 1).[3] But because Grid technology is distributed and based on industry standards, it allows many disparate services to execute on a collection of low-cost heterogeneous platforms at multiple locations, using just the amount of resources needed at any time. No matter how the demands on a service may change, we can meet the peaks or scale back during slow times, using and pay-

> Business demands, IT challenges, and the convergence of technology are reaching a critical intersection point that mandates new IT infrastructure solutions.

---

[1] "The Grid: Computing Without Bounds," Ian Foster, Scientific American, April, 2003.

[2] ibid

[3] "Describing the Elephant: The Different Faces of IT as Service," Ian Foster and Steven Tuecke, Enterprise Distributed Computing, Vol. 3, No. 6 – July/August 2005.

ing for only for what we need to get the job done—just the way we use the electrical power grid. Utility Computing, enabled by Grid technology, allows us to handle peak loads while achieving the 90% efficiency of a mainframe, but on cost-effective, highly redundant, "rack-and-stack" commodity platforms.

The flexibility provided by a Grid infrastructure is critically important to realizing the full promise of SOA. Without the ability to dynamically provision resources, it would be difficult or impossible for the physical IT plant to respond to the dynamic nature of Web Services deployment, and the unpredictable nature of workloads generated by services exposed on the Web. By marrying SOA and Grid, companies can create an efficient and agile IT environment for innovation. SOA provides a way to rapidly build and experiment with outward-looking services that create new business value at the edge of the network. Grid provides the headroom needed to support these new services, but in a manner that maintains cost effectiveness through high resource utilization, the ability to employ high-volume, low-cost platforms, and a high degree of management automation.

The Innovator's Opportunity

Grid and SOA are powerful, standards-based technologies that are clearly the future direction of IT. They can deliver unprecedented levels of efficiency, flexibility, and manageability to IT. However, SOA, Grid and Utility Computing will provide only limited competitive value if IT organizations merely upgrade their architectures—or outsource all their IT services—while running the same business processes and applications. As Nicholas Carr[4] has pointed out, utility computing using Grid and SOA will raise efficiencies and lower costs, and enable outsourcing of basic, undifferentiated services. Consolidating applications onto a virtualized IT infrastructure will lower overall costs and put everyone on an equal cost basis. But by itself, utility computing and consolidation introduce no competitive advantage—these actions will only keep companies at parity *if their competitors do nothing innovative*.

The bigger opportunity is to invest in the restructuring of business itself through global business process orchestration. By integrating devices at every level of the network—data and compute centers, mobile PCs, wireless PDAs, smart cell phones, RFID readers, sensor networks, etc.—companies can transform their external business processes from slow, error-prone manual activities into accurate, real-time, highly automated processes that can deliver more competitive goods and services.

To capture the maximum value from these new technologies, we encourage every IT organization to learn about Grid, SOA, and Utility Computing, and build future IT plans assuming these technologies. But don't stop with consolidation or resource outsourcing—learn how global business process orchestration can create new competitive advantage for you. Experiment with systems to automate your critical competitive processes using the latest business process modeling tools, SOA applications, and Grid-based infrastructures. Finally, engage suppliers and standards bodies to ensure you know where they're going and that your needs are met.

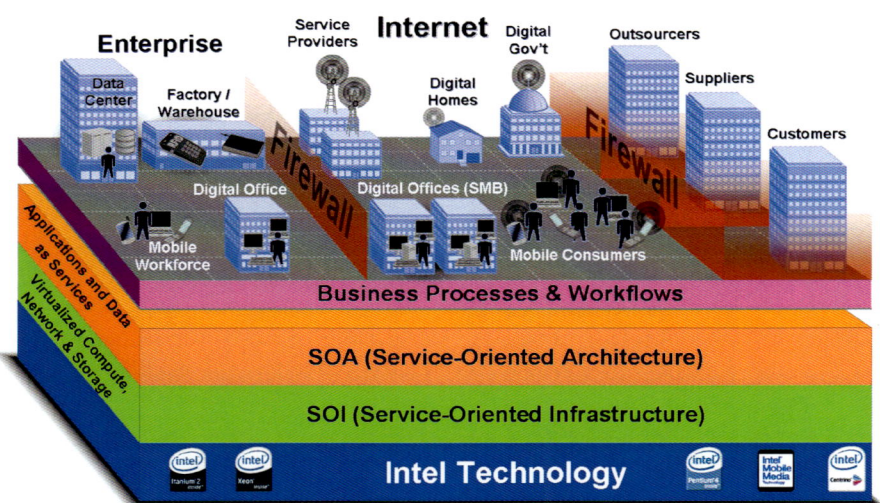

Figure 1. The Convergence of Business and IT

---

[4] "The End of Corporate Computing," Nicholas G. Carr, MIT Sloan Management Review, Spring 2005, Vol. 46, No. 3, p. 67.

From Big to Small: Moving from Monolithic Applications to Granular Services

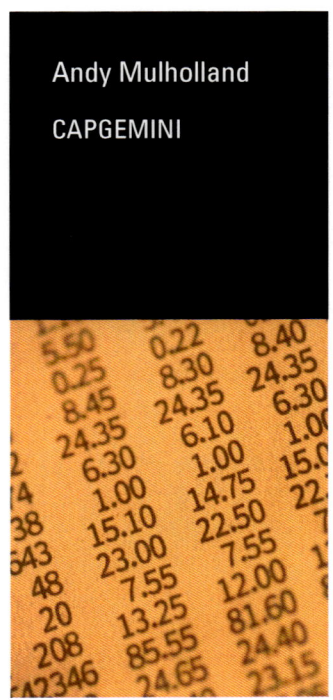

Andy Mulholland

CAPGEMINI

From the very start of the computing revolution, the direction has been from 'Big' to 'Small,' or at least smaller. Moore's Law is not only a prediction of increasing computing power, it is also the source of plummeting cost and size that has moved computing out of the data center and onto the desktop. The migration continues as a wide range of devices, from cell phones to personal digital assistants, as well as automobiles, entertainment centers, sensors, and myriad other 'things,' benefit from the incorporation of computer intelligence and communications.

Now a similar evolution toward 'the small' is starting to happen in software. After years of capturing more and more complex functionality into ever-larger 'monolithic' applications, almost all enterprise software vendors are struggling with huge code bases filled with proprietary interfaces that are inherently difficult to maintain and integrate. Although Enterprise Resource Planning (ERP) and other enterprise solution vendors have tried to address the integration problem, unfortunately the result has been even bigger and more monolithic applications!

However, the Internet, as in so many other areas, is beginning to fundamentally change the ground rules of software application architecture in that:

- WAN charges are no longer a barrier—everything can be assumed to be connected by the Internet, so there is no cost burden for a project to make use of this connection.
- Simple, standardized 'service interfaces,' made externally available, are proving to have more business value than complex, proprietary internal functions (this came with the advent of the Web).
- These changes have spawned a new architectural model called Service-Oriented Architecture, or SOA.

This sea change has been amply validated in the marketplace. In spite of immense efforts and sums of money, 'Big,' function-rich, monolithic, e-commerce hubs failed, whereas constantly changing 'Small' service collections, such as eBay, have become worldwide trading centers. Application Service Providers (ASPs) offering low-cost access to their 'Big,' functionally rich applications failed, while products based on the 'Small' model, such as Salesforce.com, have succeeded.

In contrast to monolithic applications, the emergence of SOA has made it possible to leverage the Internet by connecting small, granular pieces of software that can be dynamically recombined to support rapidly changing business needs. The industry is in the early days of building and deploying Web Services based on SOA, an evolution we call 'Moving from Big to Small.' This paradigm shift will ultimately affect all information technologies, their deployment, and their management, as profoundly as the PC and Local Area Network technology waves of the 1980s and '90s. As the SOA wave matures, it will even change the nature of human business relationships from traditional hierarchal structures to 'personal matrix' structures.

The use of Web Services for both internal and external processes linked by the Internet establishes a new model for competitive advantage by improving interaction with the marketplace. Since all businesses exist to buy and sell goods or services, it's not surprising that by shifting IT priorities from supporting internal departmental operations to facilitating key market interactions, the competitive advantage is enhanced. However, to do this successfully requires that IT be responsive to external drivers through the rapid creation of information services to address market needs and business strategies. This is the business mandate for replacing huge, rigid applications with more adaptive, easily changed service components. In turn, new externally useful information processes tend to suggest additional improvements in a 'virtuous cycle' that accelerates a competitive advantage. The lesson of SOA is that small pieces of software are easier to standardize and make interoperable among multiple trading partners than large and complex applications.

The competitive business case for moving from client-server to 'client-services' is clear. Interestingly, the need for compliance is another key driver for restructuring our information systems. Compliance regulations addressing new risks require collecting and holding data associated with trading 'threads' (which include external interactions) in addition to traditional internal departmental transactions.

To meet these challenges, our approach to defining, building, and managing information systems has to change. It means employing protocol-based interchanges driven by small pieces of software created as services, where interactions are defined as much by the external market (customers) as internal business processes (operations). This requires rethinking and transforming the development processes, as well as breaking application systems down into small, distinctive transactional elements. This is a major challenge for almost every aspect of Management Information Systems (MIS) including:

- Training business analysts to think 'small' when scoping projects and functions.
- Moving from firewall perimeter security to securing end-to-end processes.
- Authenticating data and users within processes.
- Employing semantic tags to make runtime decisions about data.
- Creating new approaches to governance based on shared services rather than central ownership of big, monolithic applications.

> The competitive business case for moving from client-server to 'client-services' is clear.

Understanding the Concept of 'Small'

Cutting down 'Big' functions into 'Small' pieces that are defined and built incrementally is not the complete answer, though it's a move in the right direction. Even more important is gaining an understanding of the overall SOA concept, its goals and values, and how to achieve them within an MIS organization. Without this unifying framework, not only will individual services fail to interoperate properly, but it's likely our organizations will not even build the right services in the first place. This will become increasingly important over time as the global adoption of client-services raises expectations that individual enterprises will be integrated into multi-company business trading threads. Challenges will not be limited to technical integration, but will include how information is presented by a browser or a Web server, how transactions are handled, how policies are communicated, how security is implemented and managed, and so on.

For example, a crucial aspect of the 'Small' paradigm relates to how the *transition* to SOA will be managed. The time and cost that went into retrofitting and standardizing in the PC-LAN era is a burden that no enterprise would willingly face again. Unfortunately, current enterprise applications reinforce the 'Big' mindset that started with mainframes and encouraged IT professionals to ensure 'complete' functionality specifications before implementation. How does the 'Small' paradigm change the approach to information system deployment?

For a realistic vision of how 'Small' can be introduced with minimal disruption, we can consider one very successful phenomenon called eBay. In April 2004, electricnews.net reported eBay revenues were up nearly 60% from the same quarter a year ago. They added 9.9 million users in the quarter for a total of 105 million members. More importantly 45 million users sold an average of US $550 each in the preceding 12 months, by any standards an outstanding success for a business and a business model that only came into being in 1996! In comparison, eCommerce (EC) hubs were, by-and-large, failures, with much money lost by even well known, long established enterprises with existing successful business models.

Is this a fair comparison? Well, in the case of eBay, catering for the trading needs of millions of individuals selling thousands of different items in many different countries would certainly appear more difficult than trading one type of goods within a single defined market, as most e-trading applications

> The emergence of SOA has made it possible to leverage the Internet by connecting small, granular pieces of software that can be recombined to support rapidly changing business needs.

attempted to do. Yet e-Bay has done it. It works, and more important, it scales! Given the size of eBay as a global marketplace, isn't this a classic example of 'Big'? Actually, it's an example of the efficiency of the aggregation of 'Small.' Each buyer or seller is interested in only a small part of the market, but the small markets aggregate to provide an overall high chance of finding your 'small' piece and being satisfied enough to keep returning. It's the same principle that created the Web in the first place!

There are some other key lessons to observe as well. First, e-Bay is easy and intuitive, requiring no user manuals or training. It provides a user interface that hides the complexity of the services behind it. The services are all granular and adaptable to change, from simple process improvement to the introduction of a whole new set of services for a new market category. But these upgrades occur incrementally, in a manner that accommodates continuous change, mostly without causing outages or user problems. Development, regression testing, and launching all happen in parallel with, and yet without impacting, existing services and activities. It's a different model in every respect, all based on 'Small' working as a granular whole by virtue of SOA.

What about the all-important question of differentiation? e-Bay clearly passes the test, but what is the core intellectual property that enables eBay to create value for investors? Clearly, eBay's IP is not the Web standards themselves that enable its system to interact with users and other software around the world. It's the unique method of binding and orchestrating externally facing, standardized technology interactions, i.e., a proprietary assembly of Web-based services. Perhaps it seems strange to think of integration as a competitive differentiator, rather than a problem and a cost, but consider that integration is the common principle that underpins all trading activities. That is, *trading* is providing value through the integration or acceleration of buying and selling activities. Other examples abound: Expedia.com—now the world's largest travel agency; Last Minute.com—an 'e-Bay for experiences,' and Dell—the world's largest PC integrator, just to name a few. In fact, Harvard Business School's *Working Knowledge* magazine described the Dell model as 'managing profitability, not inventory,' going on to say that Dell matched supply to demand by using its unique systems. Dell manages other businesses external to its own for most aspects of its business, perhaps qualifying it as a trading business more than a manufacturing business, with margins to match. Are its actual products (PCs, Servers, etc.) differentiated from competitors? No, but its way of doing business in the market is differentiated, and that comes from its ability to integrate myriad smaller services into a large, coherent business process.

If these companies had tried to create their current advantages in flexibility and low cost through big functional applications, they would likely still be enmeshed in requirements gathering, just trying to keep up with the rate of changing business demands! It's not that large operational enterprise systems are no longer needed, but they will have to interface with more nimble, customer facing systems assembled as Web Services and linked into traditional enterprise databases. Figure 1 is a good way to understand the differing IT 'zones' and their characteristics, as well as the direction of various suppliers. Taking two ERP vendors as an example, SAP uses Net-Weaver tools to link R/3, its back-office application suite, to small Web components for front office or cus-

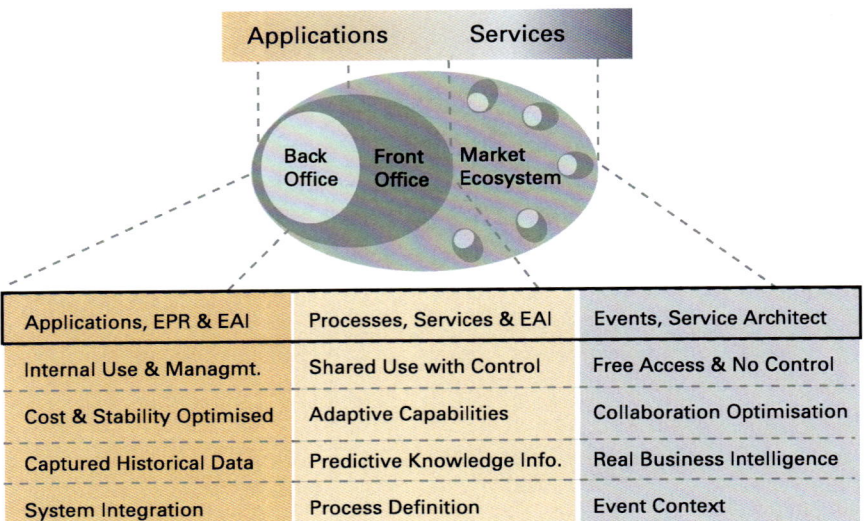

Figure 1. Integrating Enterprise Applications with New Web Services

tomer-facing services. Oracle also has its back-end suite linked through its Web-based 'technology products' that provide the capabilities to build small Web Services.

Key Drivers: Cost, Competition and Compliance

Business is looking to its MIS departments to provide new capabilities centered generically around three core issues: compliance, cost, and competitive advantage, as well as continuing to provide 'business as normal IT.' These drivers are increasingly external in nature, so at least two, compliance and competitive advantage, are likely to be best delivered through the 'Small' model, and in doing so are also more likely to deliver at lower costs. But where do IT professionals start to get a handle on meeting these new challenges? There are numerous well-supported Industry groups working diligently on various standards, while technology vendors, large and small, flood the market with information on current and future products. With so much data on individual aspects of SOA, often from a particular competitive point of view, it is very hard to get a sense of perspec-

tive on the overall model. Once again, it is easier to see with an example.

Consider a supermarket trading with many suppliers and having the following requirements:

- Cost reduction—looking to reduce the cost of 'book to bill' trading transactions.
- Competitiveness—wanting to manage 'stock outs' on the shelves better.
- Compliance—needing to show the processes to be complete and safe.

Referring to Figure 2 and starting with the 'Mobility' block, a pallet arrives in the warehouse with an RFID tag that is read automatically by a reader that senses the pallet passing into the warehouse over the loading dock. The reader uses the unique code from the tag to identify what type of goods and to pass the information to the 'goods inwards (Web) service.' There could be multiple goods inwards services to handle different types of stock that may require very different processes to be followed—frozen food versus canned food, cigarettes versus chocolate, even goods for the onsite canteen. The fact that any tag and any reader can work with any other device as the 'event' demands (in the same way a browser will work with any Web server) is why such 'clients' are grouped under the heading of 'mobility'—they are *not* permanently tied to any other device in the traditional manner of "client-server" protocol bindings.

The 'goods inward service' uses its rules structure to determine which other 'services' to notify, maybe even to pass information to an existing legacy 'application' to record the transaction into warehouse stock. One set of services deals with the 'book to bill' process notifying the supplier of the goods' arrival, matching the tag with goods dispatched, then with the order and the invoice to automate a payment. This automation reduces cost, and ensures that the process is 'safe' or 'compliant' with auditing requirements to ensure that safeguards exist to manage payments against orders, goods received, and invoices. Other services are also notified, such as those supporting merchandising and shop floor managers.

Event-driven Services, Agents, and Dynamic Provisioning

With the length of supply chains growing, often spanning halfway round the world, there are increasing problems with attempting to manage synchronized activity based on rigid processes. It's better to be able to respond tactically to optimize the real circumstances in many cases. This is where the 'event-driven' nature of Web Services becomes important. Responding to what really happens instead of an application's expectation of a 'nominal' process helps when, by accident, a pallet is reloaded back onto an outward-bound lorry one hour after arrival. In this case, the 'reader' notifies an 'outward-bound service' that, upon finding there are no instructions for dispatch, orchestrates a set of other services to recover the situation. Perhaps a service directs the forklift truck driver via his wireless station on the forklift to remove the pallet from the lorry, allocating a warehouse bay for safe storage, and so on. It's this event-driven flexibility that so characterizes the difference between fixed function applications based on idealized requirements, and 'Small' services dynamically orchestrated to respond to real circumstances based on policies.

In the past, there was a good reason why application specifications had to be comprehensive and complete. Sizing and provisioning an application with the right amount processing power and storage were key tasks that were difficult to correct later if under-provisioned, hence the common and costly practice of over-provisioning! The unpredictable nature of event-driven responses with constantly changing services orchestration requires the ability to provide millions of instructions per second (MIPs) on demand from utility- or Grid-based infrastructures. In a similar way, data storage has moved from dedicated Direct Attached Storage (DAS) to virtualized Storage Area Networks (SAN) that can be provisioned dynamically. Unfortunately, there is confusion over the meaning of technology-based definitions of 'virtual servers' and 'Grid computing' versus business-oriented definitions of 'on-demand' and 'utility' computing coined by IBM and HP for their commercial offerings. But all these technologies and solution initiatives boil down to one overall objective—making optimal use of available resources and meeting unpredictable workload requirements by allowing dynamic allocation from an aggregate pool of available computing devices,

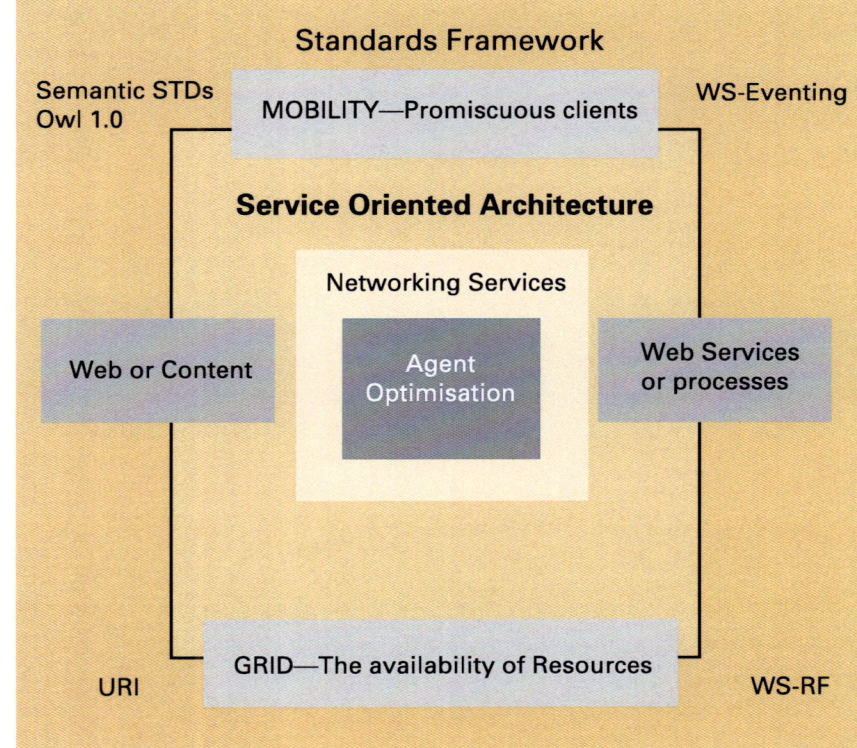

Figure 2. An Overview of the SOA Standards Framework

whether they are PCs, servers, minis, or mainframes. Hence, technologies like virtualization and Grid are vital complementary technologies that enable the practical realization of the SOA model.

In addition to managing raw computing and storage resources, an SOA environment automates the provisioning of higher-level services such as security and directory services. In essence, the trend started by N-tier architectures to consolidate and share services replicated by multiple applications, such as 'directories,' security, etc., has been broadened to provide an even more comprehensive set of services. Indeed, a single infrastructure service may expose a different set of capabilities through a different interface, depending on the context of the requesting service. The importance of locating these kinds of versatile infrastructure services in the network has not been lost on Cisco, which is moving to become a leading supplier of security and storage software, integrated into its network hardware, as part of its vision of a 'network services'-based future.

The level of complexity implied by the potential interactions described here exceeds the capability of business analysts using programmed rules alone to manage all the resulting events. This is the role of 'agents'—not a new concept, but one that is now coming into its own due to a good fit to the requirements of managing myriad small services. An agent is distinguished by its ability to deal comprehensively, unambiguously. and quickly with a single issue. Coupled with a mechanism for groups of agents to delegate decisions and actions to each other based on their relative areas of expertise, agents provide an elegant, powerful, and highly scalable way to manage large numbers of interactive Web Services.

De-perimeterized Security and Boundary-less Information Flows

In the IT world, security has a poor image. It is seen as a costly drain on limited budgets and yet, regardless of the sums spent, all too often fails to stand up to an attack. Most people experience frustration every day when spam and viruses create constant distractions. Expenditures on security are at an all-time high, yet IT executives have low confidence in the overall effectiveness of security in their business. Why is this?

The change over the last few years from internal application-centric IT to external communications and information sharing has made it very difficult to have an impermeable 'fence,' or firewall, around the outside of the enterprise to limit access. Any-to-many email extending across firewalls is a fact of life for most enterprises; indeed email is often a crucial part of the business process! So the move from applications that can be protected by denial of access—the key principle of perimeter-based security—to Web Services where standardized 'open' access is a key advantage, is a significant and inherent part for the problem.

'De-parameterized security' is a way to deal with these changes. Instead of assuming that controlling access is the best way to ensure security, de-parameterized security allows access, but uses a 'trust factor' associated with the user to decide which activities should be allowed and which information can be accessed. This is an extremely flexible approach, since any combination of users, processes, data, devices etc, including wireless devices, can be accommodated, and it supports ongoing development of electronic inter-business trading. Demonstrating the attractiveness of this approach, more than 40 global enterprises, including Proctor and Gamble, Unilever, HSBC, HBOS, Boeing, BAE, Pfizer and GlaxoSmithKline, have joined forces in the Jericho Forum to help define de-parameterized security requirements. Complementing the Jericho Forum, the Open Group is developing business models for interactive trading. Its goal is to enable 'boundary-less organizations' to improve operational efficiencies. These organizations represent a business community that in some ways has changed places with the technology vendors by becoming the drivers for change.

Clearly, information security is a sensitive issue and a phased implementation approach is called for. Many organizations are in the first phase, 'moving outside the perimeter.' In Phase 1, the organization moves public-facing Web applications outside the corporate perimeter and closer to the people using them. This enables more seamless Internet-based communications with

> A 'Small Model,' service-centric approach enables innovation by delivering new business capabilities and improved operating efficiencies incrementally, at low risk and cost.

consumers, customers, and business partners, while freeing the corporate IT staff from the pressures of securing data via the perimeter. In the Phase 2, 'soften the perimeter,' organizations drop the pretence of supporting a hardened perimeter, and instead focus on providing encrypted transport with authenticated access to internal data. The members of the forum are pledged to achieve this within two years. In the Phase 3, the perimeter ceases to exist at all. Organizations in this phase will move to data-level encryption and connection-level authentication, removing the need for the perimeter. Look for these kinds of changes in member companies in the 2006–2007 timeframe.

De-parameterized security will employ security standards that are already under development. For example, verifying user identities is handled in the Liberty Alliance trust model. The Liberty Alliance is a consortium founded by Sun Microsystems that now includes most major technology vendors, as well as a significant number of global businesses in a variety of vertical sectors. The Alliance is affiliated with other major standards bodies to coordinate effective models for user identification. Identities are based on a trust model that uses a reference identity in one interaction as a basis for providing a trusted identity for a different interaction with a previously unknown partner, similar to the way eBay fosters trust relationships between its buyers and sellers. The common principle in all these approaches is that security must be based on trust relationships rather than perimeters.

Organizing Structures for MIS

With the fundamental changes in architectural approach represented by SOA, there are accompanying potential changes in human roles within the MIS organization. Increasingly, busi-

> As the SOA wave matures, it will even change the nature of human business relationships from traditional hierarchal structures to 'personal matrix' structures.

ness and compliance (financial) managers are looking for data to be cut, chopped, and recombined to suit their needs for business trading threads, rather than being defined by the big applications (e.g., ERP, CRM, etc.) supporting operations. They require high-value information specific to a desired business context. So MIS needs to restructure itself to be accountable both for technical competencies and for responding to targeted business drivers. Capgemini has developed a simple matrix (Figure 3) that provides the needed focal points by associating business improvement targets with technology areas to support them. The significance of this view of MIS planning is that the emphasis is on business objectives and supporting technical competencies, rather than on application centers, such as ERP, Web presence, technical computing, or corporate messaging. Some of the intersections are immediately recognizable for their

Technology Units \ Business Targets	Compliance	Cost Mgt	Competitive
Innovative			
Information			
Integration			
Infrastructure			
Industrialisation			

Figure 3. Focal Points for Using Technology to Achieve Business Improvement

importance, though a business target usually has implications for more than one technology area. For example, compliance and Information are obviously connected competencies for meeting Sarbanes-Oxley requirements, but integration will also be a key to tracking data from multiple applications, and the Infrastructure will need to accommodate secure access across these domains. Table 1 provides some definitions for the technology areas and the potential business value supported by each area. We have broken out industrialization and innovation as separate dimensions because they will frequently be at odds with the status quo or self-interest of those working in the other three core delivery areas of information, integration and infrastructure. This is something to pay close attention to as part of planning and organizational governance.

Managing Standards

There are so many Web-related standards under development; they seem to form an almost impenetrable thicket hindering the ability to make necessary decisions. While it is undoubtedly true that there are many standards, it is possible to view them in two broad families—those impacting some form of business data, and those that deal with some form of business process, as shown in Figure 4.

There needs to be a consistent approach around these two standards axes to ensure the right building blocks for globally integrated solutions. Accordingly, the vertical axis should be managed by the 'Information' team

Technology Area	Definition	Value
Innovation	Understanding new technologies, products, and practices, to build propositions on how to improve any technology or business area	The ability to be able to make decisions on the best time to adopt, and in the value of changes, to ensure a persistent rate of improvement in all areas
Information	The form, content, and context, of data management to actively support business decisions and record both business and technology transactions	Current information on key business processes is becoming increasingly important with faster moving markets and the demands of compliance
Integration	The definition of all standards, naming conventions, practices, and architecture reference models, to support cost effective integration technology aspects	Creates the ability to be 'adaptive' and 'collaborative' in terms of creating business flows internally and externally, to quickly meet business requirements
Infrastructure	Provisioning 'shared service' capability to support common IT elements; networks, directories, security, and increasingly MIPs and storage	Provides low cost flexibility with high reuse of expensive fixed assets, together with high reliability and the provision of charge/management metrics
Industrialisation	The awareness of method and practices, even suppliers, that can be used to reduce operational and maintenance costs and time	Ensures a market competitive provision of IT by matching and maintaining the best, or at least optimal levels, of cost, manning, or time for operations

Table 1. New Technology Areas and their Business Value

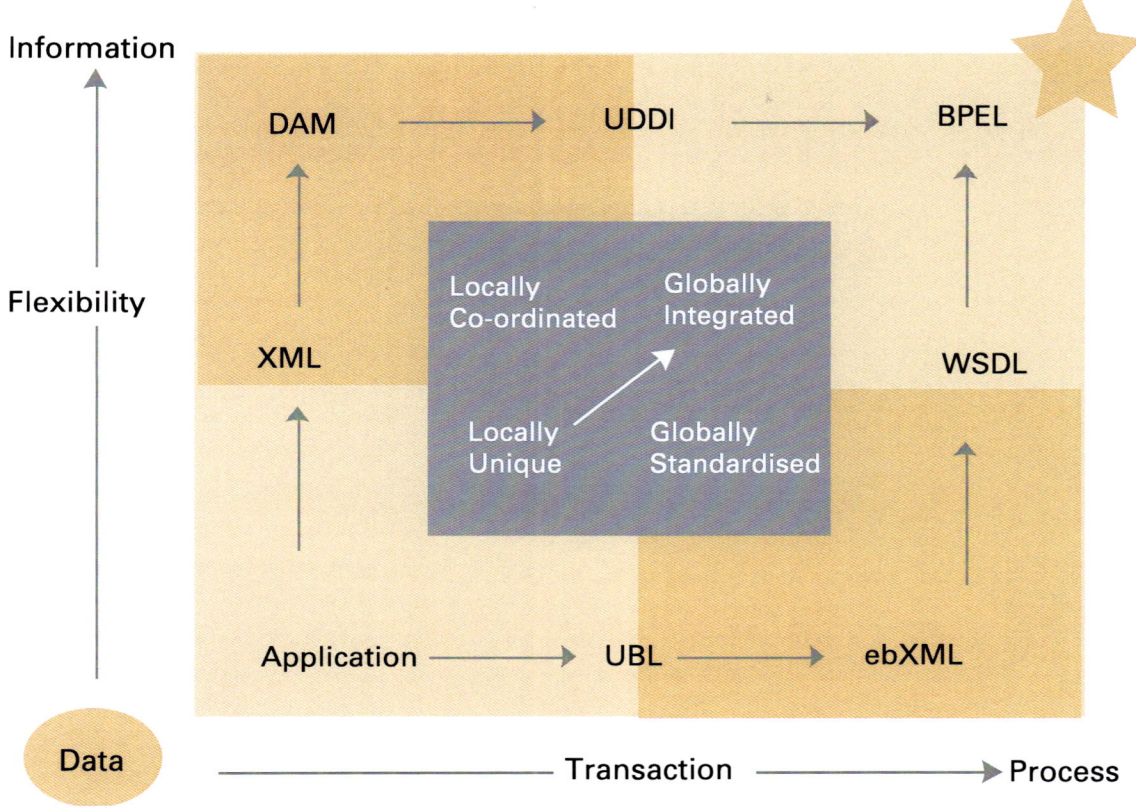

Figure 4. A View of Service Standards in Terms of Business Information and Process

within MIS, around the local use of information as well as the external market definitions and use of data. The horizontal axis requires a similar approach to processes managed by the 'Integration' MIS team. Determining how to design, build, and implement with new tools, techniques, and methods is the task of the 'Innovation' and 'Industrialization' teams with the role of challenging the status quo in order to find better solutions both for the business in terms of performance and for MIS, around cost. Many of the decisions on both axes cannot be made based on internal issues. The marketplace is the key influencer, and in particular this means that standards must be chosen in light of the practices of the target vertical marketplace, or trading partners. Many vertical industry sectors such as the retail sector have already seen major enterprises sponsor associations to make decisions on data formats to allow readily understood information exchanges.

Conclusions

A new technology generation is making use of the Internet and World Wide Web to create new capabilities for 'inter-enterprise' trading and direct interaction with target markets. The potential for business differentiation based on IT has been reinvigorated, but not through the traditional application-centric model. Rather a 'Small Model,' service-centric approach enables innovation by delivering new business capabilities, as well as improved operating efficiencies, incrementally, and at low risk and cost. The technology and associated industry standards are now available. The key challenge is for IT to define a consistent overall direction, and implement a cohesive management approach that will successfully embrace all projects and drive toward common corporate goals and standards.

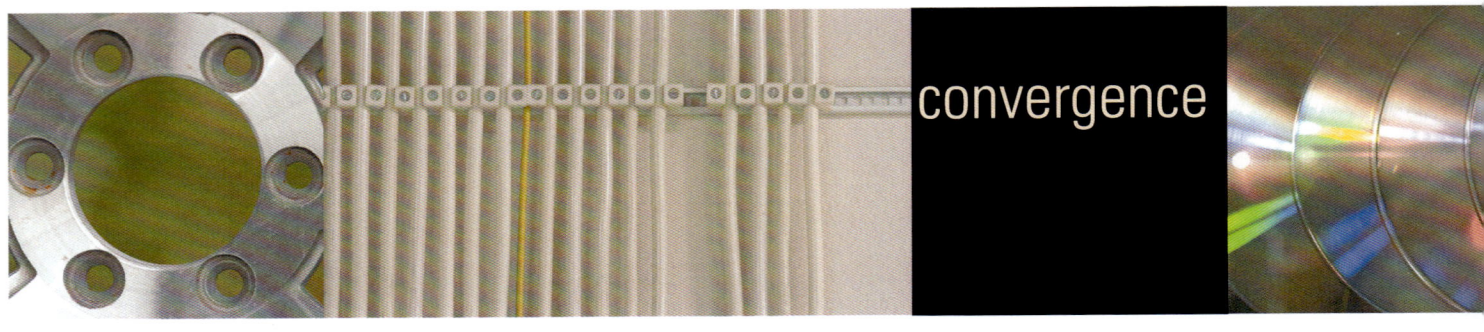

Adaptive Computing: Thinking Beyond the Box

Amit Sinha

SAP

Rapid implementations of business imperatives are driving the adoption of Service-Oriented Architectures (SOA) such as Enterprise Services Architecture (ESA). ESA is the blueprint of a SOA that combines the reliability and functionality provided by SAP's extensive enterprise applications with the flexibility of Web Services based on open standards.

This transition to SOAs can be greatly eased—and simplified—thanks to an approach to hardware virtualization known as *adaptive computing*.

In effect, adaptive computing does for the hardware IT infrastructure what SOA does for software: it makes it more flexible by permitting reuse of basic components. Just as SOA lets you expose functionality from your existing enterprise applications into standards-based Web Services for greater reuse, adaptive computing lets you turn your existing hardware infrastructure into a virtual computing resource for a more dynamic model. In both cases, you don't have to jettison your existing resources, since you're really finding new techniques for using them.

As a result, adaptive computing reduces the complexities of the conventional IT hardware infrastructure and increases utilization efficiency. Essentially, you get more application handling horsepower, but at a savings in total cost of ownership (TCO), so you can re-invest in product innovation, rather than having to worry about your IT infrastructure. Sound too good to be true? Companies such as Colgate-Palmolive and Hella KG have already used adaptive computing to reduce TCO by 30 to 70 percent.

A Break with the Past

Adaptive computing represents a significant change from the conventional enterprise computing paradigm. Traditionally, organizations have used dedicated hardware to run application software. With this approach, adding new applications, or users, or upgrading the software in general, often means having to upgrade hardware as well.

Many organizations have had to overdesign their hardware to be able to handle major traffic peaks. This means that in addition to adding servers for temporary capacity demands, organizations have also had to add peripheral systems, backup facilities, and supporting maintenance—something that adds greatly not just to cost, but to complexity as well.

In an age of services-based applications, the traditional hardware approach simply won't work. Today, an organization may be running 1,000 core applications. In five years, that same organization may be running 10,000 independent business processes, powered by business-oriented Web Services called *enterprise services*.

Enterprise services will be easy to build because they'll be reusing basic application components, so in many cases organizations won't have to write five new applications for every five new business processes (see sidebar: Mirroring Software with Hardware). Instead, their basic functionality will be reused by the business process-oriented enterprise services, as illustrated in Figure 1. Also, tools for constructing composite applications—which are built from Web services—will be extremely easy to use, and therefore will encourage the rapid creation of new business processes.

This combination of easy creation and re-use means there will be a near-exponential growth in new Web Services. The successful organization will have a hardware infrastructure in place to support this growth, and so will be able to take advantage of the greater flexibility in building, modifying, and supporting business processes.

Adaptive Computing: Virtualizing the Hardware

The concept that drives adaptive computing is simple: by decoupling the application software from the underlying hardware, adaptive computing puts all hardware resources in the service of all software applications.

In operation, adaptive computing does several things. It establishes intelligent links between all hardware, storage, and operating system resources, and creates a transport layer to insulate them from upper-level applications. It also adds controlling software—the Adaptive Computing Controller, which is part of the SAP NetWeaver open integration platform. The Adaptive Computing Controller tool provides a single point of control for observing, operating, and managing the

Mirroring Software with Hardware

Adaptive computing is a way to reuse hardware resources in much the same way that the SOA reuses software functionality. For example, enterprise services might use the same core credit-check functionality for validating customer demographics, for performing loan checks, or for pre-approving credit in a Customer Relationship Management (CRM) system. Likewise, with adaptive computing, a server might be used for running an Enterprise Resource Planning (ERP) application in the morning, and then might share the load with another server to run a demanding CRM application in the afternoon.

> Companies such as Hella KG and Colgate-Palmolive have already used adaptive computing to reduce total cost of ownership by 30 to 70 percent.

adaptive computing resources. It also employs robust underlying functionality for establishing compatibility with different hardware and operating system platforms, for load balancing, scheduling, and other management tasks.

For the IT administrator, the Adaptive Computing Controller tool creates a cockpit that greatly facilitates managing the underlying resources. For instance, in a single management screen, an IT administrator can view all applications that are running, as well as the servers they're running on If the administrator wants to send an application to another server, it takes about two seconds for the complete relocation. Compare that to the day or so it would take to re-orient applications on dedicated hardware.

And if the administrator wants to link an enterprise application with a second, dependent application, that's easy, too. That way, the two applications will behave as one, in terms of the adaptive infrastructure.

Adaptive computing carries another major benefit: it serves as a vendor-neutral platform for supporting the applications from partners. This way,

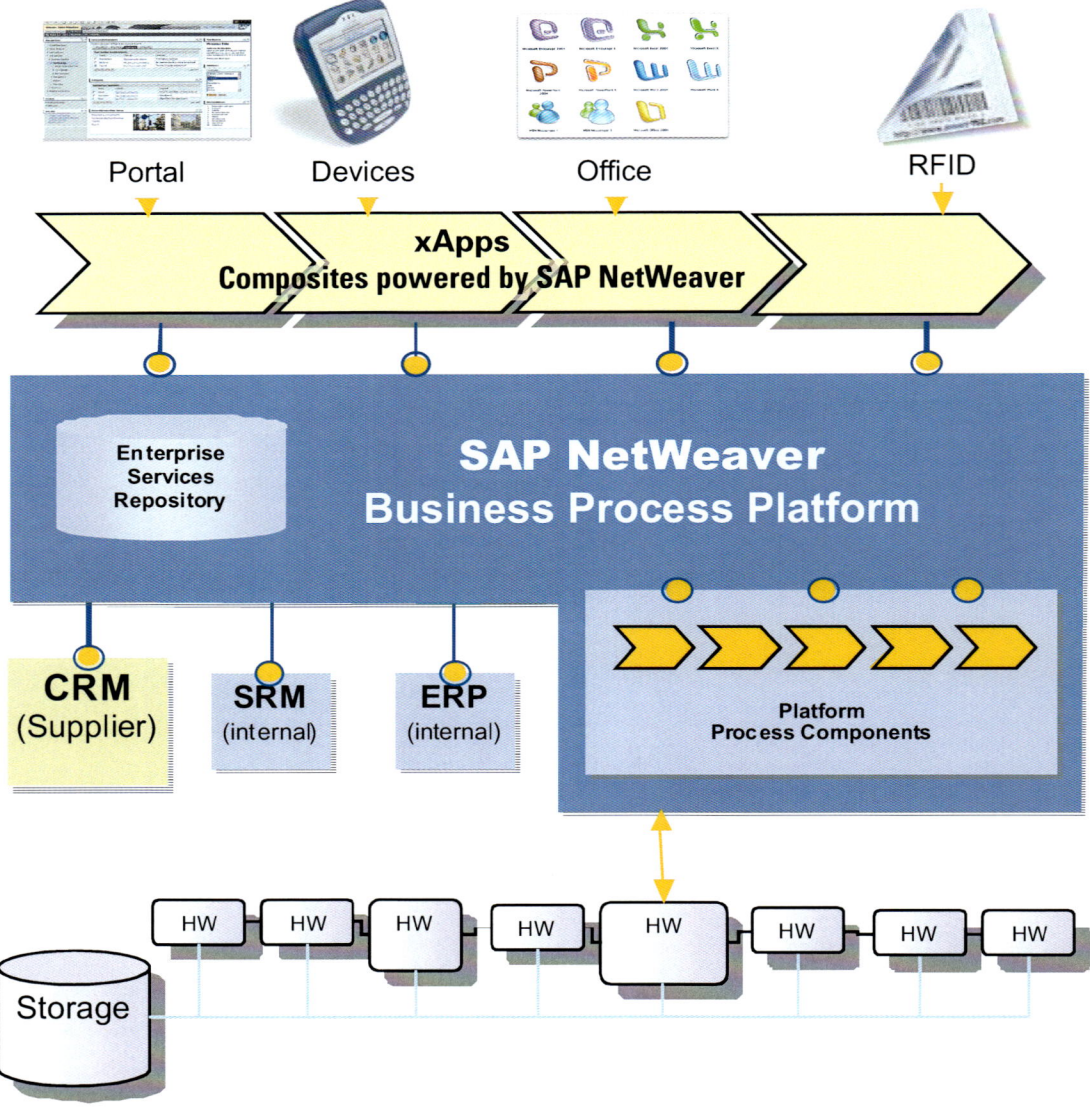

Figure 1. SAP NetWeaver Business Process Platform: Integrating Applications Functionality with a Technology Platform

convergence

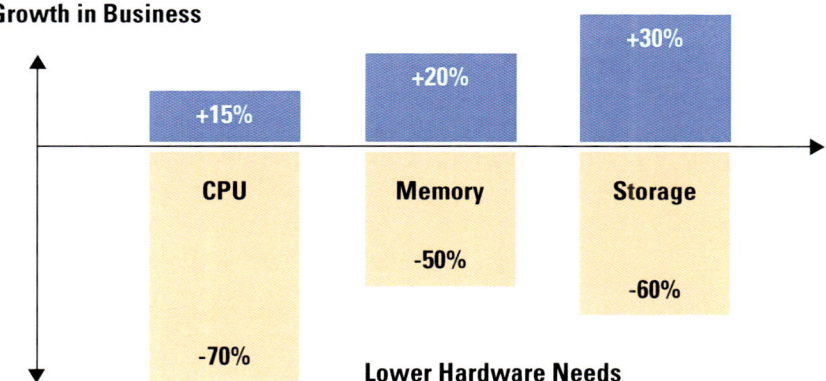

Figure 2. Colgate-Palmolive: Growth and Total Cost of Ownership Results Using Adaptive Computing

your organization can receive a continuing flow of leading-edge Web Services to evaluate, and perhaps to use. Not only does adaptive computing help you distribute applications across your hardware resources more effectively, but it can also be a catalyst for application innovation will help your organization make the most of services-oriented computing (see sidebar: Building Partnerships).

Case in Point: Colgate-Palmolive

The story of Colgate-Palmolive illustrates the real-world benefits of adaptive computing. A $10 billion company with operations in 223 countries, Colgate-Palmolive is using adaptive computing to improve business-process flexibility, simplify their IT landscape, optimize server CPU utilization, and increase application software availability—while at the same time lowering TCO.

Sounds like a tall order, but the company is succeeding, with significant savings demonstrated on SAP-specific IT infrastructure (see Figure 2).

"With the adaptive computing capabilities from SAP, Colgate has reduced the total cost of specific IT infrastructure by 70 percent," said Jim Capraro, director of global information technology for Colgate. "In addition to these savings, it also simplifies the system landscape and reduces overhead required to manage such complex IT landscape as ours."

Perhaps most important, Colgate-Palmolive is well on the way to implementing ESA—SAP's blueprint for a SOA for enterprise applications. By adopting ESA and adaptive computing, Colgate-Palmolive is transitioning its existing IT infrastructure into a strategic environment that enables the company to respond more quickly to changing business requirements.

Building Partnerships

Not only is SAP delivering software, courtesy of SAP NetWeaver, that will coordinate and manage an adaptive computing hardware infrastructure; the company is also building partnerships with key third-party infrastructure vendors.

As part of this effort, SAP and its partners abide by a two level-quality assurance code that covers compliance testing and interface certification for adaptive computing. SAP's adaptive computing partners include Dell, EMC, Fujitsu and Fujitsu-Siemens Computers, Hewlett-Packard, IBM, Intel, Network Appliance, Redwood Software, and Sun Microsystems.

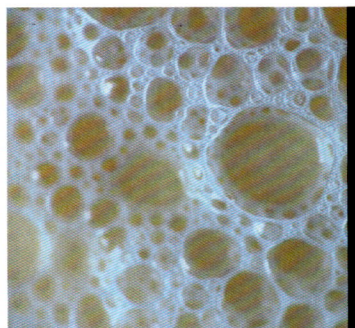

With the adaptive computing capabilities from SAP, Colgate has reduced the total cost of specific IT infrastructure by 70 percent.

The Evolution of IT Infrastructure into a Service-Oriented Model: Grid Computing and a Moore's Law for Services

Robert B. Cohen

COHEN COMMUNICATIONS GROUP and the ECONOMIC STRATEGY INSTITUTE

What economic factors are behind the transformation of IT infrastructure from the decentralized, but very distributed and "walled-off" structure of the past ten years to the services-oriented model that IT infrastructure is moving toward today? How are the development and more widespread use of Grid computing shaping this evolution?

To look at the economics of this change, we need to focus on the economics of services, because for computing, the shift to Service-Oriented IT (SO-IT) means that changes occur in the cost of delivering services. In the economics of services, the time to create a service is a major determinant of its cost. Think of it this way: when services were in silos, each department needed to purchase hardware and employ programmers to create services. While the hardware was amortized over a long time period and many functions, the amount of programming required to develop a service largely determined its cost. The economics of services remained this way for a long time, and the fact that the costs to integrate services were high (and the technology offered very cumbersome integration) meant that the economics of services did not benefit from anything resembling Moore's Law.

The move to SO-IT has begun to alter the old economics of services. SO-IT offers firms a way to use new Web Services technologies in a way to create services that break the old economic framework. Applications or services now work across a number of departments so that they can be shared within the firm, and can be modified without a great deal of additional programming cost. The result is that these services cost far less. In an economist's terms, the new technology has expanded the scale—areas where a service can be used—and the scope—ability to add new functionality—of any service.

In a nutshell, the technologies of SO-IT let firms take advantage of economies of scale and scope that they could not realize earlier. Today, a firm can take the services it develops and apply them to a number of issues, calculations, and service offerings. In manufacturing, the parallel world would be that when computers were first created they focused on extremely large-scale computing. Most forecasters believed that a handful of computers would satisfy demand (assuming they would be high-priced and highly complex). As we know, once applications made computers essential for many roles, the market size exploded.

In the services, the historical assumption has been that services had a limited market. Each firm had certain services matched to its operations. With the Internet and new Web Service technologies, it is possible to create more flexible and adaptive services. This changes the scope and scale of the market for services, and changes how we look at the economics of services.

Today, in the more extensible market for services, built with Web Service technologies and Service-Oriented Architectures (SOAs), it is possible to create services that support functions across far larger parts of the enterprise. As a result, we have a new economics of services based upon SO-IT. Functions for specific services (or applications) can be expanded without a great deal of difficulty. With SOAs, it is possible to "snap together" a series of services that can work as part of a functional whole.

This brings the use of services to an en-

> Service-Oriented IT offers firms a way to use new Web Services technologies to create services that break the old economic framework.

tirely different level. Prior to SO-IT, it was rare to find "joint economies of production." In manufacturing, these economies indicate that a producer benefits because other producers can use the product produced as a substitute, usually as an input in their own production. The result is to increase the market size and lower marginal costs. In services, there are similar impacts, but they initially have greater impacts within the operations of a single firm, with new services creating joint economies that lower the cost of creating services. This dynamic begins to create some of the benefits of Moore's Law by offering firms a way to reduce the cost of services because new technologies enhance the scale and scope of services that firms use.

The connection to Grid computing arises because advances in computing and storage are so intimately tied to further efficiency gains in the use of services. In other words, without gains in computing and storage, SO-IT and SOAs can take the economics of service use only so far. Since Grid computing enhances the way that firms employ services, it provides an avenue that lets firms capture greater efficiencies in their use of services. Grid computing does this by providing a more flexible and efficient framework for the use of hardware and storage that underpins the operation of services and upon which services depend for their efficiency. So in a sense, as hardware becomes more efficient, the delivery of services becomes more efficient. This suggests that we need to recognize that there are also joint economies between computing and storage and services.

We are only beginning to see the economic benefits because they are being captured at a department or R&D group level. This is too limited to have a big impact on the enterprise. Once there is a large deployment of SO-IT in certain industries there could be formidable economic benefits. For instance, in financial services, SOAs are helping firms create new investment vehicles and risk analysis instruments. As a consequence, European hedge funds are increasing IT spending by more than 50 percent a year over the next few years to use IT to enter new, profitable markets. With this level of investment, it is likely that these hedge funds are achieving benefits that far outweigh their cost.

Thus, the industry-wide or firm level gains from SO-IT are likely to be significant, primarily because of the joint economies that we discussed above. These are only possible because firms are linking services together with SOAs and utilizing services more efficiently by using them on top of a Grid computing or cluster computing infrastructure. This should open the way for a Moore's Law in services that indicates how efficiency gains will greatly enhance the scope and scale of services every 18 months in the future.

integration

On the Edge of the Grid: Using the Grid to Digitally Enable the Point of Action

Tom Gibbs

INTEL CORPORATION

The application of Grid computing and communications is moving to the edge. I mean that in two senses. Grid is on the edge or "knee" of the technology adoption curve—it is starting to "cross the chasm" from the early adopter stage, to the "tornado," or high growth stage, and in the process it's becoming a key component of IT architecture. In another sense, the use of Grid is also expanding from the data center to the edge of the enterprise network, where it is digitally enabling users so they can make better use of distributed information technology. New usage models enabled by Grid offer the potential for structural business improvement at the point of action, i.e., near customers and value chain partners, in ways that were not possible in the past.

At the outset, I want to establish a definition of what "the Grid" is so I can clarify some of the confusion that is natural at this phase of technology adoption. Once we have a common perspective on what Grid is, I want to discuss why I think the adoption of Grid is crucial, if not inevitable, and offer a few suggestions to help users maximize the benefits of Grid.

To start, "the Grid" doesn't exist. It's not a thing. You can't buy one and it can't hurt you. Grid is a metaphor that describes the evolution of IT to an architecture that is completely distributed, fluid, and shareable. The Grid metaphor is a useful reference to a more familiar scenario—the way electrical power is delivered. In the electrical utility grid, the use of electrical power is not constrained by where the power is generated or where and when the user wants to use it. The Grid metaphor is powerful for IT because it forces people to think about computing and communications in a way that isn't tied to specific physical assets located in a specific place or plugged into a specific socket. In a Grid infrastructure, resources can be shared in the same way that electric power is generated in one region and consumed in another. Users don't think about the details; it's a utility service that's always there when you need it. So it's not surprising that IT infrastructures based on Grid are sometimes referred to as "utility computing."

Ian Foster, of Argonne National Lab and the University of Chicago, and his colleagues in the scientific community conceived of a worldwide Grid to parallel the worldwide Internet, and have developed a good deal of the technology needed to realize the vision. While the Grid was developed in the realm of scientific research, there are huge commercial applications and benefits of Grid, in much the same way as the World Wide Web, Web browsers, search engines, and other information technologies have moved from research lab to widespread commercial use. In fact, as is often the case with emerging technologies, it may be that the market has been tempted to expect too much too soon from Grid, which could lead to some disappointments in the near term.

For one thing, information resources are not quite as undifferentiated a commodity as electricity flowing through transmission lines. Information has context, semantics, security requirements, and a host of other issues that make its delivery as a utility an extremely complex challenge. In fact, some of the components of Grid haven't been invented or are not yet commercially available. You can't buy a solution tomorrow, or the day after, that fully realizes the entire Grid vision—no one has completely implemented a fully functional Grid yet. However, that's no reason to stand at the sidelines. In the same way we couldn't deliver on the ultimate vision of intercontinental travel until the airplane was invented, that didn't stop far-sighted leaders from investing in roads, canals, and railroads. While Grid will take years to fully mature, there are already a number of proof points up and running, where companies are sharing resources across multiple geographies and business units to gain real business advantage.

The fantastic thing about the Grid metaphor is that it clarifies how limitations of locality and dedicated physical assets can inhibit our ability to develop, deliver, and use information. As in the case of electricity, the Grid paradigm clearly suggests that we eliminate all artificial boundaries in our computing and communications capabilities. Rob Pennington and the folks at the University of Illinois—pioneers of the Grid who have been working for years to make Grid a reality—introduced me to a cool slogan that reflects this new perspective: "Develop Locally, Run Globally."

A Grid approach to IT allows digital computing and communications to be used in a wide variety of new ways by a whole new class of users who work at "the edge of the enterprise," that is they may be in the field at customer locations, in remote offices, in dispersed R&D labs, and so on. Grid allows IT to cross the digital divide in the workforce by providing whatever computing resources are needed at any point in the enterprise at any time, thereby unleashing new levels of productivity and worker job satisfaction. The fact that Grid can also reduce the total cost of delivering information services, through higher utilization and more automated management, is a bonus.

The Impact of Globalization, Outsourcing, and New Organizational Models

I believe that two trends in business today—globalization and outsourcing—actually combine and reinforce each other to form the single biggest megatrend influencing information technology and overall business today. Many of the technical underpinnings of Grid have been around for well over 20 years, but it is changes in the overall business environment that are driving the changes in IT architecture today. The concepts of modularity, service orientation, distributed memory and data, componentized applications,

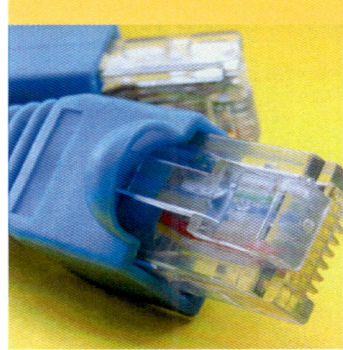

> Many of the technical underpinnings of Grid have been around for well over 20 years, but changes in the overall business environment are driving the changes in IT architecture today.

stateless compute models and object orientation have been with us for a long time. Although we have new standards, and have seen continuous advances in device technology, what's revolutionary is that business itself is changing in fundamental ways, and this is forcing information technology architectures to evolve or perish. Business leaders need information technology to hurry and catch up to meet emerging requirements.

In the "global economy" the competition is fierce, and is becoming "boundary-less." Yet new regulations require keen attention to ethical business and reporting practices. Businesses need information technology that provides more automation and control of business processes, without geographical, temporal, or configuration limitations. And they need these capabilities at the lowest possible total cost of ownership.

The trend toward outsourcing should be viewed as a logical reaction to the new competitive environment. Companies large and small are outsourcing those parts of their business that aren't a core competency to suppliers offering the right expertise at the right price, no matter where they may be physically located. Companies routinely have functional teams distributed around the globe, and in many cases they have formed partnerships in which other companies supply key elements of the product or service.

Globalization and outsourcing are forcing business processes to be physically distributed and reorganized into "webs" of interacting workers, customers, and business partners. The hierarchical, command and control, vertically integrated business model is giving way to complex value chain networks. The speed with which the structure of business is changing is unprecedented. For example, Ford Motor Company has turned the organizational pyramid in their manufacturing operation upside down. Decision making is certainly guided by business objectives from senior managers, but many day-to-day decisions are made by cross-functional teams on the manufacturing floor using data that is provided throughout their shift. There is no longer a divide between knowledge workers and "non-knowledge workers." In the new economy, the entire workforce needs to be knowledge workers, and IT needs to support them as they adapt to a continuously changing competitive environment and customer base.

A recent book by Tom Friedman, the foreign affairs correspondent for *The New York Times*, titled "The World is Flat," highlights this change across multiple industry sectors and multiple geographies with some wonderful anecdotes. One that I found compelling, based on my own personal experience, was his description of the changes at Boeing as they adapt to develop their new *Dreamliner* airplane. In the past "vertical era" Boeing did the design, simulation and testing, and the majority of the manufacturing in house, with most of the labor and intellectual capital located in the Puget Sound region around Seattle. Today, in the "flat era," Boeing relies on scientists in Russia to develop key modeling algorithms that are turned into software in India. Airplane wings are manufactured in Japan, and the final assembly is completed in Everett, Washington. Boeing even developed a special cargo plane to fly the subassemblies built around the globe to the final assembly site. Just as Boeing needed to build a new logistics infrastructure to construct their latest airplane, IT worldwide needs a new information infrastructure to support their new business models.

If business processes themselves have no boundary, then it follows that the information technology that supports them should have no boundary. Otherwise IT will constrain the potential to achieve new business value and to create more effective and efficient value chains. The new economy needs a new IT architecture that eliminates physical constraints. This is why an IT architecture based on the Grid metaphor is so important, and in my view inevitable—business will quite simply demand it.

The Impact of Convergence

When most people in or out of the Grid community talk about "Grid" they often refer only to high-performance computing. They tend to ignore communications and storage. But access to processing power alone is the key factor in only a fraction of modern use

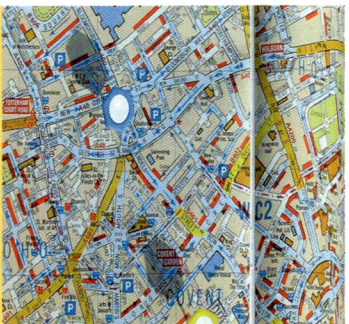

A Grid approach to IT allows digital computing and communications to be used in a wide variety of ways by a whole new class of users who work "at the edge of the enterprise."

integration

cases, while access to data is critical in nearly all of them. An IT architecture based on the Grid metaphor removes the physical constraints in the development and delivery of information that benefit from a boundary-less approach to *storage, communications,* and *computing*. In recent years the basic building blocks for computing, storage, and communications have been converging, that is, all devices or platforms that compute also communicate and store data, and vice versa. So the implication for commercial enterprises is that there are really two parts to the Grid solution—the compute Grid and the data Grid, both supported by high-bandwidth communications. While these have often been developed and deployed separately in the past, the current trend is for these to be fully integrated into one information Grid.

Platforms are also getting smaller, more personal, and more mobile. More computing, storage, and bandwidth are available at the point of use no matter where the user may be located. At Intel we found that these changes led to the emergence of a new category of users when we introduced Intel® Centrino® mobile technology. They weren't traditional office workers. They worked in the field as construction and maintenance employees, or on the factory floor, in a distribution center, or in a hospital at the point of care. Grid technology promises real advantages in the ability to manage and share these mobile resources, and to provide additional resources to mobile users whenever and wherever they need it.

Moreover, a new class of devices that sense (gather data), compute, store, and communicate on their own is emerging that requires no human in the loop. Common examples are the ubiquitous Radio Frequency Identification (RFID) devices, and there are many more so-called "autonomous data sources" coming on line. These new data sources plug information gaps in the supply chain, helping manufacturers track goods, and hospitals to track critical equipment. In general, these new devices will be crucial for closely monitoring and automating global business processes throughout the enterprise and global value chains, and they will drive a huge increase in the volume of data that will be moved, stored, and processed in our enterprise networks. An IT architecture based on Grid is critical to be able to effectively mange these new sources of data, to turn raw data into information at convenient locations, and then move information to where it can be applied at the point of action (i.e., the edge of the network) to maximize ROI.

> **This is why an IT architecture based on the Grid metaphor is so important, and inevitable—business will quite simply demand it.**

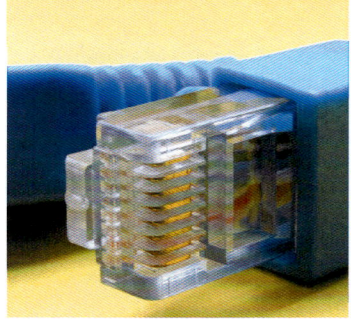

We Need to Move Faster

The global economy is moving at high speed, and companies require new business models and information tools to compete. The legacy architectures of the past will not support the new models. Customers need to examine their business imperatives and determine the key areas where they need to invest in structural improvement. It may be supply chain, customer service, on-line service delivery, product design, or manufacturing. They should aggressively engage their vendor community, invest, and communicate.

"The Grid" is a metaphor that describes an information technology architecture that is distributed, removing physical constraints and allowing multiple users and intelligent devices to share resources wherever they are located. Grid enables new usage models that can have a crucial impact on business. After a little over a decade of hard work, there are exciting Grid proof points coming on line in multiple industries around the world. As an industry, we aren't able to deliver the full promise of Grid yet, but we are making steady progress.

Hopefully, users doing early Grid implementations will communicate the strengths and weaknesses of the current technology to their peers and their technology vendors. I also encourage users to lobby for a robust set of Grid standards that can be used by the worldwide software developer community. Finally, I would suggest that Grid technology is mature enough now for the majority of companies across all industry sectors and geographies to start pilots if they haven't already done so, in order to test and to learn. I encourage you to join the growing community of users who are seeing real ROI today.

Virtual Application Infrastructure (Grid) and the Migration to SOA

Kelly Vizzini

DATASYNAPSE

The global marketplace is forcing companies to respond quickly to dynamic market conditions while reducing costs. When faced with the need to increase scale, improve application performance, and improve quality of service (QoS), corporate environments are exploring Grid computing and application virtualization as proven and cost-effective technology strategies. Not surprisingly, industry analyst firm Gartner Inc. placed virtualization and Grid at the top of their *Top Ten Strategic Technologies* for 2006, followed by service-oriented business applications.

A virtual application infrastructure aligned with Service-Oriented Architecture (SOA) objectives not only yields significant savings in IT spend, but delivers increased ability to process information on demand—improving service levels without adding hardware, software, or headcount. All of which yields a more agile, responsive, and competitive enterprise.

Application Silos Create Operational Inefficiency

Static business systems, distributed across siloed, static processing channels have constrained the evolution of IT, resulting in an infrastructure that is not aligned with business needs. Workload distribution is segmented and sprayed across fixed sets of resources that scale poorly and prohibit service-oriented control. Data access requests are restricted to a fixed set of connections to data stores, resulting in I/O bottlenecks and severe penalties in business system performance, cost, and QoS. As a result, each of the following key business computing objectives has gone unmet:

- Delivering service as needed, when needed.
- Optimizing performance, reliability, and total cost of ownership (TCO) of critical business systems.
- Establishing control and discipline over service delivery and resource consumption.
- Implementing SOA runtime execution control.
- Delivering IT as a service.

Most enterprises are losing the battle to continually harvest the growing speed of computers and the availability of distributed data. IT organizations are so burdened with maintaining lights on that strategic IT initiatives flow bottom up from the systems layer (the supply side), rather than top-down, as they should, from the business layer. Narrow, tactical distributed processing techniques enable short-term performance gains, but these options are often costly, complex, and difficult to scale with business demand. The real goal—the right service, delivered at the right time, to the right user, at the right performance and cost levels—remains well out of reach. SOA and Service-Oriented Infrastructure (SOI), similarly, never escape their positions on IT to do lists.

An important step in IT evolution, distributed computing, has offered limited relief to some large enterprises. Its layered collection of tools and strategies including segmenting, partitioning, clustering, queuing, and load balancing become fixed and costly to maintain.

Moreover, while distributed computing has existed for several decades, it has been largely confined to high-performance computing applications. Administrative complexity and high maintenance costs make it unsuitable for most mainstream corporate computing tasks. In addition, because the types of applications and operating systems they support are limited, traditional distributed solutions cannot be deployed enterprise-wide.

In the constantly shifting and evolving world of enterprise IT, the age of virtualization technologies and Grid computing is underway.

A New Alternative: Virtual Application Infrastructure for the Enterprise

Through standards-based Grid technology, virtual application Grid infrastructure software creates a real-time, application-operating environment that:

- Completely decouples application processing from dedicated hardware.
- Intelligently and adaptively distributes work across the appropriate resources.
- Dynamically scales applications over a virtualized, heterogeneous, enterprise-wide computing infrastructure.
- Provisions the application services and dependent components dynamically on Grid resources.

Business needs are met by optimizing performance and utilization on currently underutilized resources available anywhere in the enterprise. A virtual application infrastructure extends an application's existing architecture—whether it's stand-alone, client-server, Web Service, mainframe system, spreadsheet-based, or application server-based—embedding distributed computing capabilities so any application can leverage existing, underutilized resources. A virtual application infrastructure helps enterprises realize the following, previously unmet business computing goals:

Deliver IT as a service with a variable-cost model—without fixed provisioned resources, radically improving application response time by creating an environment where heterogeneous system resources are pooled, virtualized, and allocated as needed to eliminate IT constraints and processing bottlenecks. Having made virtualized, non-dedicated IT resources a reality, IT managers can now establish variable cost, pay-as-you-go charge-back systems that can track computing resources actually consumed.

Deliver service as needed, when needed, with dynamic service provisioning. Eliminate silos, any number of desktops, servers, blades, clusters, or even mainframes—these can be conceptually virtualized into a single resource. Applications can then access this aggregated system resource pool as needed, when needed—on demand—without being tied to any specific resources. Application service requests are assigned to the most appropriate available resources in the virtualized resource pool, based on the organization's required service levels, cost structure, policies, and priorities.

Establish control and discipline over service delivery and resource consumption using policy-based adaptive provisioning, dashboard monitoring, and administration tools. A virtual application infrastructure provides a highly scalable IT infrastructure that enables organizations to quickly and effectively respond to changing business requirements, while satisfying the volatile and unpredictable demand for computing power.

Implement SOA runtime execution control by being application-centric and demand-driven, not resource-centric and supply-driven. With an adaptive infrastructure, limiting legacy applications can be virtualized and scaled creating a real-time, application operating environment. Once Grid-enabled, legacy applications can quickly and efficiently realize the benefits of Service-Oriented Architecture without having to undergo exhaustive and costly application rewrites or re-architecture. Flexible integration strategies make it easy for a breadth of business-critical applications to take advantage

> The performance, total cost of ownership, and quality of service benefits directly attributable to virtualizing resources, data and application services are proving to be irresistible for IT decision-makers.

of all the benefits of a virtual infrastructure: improved application performance and resiliency through the automatic sharing and management of computing resources across the enterprise. Business needs are met by optimizing the available, yet underutilized, resources across the organization.

The top-down approach to brokering business application demand, combined with self-managed allocation of the runtime IT resource supply, helps an organization implement a service-oriented computing utility that optimizes application performance and utilization of computing resource investments already made.

Accelerating the Shift to SOA with Grid

By distributing application workload across shared system and data resources, the service execution platform inherent in a virtual application infrastructure drives new levels of business performance. This virtualized infrastructure allows applications to non-invasively leverage heterogeneous resources across the enterprise. It also manages the execution of services as required to meet the service levels and cost structures of the business.

Aligned with SOA objectives, a virtual application infrastructure serves as a fabric and service execution platform focused on application, hardware and data virtualization (Figure 1). The result is a service fabric that can dramatically accelerate an organization's shift toward SOA. Some of the key benefits that enterprises can achieve by deploying a virtual application infrastructure to support their SOA strategies are:

- ***Application performance:*** Some Grid users have documented 25 to 50 times improvement in application performance speed, measured by response time and throughput benchmarks.
- ***Resilience and reliability:*** With guaranteed task execution and mechanisms to ensure recovery and migration in the event of system error, application failure rates can drop by up to 90 percent or more.
- ***Flexibility and API independence:*** Forming an application execution environment, the Grid layer supports a wide variety of clients that can be quickly virtualized, including Java, .NET, SOAP, C++ and binary executables.
- ***Service-oriented control:*** Grid enables the global management of services, and administrative control of

virtualization

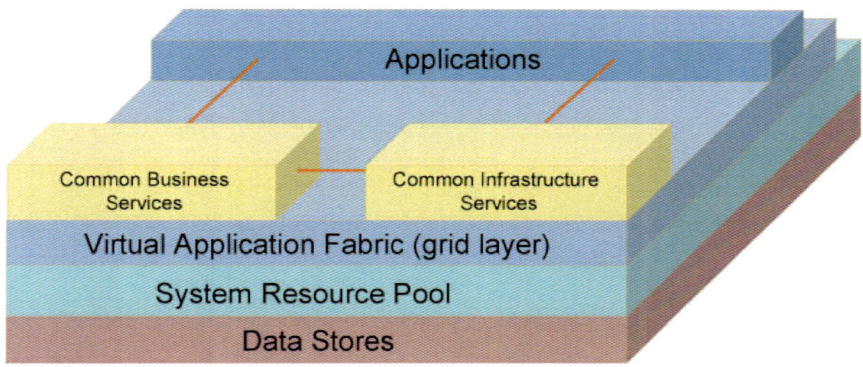

Figure 1. Virtual Application Infrastructure: SOA Fabric

operational parameters, including policy-driven service, resource assignment and workload distribution rules.

- *Rapid development and deployment:* Providing a standards-based, flexible, and intuitive programming model, the Grid layer can simplify development and streamline deployment.
- *Usage-based accounting:* With centralized administration tools, the Grid infrastructure can help IT managers establish variable cost, pay as you go charge back systems and measure service level agreement compliance.
- *TCO reduction:* With all of these benefits together—performance, utilization, reliability, flexibility, service-oriented control, dynamic provisioning, rapid development and deployment, and centralized accounting—Grid can yield a more efficient, cost-effective enterprise.

Summary

In the constantly shifting and evolving world of enterprise IT, the age of virtualization technologies and Grid computing is underway. The applicable business value propositions and value impact benchmarks are extraordinary. The performance, TCO and QoS benefits directly attributable to virtualizing resources, data and application services are proving to be irresistible for IT decision-makers.

DataSynapse, Inc. is a leader in this new age of computing. Its adaptive Grid infrastructure software delivers the highly reliable, scalable and dynamic capabilities required by companies embracing Grid technologies. DataSynapse customers are achieving higher levels of resource utilization and application performance while reducing their operational and capital expenses. Their business operations have become more agile, readily responding to changing market demands and competitive threats.

By distributing application workload across shared resources, the service execution platform inherent in an adaptive Grid infrastructure drives new levels of business performance.

collaboration

The Global Grid Forum: Leading the Journey to Pervasive Grid Adoption

Mark Linesch

GLOBAL GRID FORUM
and HP

In today's dynamic business environment, enterprises around the world are aggressively working across organizational and geographic boundaries to deliver greater customer value and competitive advantage. Working horizontally places increased demands on organizations to break down existing barriers that inhibit the flow of information, innovation, and commerce in our increasingly inter-connected economy. Individuals are challenged to work in new ways—often in collaboration with other departments, disciplines, and/or organizations. IT is challenged to deliver increasing value to the organization while reducing costs and maintaining stability as they transform their organizations to support this more dynamic, global business environment. Solution providers are challenged to deliver practical real-world solutions that deliver value today while helping to cut through jargon and provide direction on future IT investments

To support this growing trend to focus horizontally, we are likely to observe a set of profound changes within enterprise IT over the next few years, including:

- Processes will be transformed from specialized and unformalized to digital representations that can more easily be linked to partners and customers, and instrumented to the supporting IT infrastructure.
- Software will increasingly be architected as services, providing standards-based integration and increased organizational flexibility.

- Information will continue to move from analog to digital, enabling more real-time decision-making and more collaborative problem solving.
- Infrastructure, inspired by Moore's Law will continue to become more powerful, lower cost, and standardized—providing an increasingly ubiquitous distributed computing environment.

Industry visionaries speak of a new world of distributed computing where application services execute on shared resources that are dynamically allocated and managed in an automated, efficient, and utility-like manner.

Organizations journey to this new world of distributed computing as they work to enable their business and the supporting IT infrastructure to become responsive to the constantly changing business and competitive environment. In this increasingly dynamic environment, leading IT organizations are exploring and increasingly adopting service-oriented, Grid solutions.

Adopting Grid solutions is a journey that includes significant people, process, and technology challenges and opportunities. From a technology perspective, Grid solutions enable IT organizations to deliver IT as a flexible service to the business while continuing to reduce costs through better resource utilization and increased automation. However, moving toward shared, service-oriented, Grid environments introduces a variety of interesting people and process questions. Does the organization have an effective IT architecture and formalized IT governance structure? For instance, assessing, prioritizing, and developing the justification for Grid-related projects across budgetary and/or organizational boundaries can be challenging. Managing the transformation to a shared environment may also require training of IT staff and users in new tools, technologies, processes, and roles. Finally, formalization of ongoing funding, operational, and security policies and processes are critical to capture anticipated benefits and provide for ongoing operation and expansion.

Today, Grids are the foundation for collaborative research and advanced scientific discovery worldwide. They also power compute- and data-intensive applications in fields as diverse as oil exploration, drug discovery, and financial services. Grid computing enables research-oriented organizations to solve problems that were infeasible to solve due to computing and data-integration constraints. Grids also reduce costs through automation and improved IT resource utilization. Finally, Grid computing can increase an organization's agility, enabling more efficient business processes and greater responsiveness to change. Over time Grid computing will enable a more flexible, efficient, and utility-like global computing infrastructure. But many organizations are just beginning to explore the benefits of Grid technology and encountering the barriers that come with adopting any emerging technology.

Grid computing can increase an organization's agility, enabling more efficient business processes and greater responsiveness to change.

Grid adoption within the industry will likely progress in three phases: 1) early adoption, 2) proven solutions, and 3) pervasive adoption. Early adoption is primarily an exercise in handcrafting solutions. In the proven-solutions phase, you see Grid-enabled software from vendors and Grid success stories in specific research and industry sectors. In the pervasive-adoption phase, a majority of mainstream users can start to adopt Grids with packaged solutions and lower risk. The ability to move to phase 3 (pervasive adoption) will require breaking through the nonstandard barriers. Organizations can gain business advantage without much standardization as long as everyone you want to share resources with is using the same software. But as organizations begin to connect Grids to other Grids either within their organizations or with other organizations, "economic" pressure for standards begins to build. For those Grids to come together and interoperate, they need to speak the same language. That's why standards are imperative before we can reach pervasive adoption.

The "heart" of a Grid system is the standards-based, service-oriented, software architecture—enabling distributed applications and associated resources (e.g.

network, compute, storage, applications) to be operated as an integrated solution. The "soul of this new machine" is standardization, so that the diverse resources that make up the solution can be discovered, accessed, allocated, monitored, and in general managed as a single virtual system—even when provided by different vendors and/or operated by different organizations.

Standardization of Grid computing is being lead by the Global Grid Forum (GGF). As a worldwide community-based forum, GGF has a shared vision and is a rich source of Grid-related problems, use cases, and best practices for research and industry. Our members utilize this vision and practical experience to develop architectures, specifications, and standards and collaborate with other standards development organizations within the broader distributed computing environment. GGF has developed the Open Grid Services Architecture™ (OGSA) and is working throughout the international community to champion this "architectural blueprint" and the associated specifications needed to support real deployments today and to lay the foundation for pervasive adoption in the future. OGSA is in the early stages of development and maturity. The architecture is service-oriented and relies on a set of emerging Web Services specifications being developed within the broad computer industry. By aligning with the emerging industry developments in Web Services technologies, Grid practitioners are able to leverage the tools, educational materials, and experience from the Web Services community when building applications. This allows the Grid community to concentrate on building the higher-level services that are specific to the Grid application domain while the responsibility for the underlying infrastructure is left to the broader IT industry.

Grids are based on the concept of collaboration and information sharing within a fast-changing, dynamic, business environment. Although industry adoption will occur in stages, there are many practical opportunities to deploy Grid solutions to reduce costs and increase competitive advantage. Organizations should start now to focus on specific problems that they might solve with Grid technology today and let the infectious nature of the Grid lead to additional deployments as software becomes more standardized and solutions mature.

Adopting Grid solutions is a journey that includes significant people, process, and technology challenges and opportunities.

Understanding the Business Benefits of Grids and Service-Oriented IT

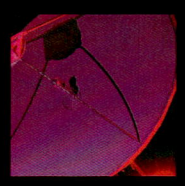

introduction

A Shifting Enterprise IT Economic Model

Although it is still early on, outsourcing, software as a service, 'pay as you go,' and subscription-licensing models point to a broad, long-term change in the economic model for enterprise IT. The desire to better align business practices with IT deployments and to automate processes suggests that enterprises will change the way they buy IT services in the long term. Utility models imply several things: an ability to move from cost centers to computational utilities run on a commercial basis; links to external service providers for peak loads; the ability to move non-core assets off the balance sheet once IT resources are logically consolidated; and paying only for resources actually consumed.

Utility Model

Accessing compute resources and data without having to own the computers is not a new idea. But accessing resources that are hosted or managed by third parties is only one part of the utility computing story. Many of the larger early enterprise adopters are developing in-house IT utilities-with utility-style access and charge-back mechanisms. Some are additionally considering the use of external resources for specific projects, but in-house utilities are fundamentally where efforts are focused today.

CONTRIBUTED BY WILLIAM FELLOWS AND STEVE WALLAGE, THE 451 GROUP

Nevertheless, a vision for the future of computing services based on the utility model is taking shape. On one side are Application Service Providers (ASPs), Managed Service Providers (MSPs), and outsourcing and hosting companies. On another are telcos and service providers, seeking roles as trusted providers of enterprise IT services. Meanwhile the major IT vendors have redrawn their strategies to suggest that the ability to provide IT resources and services on an as-needed basis is the industry's future.

It is entirely reasonable—given the loaded expectations being driven by IT vendor marketing—that enterprise early adopters should therefore want to procure and pay for their IT in different ways and indeed look forward to the day when the use of computers matches the ease of other everyday appliances and utilities.

From the enterprise customer's point of view, the business logic of metering usage is compelling: you only pay for what you use. This is brought sharply into view when considering that the use and procurement of computing services is increasingly driven by economies of scale and the effective utilization of resources. But moving from ownership to utility will still require some insight. Early adopters are going to want a way to determine the likely cost to them when the meter is turned on.

From a supplier perspective, development around utility concepts is being played out in two areas: public utilities (HP Flexible Computing Service, IBM On Demand Supercomputing Centers, Sun Grid Compute Utility) and technologies to support internally shared/datacenter utilities.

Role of Grids

Most IT vendors and enterprise early adopters that The 451 Group has spoken with see Grids and the attributes that give Grid computing its meaning —virtualization, resource reallocation, automation, and self-management—as providing a technology underpinning for new kinds of IT procurement, delivery, and usage models, the most evident of which are SOAs and utility models. As Grid computing becomes important, it may also become more transparent. By the time it is important, it will be called something else—utility computing, SOA, or datacenter automation, for example.

As far as utility models are concerned, there are a number of ways in which Grids are being applied. Grids enable a new model of internal service provisioning, where the IT provider bills early adopters—a company's own departments, and perhaps suppliers or customers as well. Enterprise early adopters may be able to earn back some charges by making resources available for use on the Grid. Because this activity is all happening over the Internet, these resources could just as well be supplied all or in part by an external hosting vendor or in some hybrid arrangement.

In this next section, you will benefit from learning how several companies approach and evaluate the business benefits of Grids and Service-Oriented IT.

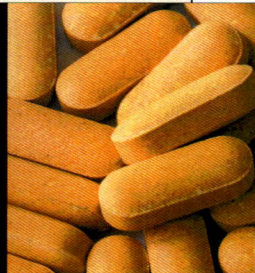

> Outsourcing, software as a service, 'pay as you go,' and subscription-licensing models point to a broad, long-term change in the economic model for enterprise IT.

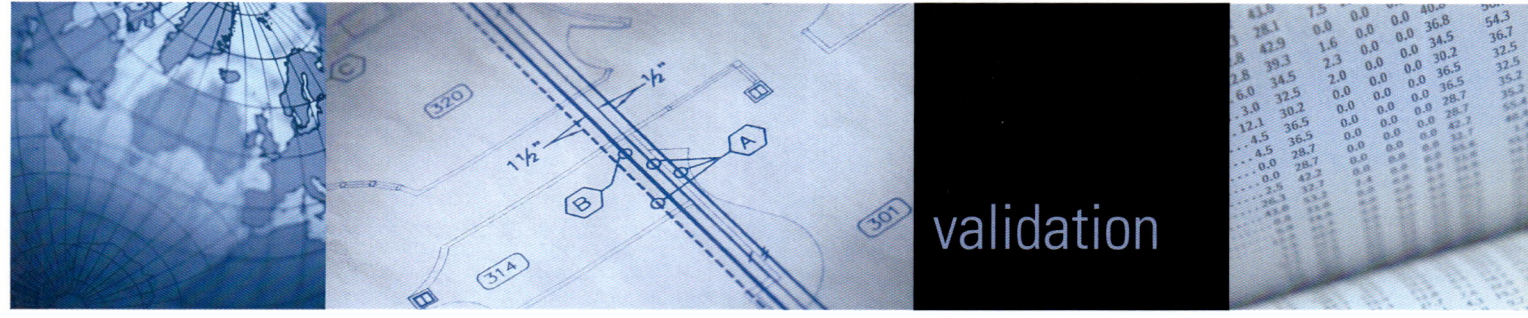

How SOA is Changing IT

SOA's Promise Is Real

The Service-Oriented Architecture (SOA) promise is real, and so is the CIO's dilemma. Although SOA offers such a compelling case for adoption, SOA's business benefits are still largely untapped as long as SOA activity is in the realm of IT.

Companies cannot expect business benefits from SOA before the IT department has been able to assimilate what SOA can do for them. The reality for IT executives and CIOs is that SOA IT benefits must precede business benefits that are a cascading effect of full-lifecycle SOA implementations.

This dilemma is real, and must be addressed by recognizing that SOA holds first and foremost a technical promise of IT cost reduction as a result of faster and easier customization, integration, and deployment of IT capabilities. The causal relationship for the business is very simple: a more competitive business environment that is able to change and react to market and customer needs without ever being bound by IT limitations.

SOA is here, but not widely distributed. A recent Aberdeen/Group/ survey revealed that only 16% of companies have had more than 24 months of experience with SOAs (21% for large companies), and 15% of respondents have managed or completed at least three SOA-related projects (27% in large companies). The larger the SOA footprint becomes, the more tangible the benefits it will yield.

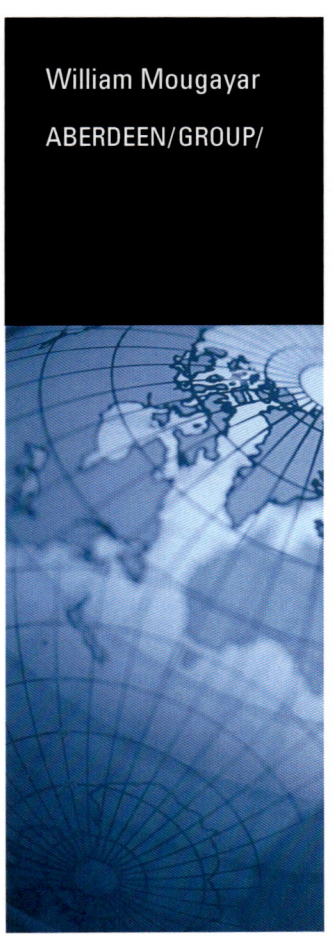

William Mougayar
ABERDEEN/GROUP/

The CIO Imperative

There is an urgent need for CIOs to more fully embrace SOA as a strategic blueprint for the IT organization. The top challenge cited by SOA adopters was "limited visibility for SOA value." This may be a golden opportunity for CIOs to focus on the end-result of SOA business benefits rather than being enamored by the technology itself. A compelling business context is much easier to sell once a well-defined SOA implementation is fully delivered.

Aberdeen is bullish on SOA. Aberdeen predicts that over the next five years, the top Global 2000 organizations have a potential to save $53 billion from their IT budgets as a result of SOA bearing fruit in reducing the costs of software implementations. This doesn't include the cascading effects of enabling the business to become more responsive to change, because IT can deliver on these changing requirements in a shorter timeframe. For example, a $10 billion company with a $300 million IT budget can save $30 million per year from a broad SOA adoption after a five-year horizon of implementing SOA in at least 75% of its applications.

Savings from SOA implementations result in two major undertakings: (1) reinvestment in new IT capabilities and (2) direct business impact from SOA enablement to generate new revenues or enable new business capabilities. It's no surprise that the top factor for implementing SOA, cited by 50% of survey respondents, was "development of new capabilities."

Companies that have had experience in the full cycle of SOA implementations have been able to quantify the benefits of their undertakings in three major categories: (1) speed of deployment, (2) easier integration, and (3) faster customization and updates. These categories carry cost- and time-savings elements that will spread into the business.

SOA is for the long term. Companies will try to balance the initial cost of developing SOA applications against the expected savings from the deployment, integration, testing, and maintenance phases. The savings are real in productivity gains, time, and costs. Whether the SOA development is done internally or outsourced, IT maintenance costs will fall. While the cost of running existing applications is low, the cost of maintaining them is high. This bodes well for justifying an SOA implementation.

SOA Demands New Competencies

Marrying the business requirements with IT capabilities using business process configuration, orchestration, and manipulation tools will become a new competency. This will contribute to a stronger alignment between IT and the business. Software deployment is moving from design/compile/run to assemble/configure/monitor. The right business services at the right granularity level can be very powerful catalysts for binding business language to IT capabilities.

By focusing on the architectural requirements behind SOA, companies can take advantage of SOA's strategic value. The architecture part of SOA is what gives the services orientation its highest value. Sixty percent of the Best in Class (BIC) companies said they are re-engineering their software architecture, versus 32% of all companies surveyed. The role of the SOA architect is critical, but not enough. An SOA competency center is needed to serve as a repository of best practices in order to efficiently master the effectiveness of SOA-related deployments.

Ultimately, the SOA promise is about giving IT a higher level of predictability in delivering IT, from technical capabilities to business value. Running IT like a service, adopting an open service architecture, and linking business to IT organically via a business services orientation will help the IT organization achieve Service-Oriented IT (SO-IT).

Can SOA Change the IT Delivery Model?

An SOA direction presents an opportunity for forward-thinking CIOs to become emboldened. The savvy CIO will know how to capitalize on the SOA shift in order to funnel the savings into more value-added activities. Fifty percent of respondents expect to be able to develop new business capabilities or new products and services and 43% expect to reuse applications via Web Services. These key benefits are after-effects of SOA. Ultimately, IT wants to spend more on innovation and new capabilities. SOA adoption will lower

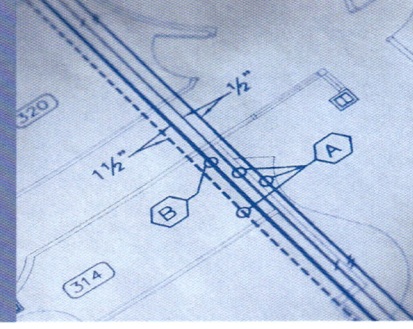

> There is an urgent need for CIOs to more fully embrace SOA as a strategic blueprint for the IT organization.

the cost of IT and enable more responsiveness to business needs. The size of the SOA budget is at stake, and it must be increased in order to fully exploit the promise of SOA.

Because SOA is still not widely deployed, it has not changed the IT delivery model yet. IT has to change its delivery model to take full advantage of the SOA promise. SO-IT is about defining and delivering IT in terms of business services that line-of-business managers can understand. IT will need to decouple these business-level services from the IT-level services, but must be able to assemble them rapidly to deliver the required functionality.

Recommended Actions

SOA is first and foremost a technology enabler for the IT organization. But it is also a catalyst of change for how IT delivers its value to the business. CIOs are encouraged to focus on the following capabilities in order to begin affecting changes within their organization:

- *Take a strategic approach to SOA planning.* Tactical SOA projects are not the only way to proceed. Multi-phased strategic projects may provide a bigger bang for raising the visibility of SOA within the organization at higher levels. CIOs must demand increased budget spending in order to bring SOA's promise to fruition. Now is the time to take a holistic and strategic approach for SOA planning that will include a roadmap, transition plans, and metrics for quantifying the value and results of SOA.
- *Invest in an SOA competency center.* Just like other innovations such as the Internet, client-server, and Six Sigma, the novelty of SOA requires a concentration of knowledge and best practices that is necessary to introduce it within an organization to achieve acceptance and effective

> SOA will ultimately tilt the IT budget toward more spending on innovations and new capabilities, versus a traditional orientation where the majority is consumed by IT maintenance and support costs.

deployments. Lessons learned from any SOA activity are best exploited when there is a centralized approach to its management.

- *Bring the network architects and network operations into SOA.* SOA is expansive and its turf will be challenged by the networking experts, especially in large, multi-national organizations. It's better to be proactive and agree on the several options that are available for bringing the network into the realm of SOA.
- *Give prominence to a senior SOA architect.* Some progressive organizations are creating a new position as a chief SOA architect who will develop the SOA blueprint and roadmap. This is an important position, but it must not be confused with SOA project management. The SOA architect is responsible for the overall planning, strategy, and choice of the various architecture elements, but not necessarily for delivering SOA deployments.
- *Redesign the role of the business analyst.* Long considered a trivial and not highly visible function, the business analyst takes a new role with SOA due of the recent increase in Business Process Management (BPM) activity. Undeniably, there is some overlap and co-existence between SOA and BPM. Furthermore, as attention shifts to the cross-process manipulation and orchestration, the SOA business analyst will become a very important hybrid, between the IT and the business units/operations.
- *Master the new SOA technologies.* Aside from trying to assimilate the several SOA product introductions from vendors, there is a handful of key SOA technology pieces that must be well understood by the IT organization. These include: the enterprise service bus, the services registry, policy governance and management, SOA infrastructure activity monitoring, business process management engines, master data management and semantics building, and Web Services/XML security management.
- *Develop SOA metrics.* There is nothing better for showcasing value than the measurement and documentation of specific outcomes. These could range from the obvious cost, productivity, and time-to-market metrics to more SOA-specific metrics such as re-use factor for a Web Service, degree of services granularity (from fine to coarse), time to change a governance or usage policy, usage statistics for a given service, value of a service, and/or linkage of IT service to business service value.
- *Conduct company-wide awareness and education on the value of SOA*

and its various implementation approaches. There is nothing better than producing several SOA experts within the organization. SOA's success will not propagate by having a single entity or single project focused on SOA.

- *Get more support and understanding from business and executive leadership.* If you haven't had the luxury to show internal success yet, there is already a wide body of external successes and best practices with SOA in the marketplace. Focus on identifying the ones that are related to your business case so you can increase the number of SOA related projects.

- *Conduct a company-wide software applications portfolio assessment.* After having secured a handful of SOA-related projects and acquiring SOA experience, it's time to fully assess all remaining legacy and existing applications, and to develop an SOA migration path for each one of them.

- *Get more support and understanding from the business side and the executive leadership.* Armed with the early results and success metrics with the SOA projects that have been realized, now is the time to raise the visibility for SOA's value within the business levels of the organization. Start waging the battle for increasing the size of the SOA budget.

- *Start implementing meaningful organizational changes to the IT organization.* Ultimately, SOA is enabling the IT organization to deliver its value as a service. The human resources side has to accompany this new orientation. Although some IT organizations have already implemented internal account management and shared success metrics with the business, SOA ups the ante even more and demands the creation of a new hybrid department that sits right in between the IT we know today and the business unit/operations. This new hybrid has skills and capabilities required to create, manipulate, design, orchestrate, and mediate a variety of business-level services. If SOA delivers on its promise, in the not-too-distant future, all of IT might look like this hybrid.

Let SOA Provide Better IT Predictability

Cost savings, closer alignment with the business, unparalleled responsiveness, predictable delivery, and ultimately customer satisfaction benefits await all IT organizations that are committed to allowing SOA to permeate their operations. Timid SOA undertakings lower IT's credibility as an agent of change for the business and do not force the IT organization to change its mode of delivery accordingly. If SOA is the exception rather than the norm, there will be a constant battle and many contrasts between traditional and progressive IT undertakings.

Ultimately, SOA is what will tilt the IT budget toward more spending on innovations and enabling new business capabilities, versus a traditional orientation where the majority of the budget is consumed by IT maintenance and support costs. In fact, the IT budget as a percentage of total revenue spent on innovations was 29.6% for BIC companies with more than two SOA projects under their belt, versus 18.5% for all participants. And software maintenance costs as a percentage of IT budget stood at 12.4% for BIC companies with SOA experience versus 27.3% for all participants.

Ultimately, the SOA promise is about giving IT a higher level of predictability in delivering IT, from technical capabilities to business value. Running IT like a service, adopting open service architecture, and linking business to IT organically via a business services orientation will help the IT organization achieve SO-IT.

Marrying business requirements with IT capabilities using business process configuration, orchestration, and manipulation tools will become a new competency.

Critical Technology Factors for the Successful Future of 'Services': How and Where to Create Business Benefit with the SOA Revolution

Andy Mulholland

CAPGEMINI

It's clear that there will need to be additional advances in some technologies to maximize the capabilities of the Service-Oriented Architecture (SOA) model as it moves from its initial stage of static configurations into one of constantly changing dynamic relationships. This article outlines technology areas that are developing in support of these future requirements.

Semantic Data

Semantic information and the associated term, 'ontology,' might be best described as technologies that allow the meaning and associations of data to be known and processed at the time of execution. In other words, allowing machines to understand nuances at the same (or at least close to the) level of comprehension as a human. This capability is being driven by the need to understand more complex things, more quickly from a rapidly rising sea of data. Therefore, tasks previously performed exclusively by humans must become automated both to support the desired flexibility of SOA, and simply to deal with the sheer volume of data. The World Wide Web Consortium (W3C) has been actively working on incorporating semantic information into its suite of Web Services standards.

As part of the solution, the adoption of eXtensible Markup Language (XML) continues to grow. More and more vertical industry sectors are coming together to agree on specific XML definitions for their own specialist data. There is also a growing adoption of XML within enterprises for their own internal data usage as part of the shift to SOA. Because XML is a 'reflective,' or self-describing data format, it allows data type descriptions to be readily transferred with the data itself, making it ideal for e-business processes such as 'book to bill' transactions between partners. However, XML conveys only content and structure, not presentation, behavior, or deep meaning. That is, XML 'tags' have no predefined inherent meaning, so while providing a standard framework for sharing information, they cannot describe the more abstract aspects of trading conventions and agreements. To do this we need other tools such as such as prose, namespace, ontology, and UML diagrams, among others. These can be grouped together as 'semantic' descriptions, i.e., descriptions of meaning.

The explosion in XML agreements makes it increasingly hard to handle the growing number of formats in use—the problem of managing complex data structures and relationships. At the same time, business intelligence and compliance requires understanding how data is used and related in many different ways around core processes, posing the challenge of managing complex queries. Neither problem is new—techniques exist to handle both individually. The new challenge is managing both at the same time in interrelated ways so that structured and unstructured data can be managed using both relational and non-relational queries. This has been referred to as the challenge of 'intelligence networks.'

So the challenge of the so-called 'Semantic Wave' is to provide any-to-any query support by extending existing data models. Figure 1 illustrates the relationship between established data models and 'Directed Graph,' a new approach using two crucial new technologies, Resource Description Frame-

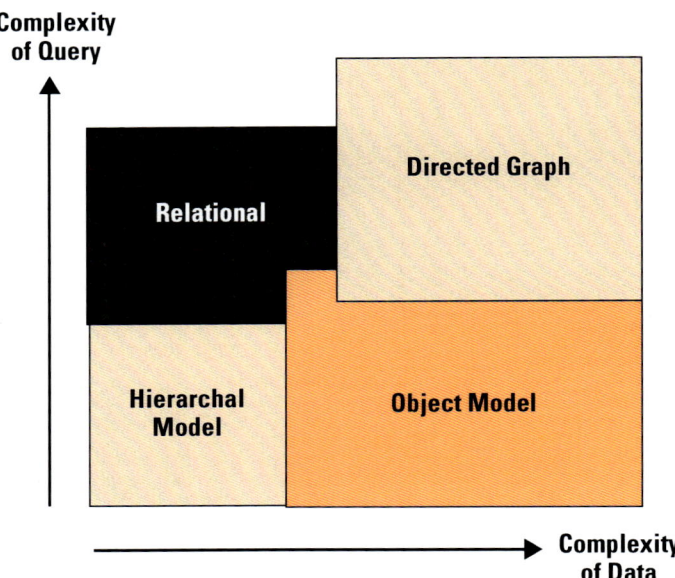

Figure 1. Using Directed Graphs to Handle Complex Data Queries

work (RDF) and Ontology Web Language (OWL), to provide the required capabilities.

RDF is a mechanism for the encoding, exchange, and reuse of structural metadata built using XML, but imposing structural constraints to ensure that there is a full, unambiguous method to express semantic meanings. In other words, a way to describe complex variables that can always be interpreted the same way by a machine. This allows XML data values to vary, but the contextual meaning to be unchanged. For example, the amount of an invoice in euros can be provided by XML, but the definition what an invoice is, and how it can be used, is given in RDF using resource headings (URIs), property types, and values which are grouped together to form descriptions.

OWL allows computers to interpret content in forms normally understood by humans by adding a further degree of richness to RDF. OWL uses vocabularies to explicitly describe properties and classes. OWL has three highly expressive sub-languages that support increasing amounts of detail—OWL Lite, Owl DL, and OWL Full—at the cost of more complexity. OWL functions analogously to a human language dictionary.

RDF and OWL add semantic detail defining collections of 'things' and their relationships. A directed graph data model uses semantic information to dynamically construct one or more queries across multiple databases to support complex data operations like building 'what-if' scenarios. Directed graphs also allow intelligent agents to make use of all available data in a contextual manner for query optimization techniques.

RDF and OWL have been quietly developing for some eight years, and appear as critical elements in six of the core WS-Standards. Commercial products are now available that use RDF and OWL. Since they provide a way to make better use of data for compliance or business intelligence purposes, these technologies will see can increasing commercial use. The technologies associated with the Semantic Wave provide the answer to how to join content to services in a dynamic manner within a Service-Oriented Architecture. Semantic approaches will also enable advanced database scaling for commercial requirements such as the Global Data Synchronization project of the United Nations Edifact trading standards.

Digital Rights Management

Related to changes in security management are challenges in managing access to specific data or content in a variety of forms. This is the work of 'Digital Rights Management' or DRM. In more formal terms DRM has been described as a way of addressing the description, identification, trading, protection, monitoring, and tracking of all forms of rights usages over tangible and intangible assets, including management of rights holders' (e.g., copyright) relationships.

For individual content creators, DRM may be as simple as setting up a spreadsheet that identifies the rights and rights holders associated with particular works, and keeps track of their use. Or it might be an online or offline rights register in which the rights and consents associated with copyright material are recorded and made available to users. For producers and publishers, more complex DRM systems can record, track, and monitor rights for a range of existing and newly created materials. Where producers, publishers, and creators are also traders, the content itself can be made available in digital format, protected by security features that are unlocked after agreements for use have been reached and payment made. All registers are based on systematic identification and recording of information about the legal 'rights holders' (copyright owners) and about the legal rights associated with the content. This is managed through the use of metadata to provide Rights Management Information (RMI) or Digital Object Identifiers. Significant efforts have been made to create enduring and universally meaningful metadata standards. Prominent among these are the efforts undertaken by the Dublin Core Metadata Initiative (DCMI) that defines 'static metadata' used to aid rights discovery.

There are a number of technologies in commercially available systems covering various aspects of DRM, listed in Table 1.

Taken together these capabilities allow data to be used as small, specialized elements rather than as monolithic blocks accessible only through specific applications or data mining interfaces. Its use can be controlled, even in dynamic circumstances, by the services using the content. This allows data to be 'trusted' in the sense that its source is known, as well as when, and who

> There will need to be additional advances in some technologies to maximize the capabilities of the SOA model as it moves from static configurations into constantly changing dynamic relationships.

Component Technologies of Digital Rights Management

Security Protection	Reduction of the likelihood of infringement through digital watermarks, etc.
Encryption	Scrambling the data so that they cannot be used without passwords or keys
Rights Management Information	Embedded information about the data, i.e., author, title, password, key, etc.
Personalization	The ability to provide a "tailored" subset of information for a particular use
Granularity	The capability to blend with other data as required to form a new format
Interoperability	The ability to be integrated in different ways around standards
Digital Object Identifier	A unique number, similar to an RFID tag to identify the data

Table 1. Component Technologies of Digital Rights Management

made changes to the data, and under what circumstances—a vital requirement for compliance data management.

Licensing Reform

If the Web is the driver for software to evolve toward small services in a standardized SOA environment, then open source has become the main channel of delivery. Linux-based open source software seems to be naturally aligned to the Internet-Web and is increasingly perceived as the safe tactic, not a 'radical' strategy. But the motivation is not just reduced cost, though that's important. Open source also aligns with the move from big applications to small Web Services.

The traditional application was a purpose-built and complicated piece of technology. Implementation required decisions about the numbers of users to be supported and the size of the hardware required in terms of numbers of processors. The more users (the more power required), the more value in the use of the software the reasoning went, and therefore the greater cost of the license, based on the formula of users and processors. License management was approached as a policing technology to ensure that the rules were not broken. But often this model did not fit the circumstance, and strange deals were done that left licenses unused 'on the shelf.' All in all, traditional licensing approaches seem to be unworkable in the dynamic world of SOA.

The whole attraction of the Web-based services model is the capability to have an 'any-to-any' interaction driven by the current need to find information, or to a service business process in response to a 'random' event. Any licensing model that restricts or defeats this responsiveness is unacceptable. Indeed, strains on the traditional licensing models are growing year by year. There has been some experimentation in this area. For example, Sun Microsystems' Java Enterprise System sells for a single fixed fee based on the number of employees. When Computer Associates (CA) made their long established Ingres database product available via an open source license, the number of registered users doubled in 90 days!

How, and why, does this work in everyone's favor? In the case of Ingres, CA had a choice to invest in expensive R & D for a product with a limited base of existing users and little hope of winning any significant new market share, or to make the code accessible under open source and grow the use base tremendously. Traditional license income is replaced by maintenance fees for managing the kernel, documentation, bug fixes, etc., which the traditional license was supposed to cover anyway. The difference is that the customer now owns the code and is free to customize it with extra functionality and is unrestricted in its use (except to resell it). Many existing Ingres users must have been frustrated trying to get new functionality from CA, hoping that the resulting release would not be impossibly expensive to license and implement. Now they are free to add what they need without changing anything else and incurring problems from unwanted changes in an upgraded release.

Adoption of open source licensing will not work for everything, in particular not for software with unique business value in a vertical sector and involving proprietary intellectual property. But perhaps there is an optimum blend of open source and licensed software in the form of 'agents.' These are relatively small pieces of software focused on highly specific functions with very high intellectual property content that can be easily integrated in an SOA context.

Conclusion

Achieving the external-facing, continuously adaptable usage models of the future requires advances in several technology areas that complement the Grid infrastructure and service-oriented software architecture. Representing the

> Achieving the external-facing, continuously adaptable usage models of the future requires advances in technology areas that complement Grid infrastructure and SOA.

meaning and relationships among data using semantic modeling technologies will be needed to enable machines to imitate the qualities of human understanding. Digital Rights Management frameworks are needed to manage the right to access or modify content and data not only within an enterprise, but more importantly across many companies and in the open Internet market. Finally, software licensing models must be changed to support the new SOA dynamic environment and to reflect the reality of shared services, composite applications, and cross-enterprise interactions.

Grid and SOA in Business Solutions

Ellen J. Stokes and
Matthew P. Haynos

IBM

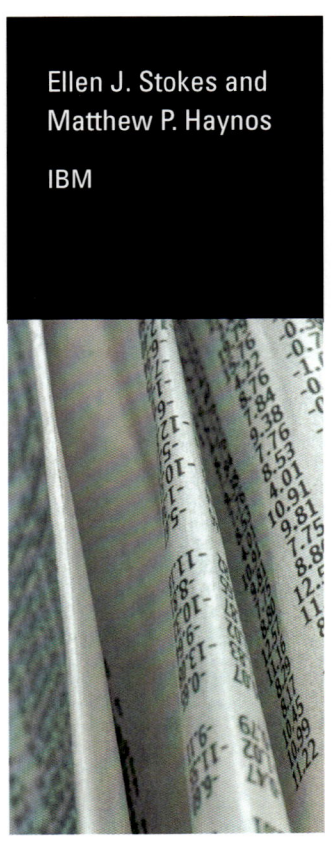

As the marketplace globalizes, new markets, new workforces, and new competitors are driving companies to look for ways to adapt more quickly. While significant changes have been made on a yearly basis, market forces are now requiring companies to make the same level of change on a monthly, weekly, or even daily basis. Business leaders who have been focused on cost-containment are now focusing on growth, which demands the flexibility to be more nimble than competitors. At the same time, companies are looking to control costs by making better use of the investments that they already have. Grid computing through implementation of a Service-Oriented Architecture (SOA) can address these needs.

A simple definition of Grid computing is: "distributed computing over a network using open standards." A Grid is a system that coordinates resources not subject to centralized control to deliver non-trivial qualities of service. Resources on a Grid are heterogeneous, dynamic, and virtualized to shield the application from the underlying details. Computational Grids seek to drive up application performance. Information Grids seek to increase productivity and collaboration via a unified view of distributed information. SOA uses widely adopted Web Services standards to ensure interoperability between services through well-defined interfaces. SOAs provide a convenient representation for things people want to do in Grids. Grid services is a particular set of distributed computing functionality using Web Services over a network using open standards. Applications and infrastructure can be defined as Web Services as well as use Web Services.

This article discusses how Grid computing can provide business value using a service-oriented architecture. Three aspects of SOA are examined that provide this business value: (1) flexibility and re-use, (2) heterogeneity, and (3) communications.

> Flexibility and re-use, heterogeneity, and asynchronous and parallel communications are important to support dynamic, SOA-based Grid applications.

Flexibility and Re-use

A service is a modular software component with a well-defined interface. Infrastructure services provide basic computing functionality such as event notification, resource state, and authentication. Business, or application, services address higher level functionality such as order tracking and point-of-sale inventory update. Adopting a services approach for applications and infrastructure leads to re-use of common functionality across business solutions. And this means determining how to define the services that will help construct a flexible environment and serve the needs of applications in response to ever-changing business conditions. Aspects that should be considered when defining services are:

- **Modularity:** A service should be able to be re-used across applications and solutions and at a level where the service can be easily replaced or updated.
- **Well-defined interfaces:** A service needs well-defined interfaces to be portable and interoperable in heterogeneous environments.
- **Loose coupling:** A service should not be bound to a specific consumer.
- **Abstraction / virtualization:** A service needs to be abstracted or virtualized based on the resources on which it will operate.

The flexibility of where to run these services increases application performance and time-to-results for computational applications, increases productivity and collaboration for a unified view of distributed information, and can maximize utilization of existing computing resources to provide a better return on investment. Harnessing the value of a Grid services SOA-based infrastructure, that is, its ability to locate resources, provision those resources, and monitor and adjust those resources to meet the required service level based on changes in business priorities or changes in resource (e.g. state) without disrupting execution of the task or application, enables increased performance, productivity, and utilization.

The following example demonstrates the business value of flexibility and re-use through a business solution that combines intensive computing and information access to meet customer needs near real-time. In the financial services industry, a common service is the ability to recommend optimal portfolios for each customer. Typically, this requires expensive and time-consuming multi-variant analysis and other advanced numerical techniques. The customer generally has to come back to an advisor's office at a later date or receive the recommendations via e-mail, fax, or mail. The optimization application can be broken into manageable pieces that can be distributed to multiple processors and then aggregated when the computational intensive work is completed. Services can be defined for the numerical algorithms needed, and those services can be run on systems that have the resources necessary and available to do the computations required. Data to drive the analysis for a single customer resides in dozens, if not hundreds, of applications and systems. Services to provide uniform access to that data to input into the computations provides portability of the data. The result is reduced processing time—from many minutes and hours to a reasonable number of seconds—while utilizing available compute time and not impacting any other financial transactions running on those systems. This now changes the character of interaction with the customer. Near real-time, the customer can sit with his advisor and make better investment decisions (having looked at more options). And the financial services firm has a better utilization of its assets and resources with no or very little additional infrastructure cost to provide this near real-time experience for the customer.

Heterogeneity

It is not uncommon for computing environments to be comprised of heterogeneous systems. A Grid environment can help mix and match these heterogeneous systems so the compute capability of these systems can be maximized. Services are benign to the system on which they run. So services can easily be implemented for different systems. Services are defined using a form of XML known as WSDL (Web services definition language); the functionality is encapsulated within the WSDL. Access to these services is via a form of HTTP known as SOAP (simple object access protocol) for uniform access.

So, for example, services can be implemented to isolate application portal servers from the system schedulers that dispatch applications and transactions into the provisioned server Grid. This is done to enable application portal servers to interact with heterogeneous system schedulers or to utilize system resources that reside outside of a given Grid. This form of flexibility enables IT infrastructure components and applications to be added or removed in a non-disruptive manner.

Building on the financial services example, heterogeneity plays a key role. The systems that perform the compute intensive computations and analysis may have hardware (such as processor(s)) that is computationally efficient. The customers' data may be stored on other systems with different hardware characteristics that are storage efficient. The optimization application may run on any general system since it is run in pieces and the results

Business leaders who have been focused on cost-containment are now focusing on growth, which demands the flexibility to be more nimble than competitors.

aggregated. And additional input data may be required from systems outside a given Grid such as current stock and bond prices. Together, this heterogeneous Grid configuration maximizes time-to-results, uniform information access, and resource utilization by scheduling the component pieces of the optimization application to run where it makes sense to run those pieces to provide the near real-time results to the customer.

Communications

To deliver results from complex applications running in a Grid environment usually requires sophisticated communications between services. Traditionally, managing this communications has been the responsibility of the application developer. Developers not only have had to construct application logic, but have also had to be concerned with the timing and sequencing of communications between entities in the distributed Grid system. While tools like MPI (Message Passing Interface) have helped mitigate this concern across tightly coupled cluster environments, managing communications in distributed Grids continues to be both challenging and error prone. However, SOA's promise to streamline this process by incorporating built-in communications primitives such as asynchronous and parallel communications allows application developers to focus more on overall application logic and flow and less on coordinating communications.

SOAs offer a level of standardization and integration in higher-level communications. There are a myriad of communications protocols and techniques currently utilized (e.g. JMS— Java Messaging System), but new approaches and architectures based on the concept of the enterprise service bus (ESB) are emerging. The notion of an ESB is an important development to Grids because it allows for easier translation of diverse communications protocols into standardized, event driven communications based on WS-SOAP and other emerging Web services standards such as WS-Notification and WS-ReliableMessaging.

Further, this type of approach to communications offers some important benefits to Grids. The first is that it is more of a peering model than the traditional communications hub-and-spoke model. This is important to support the inherent scale of Grid systems because communications processing can be optimized by isolating heavy processing tasks (such as transforming XML documents into other XML documents) on powerful machines and less intensive tasks (such as routing) on less powerful machines. In a centralized hub-and-spoke system, this would not be possible. The second important benefit to Grids is loosely coupled communications via asynchronous, message passing. This type of communications model is a natural one for supporting complex, distributed Grid applications.

Many of the interactions between the components in the financial services example can be supported by standardized, asynchronous communications. Changes in a customer's portfolio (e.g. deleting an asset) can be communicated asynchronously to the optimization application. Stock and bond prices, being inherently dynamic, can be regularly broadcast to the optimization application as well as other interested parties.

Conclusion

Flexibility and re-use, heterogeneity, and asynchronous and parallel communications are important to support dynamic, SOA-based Grid applications. SOA services can be re-used extensively regardless of whether they are based on new services implementation or existing IT assets. The flexibility of where to run these services increases application performance and time-to-results for computational applications, increases productivity and collaboration for a unified view of distributed information, and can maximize utilization of existing computing resources to provide a better return on investment. SOAs incorporate built-in communications primitives such as asynchronous and parallel communications to allow application developers to focus more on overall application logic and flow and less on coordinating communications. And finally, SOA commands organizational commitment by focusing on business-level activities and interactions rather than technical sub-tasks to deliver greater business value. Through the use of SOA to support dynamic Grid applications, the financial services example changed the character of interaction with the customer. Near real-time, the customer can sit with his advisor and make better investment decisions (having looked at more options). And the financial services firm has a better utilization of its assets and resources with no or very little additional infrastructure cost to provide this near real-time experience for the customer.

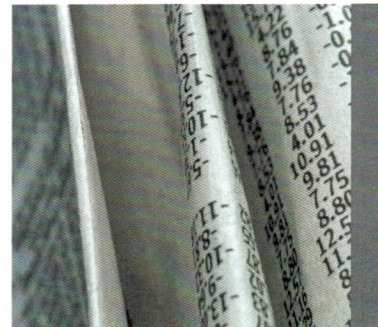

SOA commands organizational commitment by focusing on business-level activities rather than technical sub-tasks to deliver greater business value.

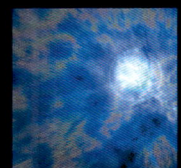

Connecting the Dots

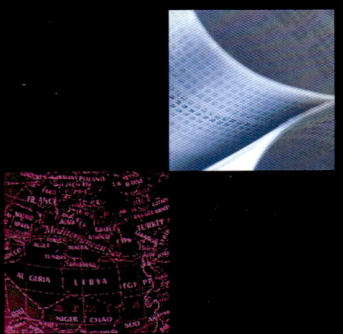

introduction

Tackling Data in an Enterprise IT Environment

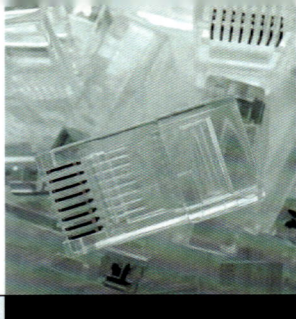

The compute Grid is well understood today, but much less time has been devoted to getting data where it needs to be, when it needs to be there, as well as to how this effort is managed.

Enterprise users say the ability to manage data on Grids is a key requirement for accelerating Grid deployments within their IT organizations. Some large enterprises are finding that limitations in data management capability mean they must hold off on developing their Grid deployments. Those that have moved forward have usually done it either through internal work or through customized or cutting-edge offerings from vendors. Most early adopters have long-term plans to extend their activities from initial beachheads to multi-application and cross-organizational Grids. But without proper data management tools in place, applications will not perform well on top of a Grid architecture, and the cost and performance advantages of implementing a Grid will not be realized.

Enterprise Grids require a data management infrastructure that allows end users and applications to share information, regardless of where it resides, and that provides secure access to heterogeneous

CONTRIBUTED BY WILLIAM FELLOWS AND STEVE WALLAGE, THE 451 GROUP

databases, middleware, file systems, and storage systems. Traditional data management techniques are well established, but they were designed to run on centralized mainframe or client/server architectures and need to be adapted and extended for Grid architectures. If Grids are to progress into mainstream commercial use, a model for transactional Grids is needed that can support the kind of transactions that underpin commercial organizations. Increasing the availability of commercial applications for use on Grids is seen as key to driving accelerated adoption. Some combination of caching, data streaming, replication, global resource namespaces, data movement, data transformation, data quality, and storage volume virtualization may be required, depending on the application and system architecture. As it stands now, no single approach—with the exception that a virtualized environment is necessary—or single vendor or group has a leadership position, and no one can address data management in every part of the IT stack. The challenge has been characterized variously as creating the data Grid, storage Grid, information Grid, or integration Grid. The 451 Group believes the ability to manage data on Grids is the key to all of these.

Many enterprises, vendors, and users have identified the transformation to a Service-Oriented Architecture (SOA) as a strategic, long-term goal that can better align business with IT and improve responsiveness to changing conditions. Financial services companies, for example, see Grids as the underpinning for SOAs, which cannot be implemented without sophisticated data management techniques. An SOA uses short transactions and large volumes of associated data elements. For many organizations, SOA is the future for their enterprise IT environments. Grid computing is seen as the infrastructure model and SOA as the application model. But SOA is not the exclusive role for Grid technology, which is also regarded as the underpinning for utility computing, a service delivery model. Equally important is how Grid technology relates to event-driven services, messaging, database systems, networking systems, and legacy assets.

A mixture of approaches—data movement, replication and data federation—will be necessary to handle the growing number of disparate data sources, including those outside the database, as well as the growing number of devices that need to access them within enterprise IT environments. The 451 Group expects to see broader use of federated data access, distributed main memory, and local disk caching techniques in future products. The 451 Group also expects to see increasing data management support for Grids embedded within application servers and databases. But because this implies a return to a more centralized application-server approach that does not fit easily into Grid architectures, an alternative development platform-oriented model supporting multiple programming language interfaces will also continue to be a requirement.

There are no doubt many possible paths to the right Grid and service-oriented IT implementation for an organization. The next section will serve as a guide to exploring many of these paths.

> Enterprise users say the ability to manage data on Grids is a key requirement for accelerating Grid deployments within their IT organizations.

The Future of HPC: Second-generation Clusters, Grid Management Software, and Greater Commercial Adoption

Donald Becker

PENGUIN COMPUTING

As the barriers to global competition are eliminated, commercial companies striving to succeed are looking to high-performance computing (HPC) to reduce cost and time to market and increase product quality. Scientific organizations are leveraging their HPC facilities to attract top talent, compete for scarce research grants, and to achieve or consolidate a reputation as worldwide leaders in their fields. And increasingly these cutting-edge organizations are recognizing that HPC is not only a key tool to improving competitiveness, but many users cannot function without it.

The strategic value of HPC is becoming more apparent to commercial organizations. To support that volume of HPC use, more new technologies such as advanced and easy to use management software will arise that will benefit even non-commercial users. The question is: how will that HPC system look and act in the future?

HPC Choices Today

Basic cluster software, a commonly used form of HPC, is mature and well tested today but there are lots of areas still to address, including ease of use. Many people are working on parts of the problem; management tools, high speed interconnects, provisioning tools, and so on, in an attempt to improve the user experience. In reality, though, these post-architecture design changes treat the symptoms of the problems inherent in first-generation designs but not the underlying cause.

The first generation cluster architecture that came out of the Beowulf project at NASA addressed the problem of getting machines to work together, making sure the networking code worked, and building the communication library layer. It did not address the problem that each node in the cluster is an independent system with a full Linux operating system to manage and maintain, making the clusters significantly more complex to use and administer than an equivalently powerful SMP system.

Most clusters need to be re-architected to address ease of use, system management, and supportability in order to deliver measurable productivity improvements. In addition, most clusters get different parts of the cluster stack from several different suppliers so customers face the additional challenge of who to turn to for support when problems occur. Second-generation clusters architected from the ground up to be "commercial-grade" do not face any of these issues, benefiting both commercial and non-commercial users.

For example, the University of Arizona Lunar and Planetary Laboratory (LPL) chose a second-generation cluster and has found that it is easy to use and manage while giving them the compute power they need. The Lab conducts astrophysical research, studying the physics of the Sun, planetary interiors and the behavior of planetary atmospheres and their work has been critical to many successful NASA programs. As a result of choosing an easy to use second-generation cluster, LPL compute resources have increased by a factor of roughly 15 and the Lab is now able to calculate an entire planet's atmosphere in about two weeks compared to the months required previously.

Before their new cluster, though, the information technology (IT) infrastructure that LPL used was very difficult to maintain. The team also wanted to make it easier to share idle resources among the research groups. However, their IT infrastructure was completely de-centralized and every research group had its own set of individual machines, making data sharing a chore.

The complexities and inefficiencies of this environment resulted in the scientific team taking months to calculate a planet's atmosphere at all the required altitudes, impacting both the quality and time-to-publication of research. Even without knowing the technical details differentiating first- and second- generation architectures, LPL knew it needed a system where everything was centralized and extremely easy to manage. The organization's goals required a solution that "took the pain out of clustering."

Their new, re-architected cluster makes this possible partly because second-generation architectures deliver a cluster environment that makes the complexity invisible to users. During normal usage, it has an "appliance like" level of simplicity while preserving system access that is transparent to administrators and advanced users when desired.

In a necessarily simplified fashion, some key elements that are required to set up an easy to use and administered cluster, by creating the illusion of a single system, include:

- A stable, reliable and observable booting system.
- Mechanisms for initial provisioning and updates of all system elements.
- A consistency model for handling dynamic updates.
- A single point of monitoring and control, for both systems and jobs.
- A cluster-wide scheduler that complements the per-machine processes scheduler.
- A file system or other storage management that suits the application.

Some non-commercial cluster systems create a partial single system illusion by requiring network virtual memory or a consistent global file system, or implementing transparent process migration. However, these designs handle failure poorly because if any of the nodes fail the system must go through a time-consuming lock recovery process or even kill all processes related to the failed machine.

For organizations like LPL using a fully re-architected second-generation cluster with these design attributes, the clean virtualization model allows greater productivity through:

> Second-generation architectures deliver a cluster environment that makes the complexity invisible to users.

- **Ease of Use:** The entire cluster looks and behaves like a single Linux workstation, which provides a familiar environment for the majority of today's users and administrators, dramatically reducing the learning curve and day-to-day maintenance tasks.
- **Dynamic Provisioning:** The dynamic, in-memory provisioning of compute slaves completes in seconds (as opposed to tens of minutes with traditional clusters) and eliminates the possibility of version skew between nodes.
- **Enhanced Reliability:** Support for diskless nodes can reduce cluster acquisition costs, increase energy efficiency, and improve overall reliability by eliminating mechanical devices.
- **Reduction in Total Cost of Ownership:** With all the benefits of second-generation clusters combined—performance, utilization, reliability, flexibility, dynamic provisioning, ease of use, and a single point of command and control—customers have experienced both enhanced productivity and up to a tenfold reduction in operational expenses.

Meeting Critical Organizational Needs

The value of these productivity increases is particularly important in light of DARPA-sponsored research conducted by IDC in the Council on Competitiveness whitepapers that found upper management viewed HPC as a cost center rather than a strategic investment. The reports identified that ease of use, the difficulty and cost of hiring computational scientists to apply tools to scientific problems, and software compatibility issues were all major factors contributing to these beliefs. These factors underpin DARPA's Dr. Robert Graybill's observation that "ease of use is as important, if not more important than compute capability."[1]

Eliminating complexity was a key driving factor in LPL's decision to opt for a second-generation cluster architecture for its 48-node Opteron-based HiPAS (High Performance Astrophysical Simulator) cluster. The simplicity of the environment meant that after about an hour of training 90% of the 30 users were up and running on the cluster.

The Lab's numerical calculations are usually run on several machines at once and the cluster has increased compute speed by at least a factor of 15.

> The simplicity of the environment meant that after about an hour of training 90% of the 30 users were up and running on the cluster.

This translates into their being able to handle larger problems, with more particles, covering a larger region of the solar system. In addition, the new facility has allowed the team to open up a new avenue of fluid dynamics research not previously possible and positioned LPL to further develop it's standing in the global astrophysics community.

Fortunately, low total cost of ownership makes clusters an option for even the most cost sensitive endeavors. In fact, one of the major reasons LPL was initially willing to consider an investment in HPC in the form of clusters is that the economics of clustering are irresistible. Just like LPL, many organizations find there is simply no other way to go financially. For $1 million you can harness well over 500 processors using leading edge AMD- or Intel-based systems. You cannot even purchase a hundred processors for that amount with SMP systems.

Standardization is an essential foundation for the cost savings portion of the equation. Clusters have become an increasingly mainstream solution due to the price/performance provided by high-volume, lower-cost commodity hardware components. In addition, there is a cost savings associated with using open source Linux software that allows manufacturers to amortize costs over multiple markets. Linux was already a familiar technology to LPL so deployment of a Linux cluster was an evolutionary rather than a revolutionary change.

Building a Better Cluster

If the combined benefits of second-generation cluster architecture are not sufficiently compelling to drive adoption

---

[1] Robert Graybill, speaking at the IDC HPC User Forum at Oak Ridge National Laboratory, September 26–28, 2005. Quoting from the "Council on Competitiveness Study of U.S. Industrial HPC Users" report, July 2004, sponsored by the Defense Advanced Research Projects Agency. Report by Earl Joseph, Addison Snell, and Christopher Willard, IDC.

of Linux cluster technology beyond academic and government circles and deeper into the commercial space, then a number of innovative developments that are on the horizon surely will.

In the near future, second-generation cluster architecture will enable users to cost-effectively manage clusters of clusters with multiple masters. They will deliver the same ease of use that they provide today, but with more sophisticated availability features, making them an even more attractive proposition to commercial enterprises. In addition, multiple masters that are able to communicate and share workloads with each other during peak demand, and are able to take direction from Grid management software, will provide an unprecedented level of increased productivity.

By their sheer size, large-scale clusters are likely to encounter frequent failures and so require a design that can handle node failures while providing continuity of the application service. Key features that will deliver an appliance like HPC environment that simply works are:

- Policy driven self-healing operations with automated fault detection and recovery.
- Seamless failover and job recovery.
- Support for virtual compute nodes.

Clusters that can expand and contract on demand to deliver compute resources when they are needed, in real time, without hardware boundaries or the need for manual intervention are the real key to mainstream adoption of Linux clustering.

Beyond clusters, though, there are additional developments on the horizon related to Grids *with* clusters that will

> **Grids are attractive because very little additional money is required for extra hardware when deploying, leaving most of the budget available for buying software applications.**

also speed adoption of HPC. Many HPC users explore Grids as a way to improve compute performance. Grids are attractive because very little additional money is required for extra hardware when deploying, leaving most of the budget available for buying software applications. And provided you can use a distributed environment where you update and maintain individual machines, this is a great option.

Grid computing differs from cluster computing by having separate administrative domains over a wide area—organization and machines cooperating through agreed-upon protocols. Grid tools focus on protocols for interaction, while cluster tools focus on booting, provisioning, controlling and monitoring sets of machines. Ideally a cluster system simplifies the details of operating many machines to the effort of managing a single system. The system should implement a version consistently model, allowing applications to be installed once and run on any machine, automatically handling updates and insuring that the application run identically on any machine in the cluster.

Having a specified, defined system consistency model simplifies many tasks: an application's communication must only be self-consistent. Differences in the OS kernel, libraries, and even library link order can change the behavior and results of an application. A cluster system is responsible for controlling potentially multiple versions of the application and maintaining a consistent execution environment.

Grid tools focus on having machines successfully interact, even when the libraries, operating systems, and instruction set architectures differ. This requires great attention to protocols and mechanisms that are backward- and forward-compatible, and constrains applications to use carefully defined, standardized interfaces.

The Future of HPC

One method of gaining greater traction of HPC is to take the advantages of both concepts and manage large pools of servers regardless of location. The catch phrase of Service-Oriented Architecture (SOA) would be a reality in this way—a small set of simple and ubiquitous interfaces would connect to multiple software agents that would be universally available for any and all providers and consumers.

Historically organizations have looked to DCOM or Object Request Brokers (ORBs) based on the CORBA specification for SOA-like behavior. However, with the strong technical development over the last several years in HPC, HPC-based SOA would offer software characteristics attractive to commercial enterprises: reliability, well-tested production environments, experienced support staff, etc, on a lower cost Linux platform with incredible ease of use. At the same time, the advanced capabilities of HPC would remove several layers of SOA complexity, both in integration and fewer interfaces.

Global Grid Forum's (GGF) Open Grid Services Architecture (OGSA) is already working on using Grids as a way to implement SOA. However, tying in the additional features of second-generation clusters will provide an even greater benefit to organizations seeking greater productivity.

Another way to gain greater traction for HPC is to focus on optimizing virtualization to a higher level and removing some of the complexity associated with using clusters. One way to accomplish this is to virtualize at the process level, creating a single virtual process space across a set of machines. This provides the application user with an unchanged model for running and controlling an application, and gives the application programmer with an already understood process management model. Important elements to implement this type of cluster being used by some second-generation clusters are:

- A controlled, reliable booting system.
- A system to provision all some or all elements of the running system.
- From the boot master.
- Diagnosibliity for failures from a single point.

Refining second-generation boot systems would take virtualization a step further. Specifically, this requires:

- Developing a program for hardware reporting at the PXE level, and establishing a *de facto* community standard for the reporting functionality.
- Creating new software and extending existing software for diagnostic reporting in the PXE environment.
- Extending the existing PXE server to understand the reporting format and implementing a general system to select an appropriate kernel and driver set from elements installed in the standard location.

In parallel with these activities, it is worth investigating whether the second-generation clusters might be suitable as host operating systems for virtualized guest operating systems. A future re-designed cluster should be able to virtualize at both the process and OS levels. If correctly implemented, it might also simultaneously be able to support both current process models, which requires a process to initiate process migration itself, and transparent process migration by migrating entire virtual machines (VMs).

Migration of VMs is initially very appealing, until the implications are considered. VMs do not exist in isolation. They have network connections to the outside world, file connections to local storage, and device drivers expecting to communicate with physical hardware. It is possible, although not trivial, to continue network connections with an immediate migration. It is difficult to maintain a connection to storage that was previously directly attached, but is now remote. And hardware devices are usually impossible to emulate, especially in the case of errors. However, if VM migration is successful, it will allow a level of virtualization that will significantly increase the level of adoption of HPC technology.

If virtual machine migration is successful, it will allow a level of virtualization that will significantly increase the level of adoption of HPC technology.

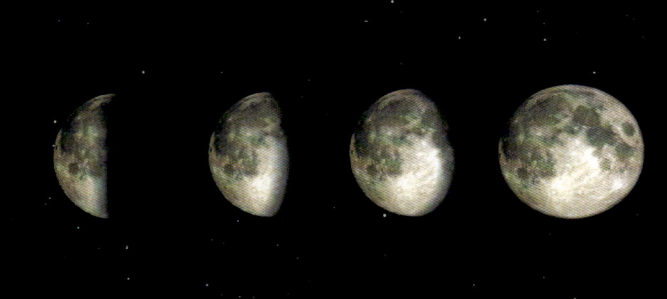

functionality

Standards Landscape in Service-Oriented Grids

Ravi Subramaniam
INTEL CORPORATION

Standards have played an important role in many aspects of human endeavor through the ages, and have been one of the foundations for many technology revolutions. They appear in nearly every facet of our daily lives, from manufacturing and transportation, to social systems and language. Though standards are not perfect, and at first may seem like an impediment to progress, they are in fact an essential part of innovation. Standards help us agree on how to talk about and build well-understood and reliable systems, which in turn serve as the platform for further innovations at the next higher level of functionality. Standards are also the vehicle for driving interoperability, which allows us to build large systems from smaller components or subsystems. In the field of Grid computing, standards are integral to the paradigm's adoption, proliferation, and the realization of its true potential.

Design Paradigms and their Relationship to Standards

As depicted in Figure 1, there are multiple paradigms or dimensions that may apply either singly or in combination to a particular solution. Since standards serve to normalize and formalize various aspects of knowledge, standardization is an activity that is relevant to each of these paradigms. Standards can take many forms, from protocols to methodology to modes of usage. However, it is important to place standards in the right perspective with respect to all the dimensions that converge in a solution. In this discussion, our focus is on Grid organization; usage paradigms (like high-performance, utility, and on-demand); Service-Oriented Architectures (SOA); the Web Services (WS) technology paradigm; and a loosely coupled implementation approach.

Grid, SOA, and Standards

A Grid (in distributed computing) can be architected and implemented in many ways. This is apparent from the many solutions that are available in the market today. Recently, there is an increased motivation to use SOA as the architectural paradigm to describe Grids. The advantages of SOA applied to Grid are many, but some of the most important are the ability to easily change implemented solutions (agility), increased reusability of implementation components, and interoperability of solutions from multiple sources.

There are many sets of standards for realizing SOA, but the most widely used and accepted is the *Web Services* (WS) family. The underpinning of WS standards is a representation and description language known as the eXtended Markup Language (XML). The relationship of Grid, SOA, WS and XML is shown in Figure 2. Often these terms are used very loosely and without qualification. For example, Grids are assumed to be service oriented, and SOA is taken to be synonymous with Web Services. For clarity and precision, the confluence of these concepts should be called *Service-Oriented Grids with Web Services on XML*. This is the topic of discussion for the rest of this article.

The Standards Landscape

Most standards efforts (especially in the Web Services and Service-Oriented Grid communities) have focused on standardizing a set of required services, with separate threads of activity centered on each specific service in isolation, often without reference to other

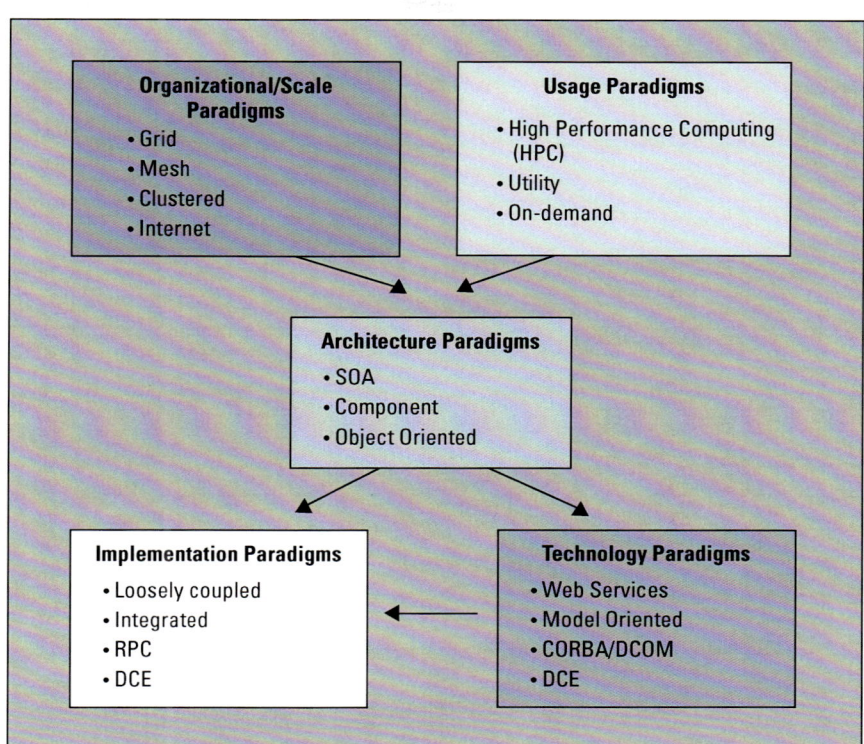

Figure 1. Standards—Inter-relationship of Paradigms in a Solution

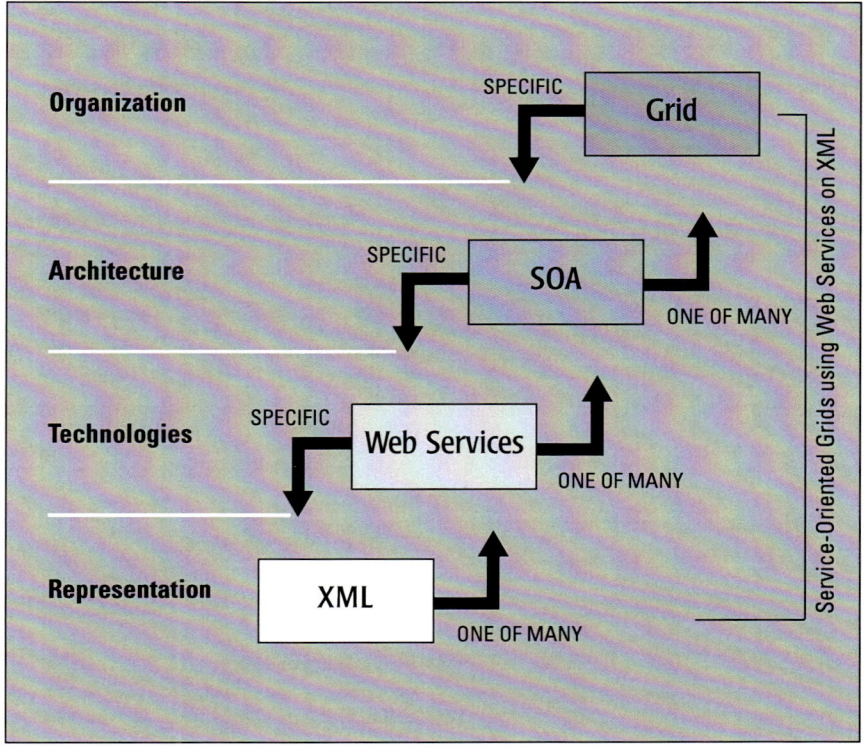

Figure 2. Service-Oriented Grids using Web Services on XML

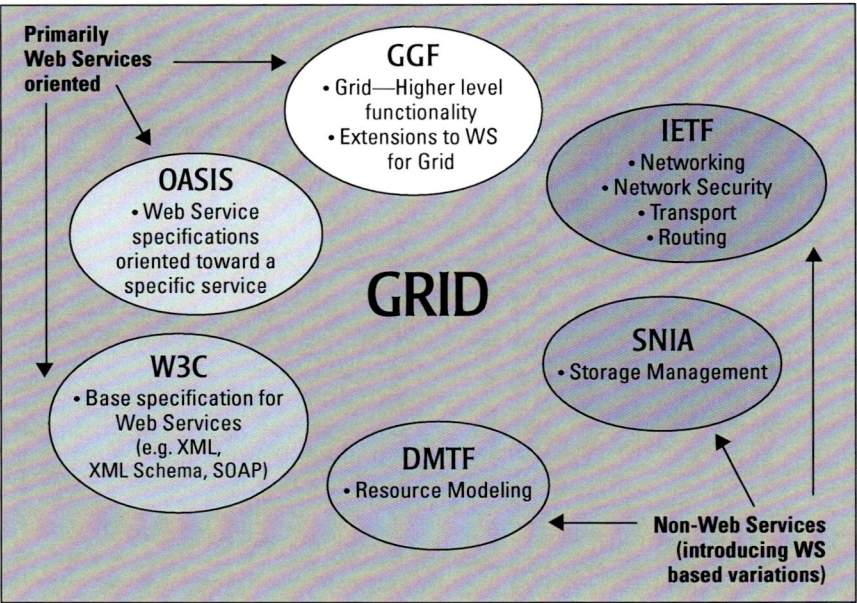

Figure 3. Standards Development Organizations (SDOs)

services. This has led to a rather large number of "granular" (small, focused) standards.

Organization: Standardization efforts have evolved in multiple *standards development organizations* (SDOs). Some of the key SDOs in the Grid and WS space are the Global Grid Forum (GGF), the World Wide Web Consortium (W3C), the Distributed Management Task Force (DMTF), the Organization for the Advancement of Structured Information Standards (OASIS), the Internet Engineering Task Force (IETF), and the Storage Networking Industry Association (SNIA). These are shown in Figure 3. Furthermore, companies or other groups with vested interests have also formed private consortia or other such multi-lateral groups to standardize services. These private parties do not always share their standards publicly, but in some cases they do, in either a fee-based or royalty-free manner. On the other hand, many SDOs have provisions in their charter to openly disclose their standards and participants in the development of these standards are required to make their contributed intellectual property available fee and/or royalty free. These publicly available standards, whether from SDOs or private consortia, are known as *open standards*. The adoption and proliferation of open standards are critical to bring multiple parties to participate in the realization of Grid(s).

For the most part, individual SDOs have charters that address specific aspects of the larger standards landscape for SOA, Web Services, and Grid. In some cases, the SDOs and private consortia have overlapping charters, but minimal mutual interaction. This has led to standards that are duplications, or at worst, in direct conflict with one another. One example of this is the WS-Distributed Management (WSDM) specification developed in OASIS, versus the WS-Management (WS-Man) specification developed by a private consortium. Experience in attempting to implement these standards as coherent solutions has made it apparent that the disjointed nature of standards development does not support interoperable solutions and easy composition of Grid implementations. To address this suboptimal situation, there has recently been increased effort to coordinate standards activities early in their development so results are synergistic and non-redundant. For example, this trend can be seen in the efforts of the "Standards Collaboration on networked Resources Management" (SCRM) working group in the GGF. Another example is refactoring of the Open Grid Services Infrastructure (OGSI) specification into a new set of specifications known as WS-Resource Framework (WS-RF) that are closer to the model and form of Web Services. The OGSI effort was divested in the GGF, and the activity moved to OASIS where a new technical committee was formed to develop WS-RF. This also led to the introduction of "state-full entities" that can be accessed and operated on within a Web Service model. Prior to this, Web Services had assumed no explicit state shared between the consumer and provider of a service. A coordinated approach allows compatibility with the implementations and tooling that were implemented using the stateless WS model, while enabling management of shared state when necessary.

Architecture and Reference Model: The "standards soup" of specification acronyms is nauseating for all but the hardiest standards advocate. It is often very difficult for developers to determine which are the most applicable, which are most likely to be widely adopted, and which are interoperable with each other. Users need a widely accepted formal framework to help them understand and describe all the standardized services and their interplay. This has motivated the development of *standard architectures and reference models.* Several SDOs have started defining such standard architectures, reference models or both within their own domain or charter. Examples of architecture standards include Open Grid Services Architecture (OGSA) in the GGF, the Utility Computing Reference Model in the DMTF, and the Service Oriented Architecture Reference Model (SOA-RM) in OASIS.

Profiles: One approach to promoting interoperable implementations for a set of protocols is to define a "profile" that specifies the protocols, the requirements on the protocols, and any extensions and clarifications that are necessary to ensure that implementations that adhere to the profile are interoperable. The profiles are usually fairly generic and focused on message interoperability. A primary organization working on interoperability profiles is the Web Services Interoperability Organization (WS-I). The WS-I is working initially on a Basic Profile focused on interoperability in the transport, invocation, and description of Web Services, and a Basic Security Profile focused on the interoperability for WS-Security standards. Other profile activities related to extensions of the WS-I profiles to Grids is being done in the OGSA work group of the GGF. Fortunately for both vendors and users, these profiles seems to be converging to a relatively small set that can provide practical guidance on how to ensure interoperability in common operational scenarios.

The plethora of specifications related to Grid requires that developers carefully assess which ones apply in the domain and scope of their particular

> **In the field of Grid computing, standards are integral to the paradigm's adoption, proliferation, and the realization of its true potential.**

implementation. Many of the standards, especially in Web Services space, are not unique to Grid architectures, but readily apply to Grid implementations that want to leverage SOA. To assist developers in selecting the right standards, there are ongoing industry efforts on standards reconciliation, standard architecture definitions and reference models, interoperability profiles, and best practices and tools. By understanding these approaches and working with vendors that define and adhere to these standards, an IT practitioner can successfully navigate this potentially confusing standards landscape.

Open Issues, Future Work, and a Call to Action

As briefly alluded to above, there are areas of standardization that are less developed at the present time, and where significant focus by SDOs could help advance the application and adoption of Grid technology substantially. Specifically, we need:

- A set of canonical (i.e., most common and representative) use cases and usage scenarios that apply to both industry and scientific communities from which standards functional requirements, interface definitions, and profiles can be derived.
- A clear definition of how a Grid infrastructure should represent, control, and manage local and distributed state (i.e., current operational status, conditions, configurations, etc.) of individual platforms and applications. Standards to identify the relevant parameters of state and the protocols to access and manipulate state have to be reconciled.
- A distributed management framework, i.e., standard definitions of resource and management functions and protocols that can operate remotely over the Internet and across heterogeneous platforms. Currently the standards available are inconsistent or duplications that partition the solution space into disjoint sets. The community should work to develop a single consistent framework, or at least rationalize and reconcile the disparate standards.
- Security, which is important to promote cross-boundary interactions on the Grid. This requires a consistent view and unified approach to distributed security. Furthermore, a clear articulation of the essential support in a ubiquitous Grid infrastructure is required.

productivity

The Scalable Enterprise Architecture: A Practical Underpinning for Grid Computing

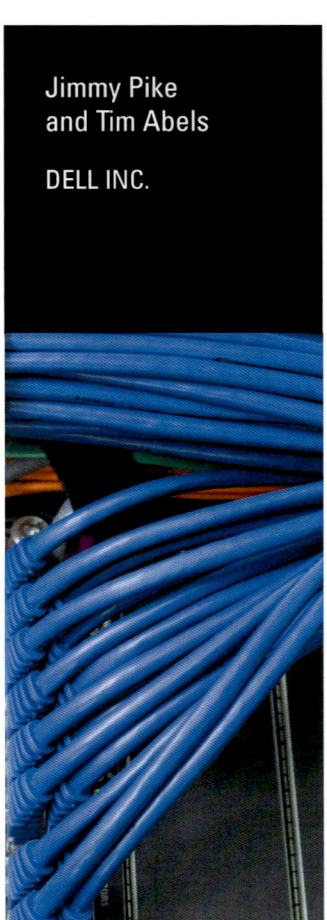

Jimmy Pike
and Tim Abels

DELL INC.

Computing architectures are expected to evolve to Grid computing, which extends clustering and distributed computing across multiple company resources. Grid computing can be thought of as a parallel and distributed computing system that allows computing resources to be aggregated and shared across administrative domains based on requirements such as quality of service.

This approach addresses three major challenges that IT organizations face. They need to improve utilization of their servers and scale cost effectively to meet increasing demands on limited IT resources. They also need to simplify day-to-day operational tasks such as deploying new systems, managing change, maintaining hardware and software security, and increasing the productivity of IT staff. In the scalable enterprise, server utilization is improved through consolidation, virtualization, and increased uptime. IT can scale cost-effectively using building blocks of standards-based infrastructure. Finally, systems management standardization initiatives will help to simplify operations through integrated, automated systems management.

Grid computing can alleviate many of the compatibility issues associated with proprietary architectures and can deliver revolutionary results when based on virtualization and industry standards. The key enabler of Grid computing is standardization. Grid environments require distributed resources to be managed and operated as a single entity, even when they are physically implemented with complex resource and business requirements.

This article presents the scalable enterprise reference architecture, which serves as a practical underpinning for Grid computing. The architecture includes a general, standards-based model that is flexible and pragmatic. This model serves as a taxonomy that IT technologists can use to develop their environments.

Scalable Enterprise Architecture

The model depicted in Figure 1 is an open standards-based architecture that applies to current data centers and emerging Grid computing. The model functions as a closed-loop management system. A standardized mapping layer provides the foundation of future systems by mapping the relationships of the following software and hardware resources to specific end services:

- Standard servers, fabrics, and storage subsystems.
- Applications and operating systems.
- Systems management software.
- Application management software.

Additional software layers provide the monitoring, operational policies, controls, and services required for the highly automated environment envisioned in Grid computing. The following sections briefly describe each of the elements shown in Figure 1.

Standard Servers, Storage, and Fabrics

These standard platforms are the hardware resources that can be applied to a Grid computing problem or service. The scalable enterprise model is based on hardware components accepted by the industry as nonproprietary.

Servers

In this model, industry standard servers are defined as Intel® x86 instruction set machines running Microsoft® Windows® or Linux. These servers are also defined with 1-to-4 CPU "sockets" that can accommodate single or multicore CPUs. Because most industry development and innovation is occurring on these platforms, it is important to carefully consider whether alternative proprietary platforms are the best choice as smooth integration becomes increasingly difficult.

Storage

In the scalable enterprise architecture, standard storage is sharable—either network-attached storage (NAS) or storage-area networks (SANs). Internal or direct-attached storage is minimized. Storage is perhaps the most mature subsystem in the scalable enterprise because key concepts such as RAID, LUNs, and LUN remapping are well established. Going forward, the industry should standardize proprietary man-

Why are 1-to-4 Socket Servers Expected to Dominate?

Larger servers with more than four sockets are expensive, generally require nonstandard components, and have very long development cycles. Furthermore, the introduction of dual-core processors with two CPU cores in a single processor enables higher-density configurations. Two CPU cores can be installed in each socket of an industry-standard 1- to 4 socket server. Thus, 2- or 4-socket, industry-standard servers can be equipped with 4 and 8 CPU cores. In the future, multicore processors with more than two CPU cores per processor will allow even higher processor densities on 1- to 4-socket servers. This trend is expected to limit the need for larger servers with more than 4 CPU sockets.

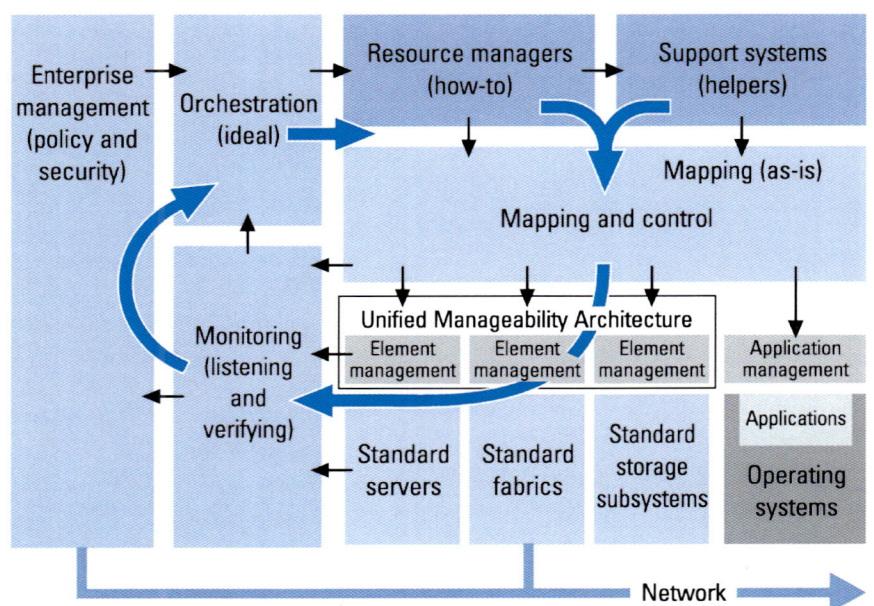

Figure 1. Scalable Enterprise Architecture

agement packages to enable flexible and interoperable storage solutions.

Fabrics

Today, different fabric technologies are preferred for compute, storage, and control functions in the overall system. There are two technologies that are prime candidates for a converged fabric: Infiniband and the emerging 10-gigabit (Gb) Ethernet over copper, with additional capabilities such as TCP offload engine (TOE) and Remote Direct Memory Access (RDMA). However, it remains to be seen if a truly converged fabric will be widely adopted. For now, the real consideration for selecting fabrics should be their impact on the ability to interact with other assets in the Grid and, most important, the applicability of management software as it fits into a specific company's management paradigm.

Systems Management Software

This layer consists of the software required to manage specific servers, storage subsystems, and fabrics. It performs all aspects of platform management, from powering up and configuration through provisioning and execution.

Currently, servers, storage, and fabrics each require specific management tools. However, Dell believes that all managed nodes will eventually support the operations defined by the Systems Management Architecture for Server Hardware (SMASH, http://www.dmtf.org/standards/smash) command line interface standard. SMASH enables a common set of systems management operations for all managed nodes. Specific management tools will only be required for features unique to servers, storage, or fabrics.

Applications and Operating Systems

These are the applications, services, and operating systems required to complete

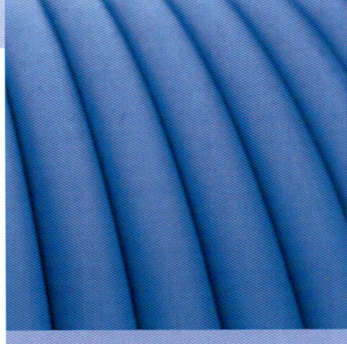

Grid computing can alleviate many of the compatibility issues associated with proprietary architectures and can deliver revolutionary results when based on virtualization and industry standards.

end-user tasks. The operating system provides access to resources and is the interface between applications and the rest of the system. As Grid computing evolves, operating systems are likely to branch into application-facing operating systems that are closely aligned with applications and infrastructure-facing operating systems that focus on internal operations. Ever-greater distinctions will emerge as server virtualization matures. Similarly, applications may branch into heavily I/O-dependent applications reprovisioned and managed in clusters, and the remaining applications reprovisioned and managed as virtual machines (VMs).

Mapping and Control

Mapping and control is pivotal to the architecture, because it manages the relationships between all resources. Figure 2 presents its major components:

- **Scalable Enterprise Resource Directory (SERD)**—Contains details of each relationship. Although largely undeveloped today, emerging configuration and management databases address some of the required information.
- **Raw Resource Pool**—A collection of objects describing available resources. An object can represent a single item such as an application, or a collection of objects such as a server with a CPU, memory, and host bus adapter (HBA).
- **Logical Resource Pool**—A collection of "logical" objects that are available, but are not bound to anything except, in some cases, other logical objects. The pool may include virtual devices and machines.
- **Physical and Logical Groups**—Optional groupings of physical or logical resources such as two physical servers that are the members of a high-availability computing cluster, or several virtual machines that are members of a virtual cluster.
- **Dynamic Bindings**—Dynamic bindings describe relationships that can be modified to meet business policies. For example, a virtual application object made up of a virtual machine with a guest operating system, agents, and an application may be bound to an object representing a physical server. If the utilization threshold defined in a service-level agreement is exceeded, the application can be bound to a new physical server.

Resource Managers

Resource managers establish relationships that govern how resources are used and, ideally, supply the mapping information stored in the SERD. A resource manager allocates and manages server, network, storage, operating system, and applications resources. The

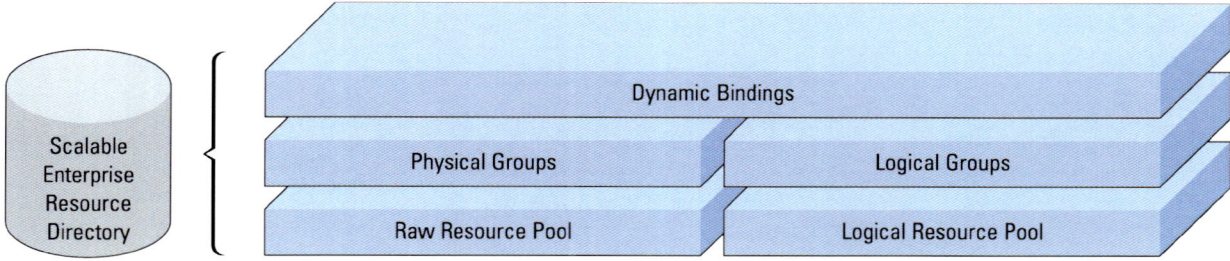

Figure 2. Mapping and Control Layer

orchestration layer's provisioning functions directly impacts resource managers.

Support Systems

Support systems provide one-time functions outside of the ongoing monitor-manage-orchestrate heartbeat of enterprise management. These self-contained utilities help the orchestration and resource managers control system-wide behavior. The utilities include backup, recovery, provisioning, updates, and help-desk support. A common framework for support systems is emerging in help-desk trouble ticketing systems and service-provider interfaces.

Monitoring (Listening/Verifying)

The monitoring software "listens" by gathering operational data describing current hardware and software behavior. This data is provided by authoritative agents from each virtual and physical resource. Today, there are many of these agents that handle tasks such as deployment, backups, virtualization, out-of-band communication, and remote access. Monitoring software "verifies" by analyzing the data to determine if operations are aligned with current policies.

Enterprise Management Framework (EMF)

The EMF provides a unified operational management view. Today's EMFs are typically higher-order management packages, although many do not include an overall policy mechanism. They provide tools that consolidate systems management data, help to interpret monitoring information, and manage workflow across resource managers. The EMF also tracks availability and response-time metrics as part of managing service-level agreements, and arbitrates resource adjustments based on business priorities.

Orchestration

Orchestration is a control level introduced by the Gartner Group as part of the emerging modern IT infrastructure. Orchestration combines operational data from the monitoring function and policy information from the EMF to describe how resources should be connected for optimal operation. A current example of the orchestration function is a manual, nonstandard script that corrects a specific operational problem. Going forward, the emerging Business Process Execution Language (BPEL) may provide a standards-based platform for the orchestration function. BPEL is a Service-Oriented Architecture (SOA) and integration platform for all operations, resource managers, and support systems.

Conclusion

Under the scalable enterprise architecture, highly automated processes enable IT managers to quickly and cost effectively redeploy IT assets to meet business requirements. The architecture's greatest strength lies in its reliance on standards-based hardware and software components. Standardization helps drive a competitive market with multiple vendors providing interoperable software tools. The competition enhances innovation and lowers prices. Standardization also helps ensure that future software tools are compatible with today's customer investments. Standards-based software, combined with standardized servers, storage systems, and switched fabrics, enables the flexible and scalable underpinning for future Grid computing environments.

© 2005 Dell Inc. All rights reserved.

Grid computing can alleviate many compatibility issues associated with proprietary architectures and deliver revolutionary results when based on virtualization and industry standards.

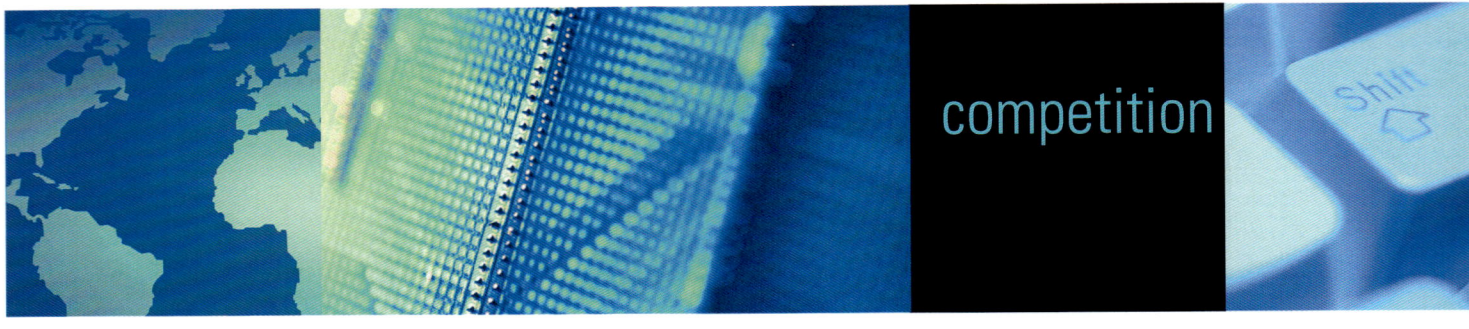

Get Started with Grid for a Competitive Advantage

Imagine if a business could increase employee productivity; analyze an investment portfolio in minutes, rather than hours; reduce design time while reducing instances of defects; unite a research team with others around the world . . . the possibilities are endless with Grid computing.

Grids are for organizations of all sizes—from large Fortune 500 corporations to small businesses. Grids can be used in a simple, homogeneous environment or across a range of heterogeneous systems and business functions.

Grid implementations are as varied as the organizations that use them. Some are large and complex, and others are small and simple. Many choose to start small, launching their Grid within a single department. As the value of the Grid is realized, the function and sophistication can be expanded to the enterprise.

Grid computing produces countless benefits, including faster results supporting better decision making, improved productivity, enhanced customer service, and faster time to market, all of which lead to competitive advantage. These benefits fall into three key categories of business value: accelerating business processes and time to market, improving collaboration, and increasing business agility and productivity.

Sherry Brewer
and Rob Vrablik

IBM

Accelerate Business Processes and Time to Market

In a typical IT environment, an application runs on a specified server, limiting available compute resources. Grid computing can remove the boundaries between applications and servers, virtualizing the infrastructure. A layer of middleware, typically called a scheduler, dispatches workload to a pool of Grid nodes. The scheduler allocates nodes automatically to an application based on business rule priorities.

In a Grid environment, benefits beyond scheduling can be gained by running concurrent instances of an application or parallelizing an application. Breaking a compute-intensive application into smaller tasks that can be run in parallel under the scheduler's management can generate results far more rapidly and accurately than in conventional computing environments.

Provisioning and orchestration middleware can be added to complement the scheduler. Provisioning middleware communicates with the scheduler to recognize when an application in a Grid needs more resources or is finished with a resource and dynamically allocates these resources to other applications. Orchestration monitors and analyzes resources in the enterprise and ensures resources are available to meet service levels. As needed the orchestrator will add and remove resources from the Grid. Orchestration also prevents the Grid or any other application from acquiring too many resources and putting other workloads in jeopardy.

An example of Grid computing accelerating time to market is the experience of Magna Steyr Fahrzeugtechnik AG & Co. KG (Magna Steyr), which provides specialized technical services to automobile manufacturers such as DaimlerChrysler and BMW. A Grid solution helped Magna Steyr improve the business processes associated with its automobile parts design. Clash analysis is used by engineers to detect when there are interferences between parts in the product design, which may cause a negative reaction. This important process had been taking 72 hours to run and therefore only performed at the end of the design cycle. Using Grid technology reduced the processing time from 72 hours to four hours. Now the analysis runs nightly, enabling timely changes to the design. Magna Steyr improved the quality of their parts and dramatically improved time to market, an obvious competitive advantage.

Enhance Collaboration

As businesses grow and evolve it becomes more challenging to locate, access, and integrate data. An information Grid provides users a unified view

Choosing the Right Partner

Because emerging Grid standards are not tied to any platform or type of system, they are paving the way to make Grid computing a reality for most businesses. Industry groups, supported by IBM and other leading vendors, are developing common standards by which any machine in any type of network can communicate and share its resources with other systems.

This makes choosing a partner all the more important—because a business needs not only a Grid, but also an end-to-end solution, with support from inception to completion.

When selecting a Grid partner, look for an organization that can demonstrate experience and success guiding customers through Grid implementations.

Ensure the partner has skilled industry experts as well as knowledgeable Grid architects to help layout a roadmap right for you.

Look closely at the potential partner's products and their supporting ecosystem to ensure they have access to the best products and solutions available in the industry.

Grid computing can remove the boundaries between applications and servers, virtualizing the infrastructure.

More specifics on some of IBM's Grid offerings can be found at: www.ibm.com/grid/solutions.

of the data enabling increased levels of collaboration and business insight previously impossible.

Three component layers comprise an information Grid: Access virtualization, file system virtualization, and physical storage virtualization. Any layer or combination of layers can be implemented to realize business value. The more layers of an information Grid implemented, the greater the value typically realized by an enterprise.

Access virtualization uses middleware for integrated access to business information across and beyond the enterprise. It reaches into multiple data sources—such as Oracle databases, Microsoft spreadsheets, and the Web—regardless of system vendor, data format, or operating environment. Users can access, manipulate, and integrate diverse, distributed, and real-time data as if that information were contained in a single source. These virtualization functions are performed via services using the principles of Service-Oriented Architecture. File system virtualization addresses heterogeneous file systems including replication and caching functions. Physical storage virtualization provides a consolidated view of multi-vendor storage.

By unifying information, organizations can increase employee productivity, enhance customer service, and quickly respond to changing business requirements, capitalizing on market opportunities and reacting to competitive threats.

Increase Business Agility and Productivity

To remain competitive, companies need an infrastructure that can dynamically adapt to fluctuating business environments, efficiently and cost effectively utilize resources, and minimize risk—again, Grid is a key element.

Grids offer a more intelligent way to manage information technology assets. A manufacturer would not let 40 percent of its assembly plants stand idle, nor would a hotel chain let 75 percent of its rooms sit empty-yet many companies are only using about 15 percent of their computing resources. Taking advantage of Grid technology can improve resource utilization and reduce costs.

Grid can enable higher levels of business resiliency. In a Grid environment with multiple applications running across multiple types of IT resources, the Grid can determine which resources the applications will use based on policies that are set for the applications. Suppose your top priority application is running on a set of resources and those resources go down, and the system crashes. The Grid scheduler recognizes a node has failed and attempts to immediately restart the application on another set of IT resources. If other resources are not available, the scheduler will end lesser priority jobs and restart the higher priority job on the freed resources. The halted jobs will be started again when resources are available. This process enables an organization to better manage business priorities and meet service level agreements.

The powerful benefits of Grid computing can be realized because of open standards and strong industry adoption. Grid middleware is available from many vendors, open source projects, and even written by customers. Since Grids are frequently built from heterogeneous collections of resources it is very valuable to be able to "mix and match" middleware from various sources to build specific solutions. Open standards like GGF OGSA, OASIS Web Services, and management standards help define interoperable interfaces and protocols that make this type of solution integration possible.

Getting Started

The first step to getting started with Grid is to determine the scope of your initiative. Will you begin with a large, complex Grid implementation, or a smaller, simple one? Factors to consider include:

- The problem to be solved. Can you realize business benefit and demonstrate success with a simple compute

> Grids offer a more intelligent way to manage information technology assets and enable higher levels of business resiliency.

Grid or information Grid, or do you need a more sophisticated solution immediately?
- Your company's political environment. Will resource sharing be accepted initially or will demonstrated success be needed to prove the concept?
- The amount of risk you are able to take.
- Your staff's skills.

If you need assistance scoping your project or laying out a plan, look for an experienced partner like IBM to walk you through the steps.

If your environment permits you to consider a stepwise approach that minimizes risk and allows for early benefits to be achieved, the following suggested steps may help you plan your Grid journey:

1. Select a single application that needs to be accelerated to improve business results.
2. Consider an integrated offering such as the IBM® Grid and Grow™ Offering.
   a. This offering is a quick and easy way to get started with Grid computing. It packages hardware, as well as industry-leading IBM and business partner scheduling middleware, along with a "get started" services package to help first-time Grid customers maximize the benefits of Grid computing at a low-cost entry point.
   b. Merchandise the business and financial benefits of the initial project and gain buy-in from others in the organization to expand.
3. Expand your Grid to multiple applications that need Grid computing to speed results
4. Apply Grid computing to information and data resources: virtualize data access using middleware such as Websphere Information Integrator to provide a unified view of data.
5. Extend the Grid across the enterprise.

The benefits of Grid computing can be extensive. Whether your primary need is to help improve information exchange, speed of computing, or both, beginning the Grid journey today can help your company gain the flexibility and productivity necessary to gain a competitive advantage.

By unifying information, organizations can increase employee productivity, enhance customer service, and quickly respond to changing business requirements, capitalizing on market opportunities and reacting to competitive threats.

SOAs and Grid Computing—A New Generation of Middleware for Grid-enabled Data Centers

Heinz J. Schwarz

SUN MICROSYSTEMS, INC.

Cluster and Grid computing are concerned with distributing compute jobs across disparate resources. Grid middleware deals with the connection between those distributed resources across firewalls and organizational boundaries. Service-Oriented Architectures (SOAs) are concerned with dynamic ways to model business processes—by connecting reusable components and integrating existing applications. The concept of SOA Grids combines these two concepts by using clusters and Grids as deployment platforms for SOAs, with middleware that takes advantage of the specific features of Grid resources relative to the requirements of specific SOA components. This article discusses the interaction between those two concepts.

Definitions and Fundamental Technology

Definitions of Cluster and Grid Infrastructures

We define, for the purposes of this article, a cluster as a collection of independent, homogeneous computational entities that are located in physical proximity, controlled by a single resource scheduler. A Grid is defined as a collection of multiple resources that can be inhomogeneous, managed by multiple local resource schedulers and located either in physical proximity or remotely connected. A Grid, however, allows access to its resources through a singular interface and provides user level code access to computational, data, visualization, or other resources.

Definitions of Service-Oriented Architectures

In a very broad and general definition, "a service-oriented architecture is essentially a collection of services. These services communicate with each other. The communication can involve either simple data passing or it could involve two or more services coordinating some activity. Some means of connecting services to each other is needed"[1]. A service is "a unit of work done by a service provider to achieve desired end results for a service consumer"[2], and finally "both provider and consumer are roles played by software agents on behalf of their owners."

Elements of a SOA are usually:

- Services that implement a contained set of functionality, for example business logic or data operation, with a defined interface. The interface needs to be lightweight and implemented in a platform-independent fashion, for example using Java™ technology, Jini™ network technology, or XML.
- A registry where all services publish their interfaces and expose their functionality. The registry is used by services to locate provider services.
- Clients, which can be other services, that locate a provider service through published interfaces in the registry and connect using the interface. (Adapted from Singh et al, 2004[3])

As a general note of caution for the reader of this article, we like to emphasize that services can be fairly complex. The concept of an SOA does not require the service itself to be lightweight, only its interface should be highly portable and multi-platform capable to represent its service in service registries that can run on entirely different platforms than the service itself. A service can be implemented in a native method like C, FORTRAN, or even COBOL. Exposing the functionality of a native method program to a public interface is called wrapping and the connector between the program and its public interface is called a wrapper. If a service is implemented in an object-oriented language, an object can be invoked from its class, but a native method program could be started by the interface. One of the key advantages of SOA is the loose coupling of elements through

A cluster is a collection of independent, homogeneous, computational entities that are located in physical proximity, controlled by a single resource scheduler.

the interface publishing and subscription method and the registry. N consumer services can connect to M provider services, which makes SOA inherently scalable. Agents are roles of services. The great flexibility of SOA derives from the fact that a workflow can be modeled by a sequence of service invocations. Once wrappers and agents exists for the service that compromise a business process, changes to the business process can easily be implemented by restructuring the workflow of the service.

In a SOA architecture, we can model a workflow as a sequence of service invocations. For our purposes it is important to note that service providers can have different resource requirements. While some might need little memory, CPU cycles, or communication to other services, others might require large amounts of memory or low latency interconnects. We can describe these characteristics in a standardized way and attach the descriptions to an interface layer for the service provider. The interface layer also describes input and output parameters. The combination of the service provider and its interface layer is called a *service*. We can use an instantiation of the interface layer to represent the service in a service directory, which allows the agents of other services to locate and connect to the service. Thereby, we have all the essential elements of an SOA, namely services, a registry and clients that connect to and use the services.

---

[1] Service-oriented architecture (SOA) definition, online at http://www.service-architecture.com/web-services/articles/service-oriented_architecture_soa_definition.html

[2] He, Hao (2003), What is Service Oriented Architecture?, online at http://webservices.xml.com/pub/a/ws/2003/09/30/soa.html

[3] Singh, Inderjeet; Brydon, Sean; Murray, Greg; Ramachandran, Vijay Ramachandran; Violleau, Thierry; Stearns, Beth: (2004), Designing Web Services with the J2EE 1.4 Platform, Addison-Wesley, Boston

Cluster and Grid Infrastructure

Cluster Design Parameters

Clusters are usually built from homogeneous components. There are several good reasons why this makes sense. One set of reasons encompasses ease of administration, software distribution, and handling. It is better to have two clusters with homogeneous components within them, than one cluster with heterogeneous components. This becomes drastically evident if nodes are provisioned with boot images, which has several advantages, but requires a homogeneous setup. Another reason to keep nodes homogeneous is application mapping. Given that a datacenter provides resources with different architecture profiles, it makes

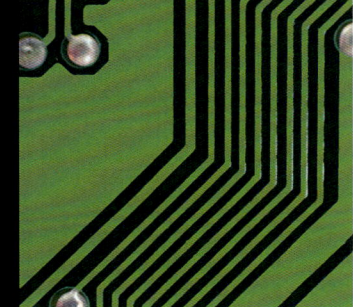

A Grid is a collection of multiple resources managed by multiple local resource schedulers and either located in physical proximity or remotely connected.

sense to allocate resources that most efficiently match the application requirements. If a cluster is built from homogeneous components, it is easy to characterize.

In order to use a cluster as a singular resource, it is common practice to define one master node that keeps track of available resources within the cluster with a Dynamic Resource Management (DRM) system like Condor, PBS, LSF or the Sun N1™ Grid Engine software[4]. Most of the common DRM systems collect jobs submitted for execution on the cluster in one or many queues and allocate resources to the job based on a policy or scoring mechanism. In the simplest form, a queue would just sequentially store and forward jobs (first-in, first out). More sophisticated systems allow policy management, advance reservation with backfilling and metering of queue and execution times per job, user, group and project. Every job is evaluated upon submission to the queue. This model creates a relatively static queue. Given a deep queue on one side and a collection of dynamic systems within a busy data center on the other side, many things can happen between initial job priority scoring and its actual allocation. Some of the traditional DRM features can be exposed to higher level management tools through the GRAM interface. The GRAM interface within the Globus Toolkit, "provides a single interface for requesting and using remote system resources for the execution of 'jobs.' The most common use of GRAM is remote job submission and control. It is designed to provide a uniform, flexible interface to job scheduling systems."[5] Higher-level services can build on GRAM to allow job scheduling across a Grid, as implemented for example in the Grid-lab resource management system[6].

Grid Design Parameters

According to our definition, we deal with Grid design parameters already when we have more than one cluster and wish to allocate jobs, or services, across multiple clusters. In reality, we could have different clusters with homogeneous nodes among them, yet heterogeneous characteristics between the clusters, and a collection of different sized single systems, for example some SMP servers with large memory. In order to be able to access resources within the Grid, the Grid offers a singular interface, which could be either a login node with a public IP address or a portal server. The login server needs to have access to some user information in order to authenticate a user and verify if that user is authorized to submit jobs to the Grid in general, or to some specific nodes. User authentication is also required to keep track of resource utilization by a user, for example for billing or bartering purposes. All of these features are required for a single system or cluster, yet the role of Grid middleware is to act as a gateway, hence handling the authentication, authorization and accounting process for all resources within the Grid. In some Grid environments, we find resource scheduling capability on a Grid level, which is desirable. However, many current Grid implementations require a user to select manually on which Grid resource the application should be scheduled. Resource scheduling at a Grid level requires a feature we will refer to as *meta scheduling*. Meta scheduling is a functionality that matches resource requests with re-

---

[4] The open source version is free and known as Grid Engine, online at http://gridengine.sunsource.net/download.html

[5] The Globus Toolkit, GRAM manual, online at http://www-unix.globus.org/toolkit/docs/3.2/gram/ws/

[6] Nabrzyski, Jarek, GRMS, online at http://www.globusworld.org/program/abstract.php?id=92

source availability of the Grid resources. We will now discuss how resource allocation and optimization in an SOA Grid can be based on economic principles and therefore optimized without user intervention much more dynamically than conventional, batch-oriented meta scheduling.

Definition of Cost

We shall from hereon refer to *cost* as a description for the consumption of any measurable resource. In order to increase efficiency within the Grid, we might have to deal with trade off decisions. Transferring data from one resource to another might make sense under the aspect that more appropriate CPU resources or storage resources can be used at the receiving resource, but we incur cost for the data transfer. Only if the aggregate benefit of a transfer from one Grid resource to another outweighs the cost, should it be done. Most current Grid middleware environments have no means to consider data transfer cost while making resource allocations, if resource allocations are made automatically or dynamically at all.

Implementation

In the previous sections of this paper we described design parameters for clusters and Grid infrastructures built from multiple clusters and other resources. We will now describe how we use economic models within an SOA framework to optimize how services are mapped to the various potential resources in a Grid environment.

Defining Fitness between Services and Platforms

We can measure and describe the resource requirements of service providers and hence determine the cost specific to different platforms. Cost, as defined earlier, is the amount of all measurable resources consumed by a

> A Grid allows access to its resources through a singular interface and provides user level code access to computational, data, visualization, or other resources.

service provider specific to a platform. The best fit between a service provider and a platform architecture will be a platform that incurs the lowest cost. This model allows us to measure the fit between a service provider and any given platform.

We can measure, for example, time, memory consumption, bandwidth consumption, and compute thread consumption on different platforms available within a Grid to determine the best fit. Some services might not need a lot of compute threads, but a lot of memory and communication. Implemented on a cluster, we would still have the same consumption of compute threads, but we'd then need additionally a lot of I/O threads to enable communication that, within an SMP system, is less time consuming. We do not correlate the cost of executing a service on a specific platform, and the cost of a platform executing a service. Instead, we create a scoring table that determines architecture match based on lowest overall resource utilization. This architecture related cost is static and therefore a fixed cost. The cost of a platform running a service, in contrast, is not fixed. It can depend on different factors and time.

Defining Cost of a Platform

Cost calculation for a platform consists of different types of costs, for example capital costs (acquisition, depreciation), operating costs (power, cooling, floor space, services etc.), connectivity costs (bandwidth of the connection, bandwidth related costs), maintenance, and so on. Most of these costs are fixed relative to utilization. A compute node running idle or at low utilization does consume measurably less power, but administration, depreciation, room, service, and many licenses are not utilization dependent. This leads to the quick conclusion that we could determine a fixed price for any utilization of that platform. But this is an overly simplistic model. Like seats on an airplane or vegetables in a grocery store, compute cycles are perishable goods. And just as the airline industry has developed a sophisticated costing model to increase utilization and therefore profitability, we argue that we need to apply a similar sophisticated model to balance the load among platforms within a Grid environment.

While cost incurred by depreciation, administration, provisioning, etc. are fixed, energy utilization actually varies not only with the level of utilization, but varies with a specific application. But for the purpose of our discussion, we assume fixed energy consumption. For the owner of the resource it would make sense to thrive for resource utilization close to or at capacity, as that would lower the price per unit of work. If it's reasonable to assume that the cluster will be utilized at 40% of capacity, the aggregate price of units (for example CPU/hour) for a period of time must equal at least the cost at that capacity. Incremental utilization would lead to marginal revenue and marginal revenue to marginal profit or return on investment. We define the point at which the aggregate of work units multiplied with the compensation yielded for the work units as the break even point. In the example, the break even point would be reached at 40% utilization. The break even point for a system can be calculated at a higher or lower utilization, based on a policy decision of the resource owner. Resource owners can implement more aggressive or less aggressive strategies to utilize their resources and maximize marginal revenue.

A cluster of 100 compute nodes with two CPUs or CPU cores per node can provide a total of 24*30*200 CPU/h, or work units, per month, 144,000 in total. If the total cost of this cluster was $25,000 for those 144,000 work units, and the target utilization was 60%, the break-even price per work unit would be (cost_period)/(work_units_period * target_utilization%), in our case $0.29. At 40% target utilization, the price would $0.43, whereas at 100% utilization it'd be only $0.17. One of the idiosyncrasies in market economies is that prices are not only a result of behavior; they have a control function which can drive behavior.

Different resources might have similar cost, yet different attractiveness. For example, comparing two clusters with similar acquisition costs purchased two years apart, the newer one likely features more memory and faster CPUs. In a conventional data center Grid environment, users would thrive to submit their jobs to the newer cluster, hence oversubscribing it, while underutilizing the older one. Traditional SOA architectures, on the other hand, would not differentiate between the two resources at all.

Policy Implementation

We established that cluster and Grid environments are dynamic, non-deterministic systems. We suggest that the connection between services should leverage and adjust to this dynamic system. Instead of determining invocation and utilization of services or mapping of service to a platform upfront, a rule-based framework, using a multi-agent system (MAS) control structure, can make these allocations *ad hoc* to optimize against a set of criteria at any given time. "The characteristics of MASs are that (1) each agent has incomplete information or capabilities for solving the problem and, thus, has a limited viewpoint; (2) there is no system global control; (3) data are decentralized; and (4) computation is asynchronous"[7]. Whenever one service provider concludes the work of its designated set of functionalities, services are invoked to determine the best possible execution platform for the next service provider. Parameters to consider are the cost of execution on platforms available within the Grid, cost of data transfer, and the platform cost, as described earlier.

Conclusion

SOAs provide a flexible way to connect services into workflow models that utilize datacenter resources very efficiently. One of the challenges of assigning service providers to a particular data center resource is a uniform way to determine fitness between the service provider and any available platform. Fitness is a function of resource consumption by the service provider and the relative cost of those resources at the time of execution. We argue that cost functions can be used for those determinations if cost is differentiated into cost of a platform at a given time and cost as a metric of resource utilization for a particular service provider. While the former is variable, the latter is static. We suggest that multi agent systems can optimize data center utilization by mapping service providers to the lowest cost resource under consideration of dynamic parameters. Further work will detail how to construct MAS frameworks with sufficient performance to perform dynamic allocation optimizing fitness by *ad hoc* lowest cost determination.

> Service-Oriented Architectures provide a flexible way to connect services into workflow models that utilize datacenter resources very efficiently.

---

[7] Sycara, Katia P; (1998), Multiagent Systems, online at http://www.aaai.org/Resources/Papers/AIMag19-02-007.pdf

Related Work

SORCER at Texas Tech[8] is related, as it creates a network of services for existing applications. The implementation uses Jini and Java technologies, wrapping existing applications and exposing them as a service. Gridlab[9] is a related architecture using existing Grid middleware while adding advanced services. Both projects contribute an extensive body of knowledge and sets of sophisticated tools.

John McClain's[10] work on building scalable and adaptive systems using Java and Jini technologies and the Rio Project[11], are related. Rio provides a framework for dynamic provisioning and the idea of dynamic containers. "The Dynamic Container support in Rio is called a Cybernode. Cybernodes embrace the recognition that the network is composed of heterogeneous compute resources with multiple architectures, operating systems-all with different capabilities. The Cybernode provides a lightweight dynamic 'agent' turning heterogeneous compute resources into services available through the network."[12]

The SeeBeyond™ ICahn suite (now Sun Java™ Integration Suite) is related, as the tools contained allow modeling of workflow and wrapping of service providers.

©2005 Sun Microsystems, Inc. All rights reserved.

Additional Reference

W3C, Mapping of W3C Web Service Architecture work to SOA RM work, online at http://www.oasis-open.org/apps/group_public/download.php/12209 Mapping%20of%20W3C%20Web%20Service%20Architecture%20work%20to%20SOA%20RM %20work_05-04.pdf

---

[8] Sobolewski, Michael; [PI] online at http://www.cs.ttu.edu/~sorcer/about/about.html

[9] Online at http://www.gridlab.org/

[10] McClain, John; online at http://www.javasig.com/Archive/lectures/JavaSIG-JiniSunTechDays-JMcClain.pdf

[11] Rio project home, online at http://rio.jini.org/

[12] ibid

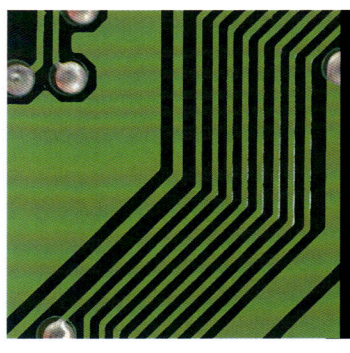

Like seats on an airplane or vegetables in a grocery store, compute cycles are perishable goods. And just as the airline industry has developed a sophisticated costing model to increase utilization and therefore profitability, we need to apply a similar sophisticated model to balance the load among platforms within a Grid environment.

provisioning

Implementing Computing Grids Using Blade Servers

Narayan Devireddy
and
Michael Brundridge

DELL INC.

The emergence of Grid computing raises a new set of equipment demands that must be considered when deploying hardware into modern data centers. Ultra-thin, rack-mount servers pack more compute nodes into a standard 42U server rack than ever before. High-density solutions such as 42 1U servers (84 processors) in a rack are gaining wider acceptance in enterprise networks. Emerging blade-server architectures could further impact Grid computing by increasing server densities and effectiveness even more. Higher server density is the foundation of a scalable and flexible enterprise architecture. In addition to the data center floor space savings, high-density server solutions provide greater flexibility for future growth. Compute-intensive environments such as high-performance computing clusters (HPCCs) can greatly benefit from blade-server architectures.

Key attributes of higher-density blade server architectures such as integrated chassis designs and the ability to consolidate servers, I/O, and cables could bring great value to Grid computing. This article presents some of the key considerations involved in implementing a Grid solution using blade servers based on the emerging Intel® blade-server architecture. The article includes a comparison of the cabling and power/cooling requirements of standard rack-mount servers and blade servers.

Using Blade Servers for Grid Computing

To meet the demands of growing data centers, many IT administrators are turning to blade-server architectures that are optimized for rack environments. A blade server contains a set of hardware components and an integrated management environment. Benefits of a blade server architecture include improved rack-space density compared to traditional rack-mount servers, server aggregation, I/O resource consolidation, cable consolidation, integrated chassis management, rapid deployment and provisioning, and enhanced manageability. By leveraging industry-standard technologies, blade server architectures can achieve high efficiency in the data center by providing an optimized rack environment. While this approach enables significant efficiency enhancements, blade server deployment requires careful planning of data center resources such as power, networking, infrastructure fabric, cooling, and management access.

Things to Consider

Systems deployment in a Grid computing environment involves several steps that must be carefully and accurately executed to achieve the expected results. Advance planning of the following data center resources can help ensure a smooth deployment of blade servers as a Grid:

- *Power requirements:* Planning for power requires a review of the overall system configuration (number of server blades, number of processors, amount of memory, number of I/O modules, and so forth); available configurations for system power supply units (PSUs); power redundancy; and data center power configurations.
- *Network infrastructure:* IP addresses must be allocated to the individual server blades, chassis management modules, and I/O modules. Access to network services such as Dynamic Host Configuration Protocol (DHCP), DNS, and FTP should be made available to the management network.
- *Cooling and thermal considerations:* The data center's cooling infrastructure must provide adequate airflow and cooling in and around the rack where the blade servers will be deployed.

Each of these aspects must be considered in a Grid environment, regardless of the particular equipment choices.

Blade Solutions in a Compute Grid

The blade solution is a practical choice for Grid computing where density, cable consolidation, operating cost, or cost per server is an issue. Figure 1 presents the results of a Dell study of the cable consolidation improvement associated with implementing blade servers, compared to a similar 42U rack-dense 1U-server implementation.

Figure 1 shows that the blade server enclosure uses fewer cables in most ar-

	Blader Server (10 blade servers in one modular enclosure)	1U Server (single server)	Blade Server (60 blades in 42U rack)	1U Server (42 servers in 42U rack)	Blade Server Cabling Reductions
Non-Redundant Power Configuration					
Required power cords	2	1	12	42	-30
Redundant Power Configuration[1]					
Required power cords	4	2	24	84	-60
Communications[2]					
Dual Ethernet pass through	20	2	120	84	36 (no reduction)
Dual Ethernet switch	12	n/a	72	n/a	-12[3]
Chassis Manager	1	1	6	42	-36
Human Interface Device[4]					
PS2 keyboard	1	1	6	42	-36
PS2 mouse	1	1	6	42	-36
VGA video port	1	1	6	42	-36

Note: This study is based on Dell PowerEdge 1855 blade servers and PowerEdge 1850 1U servers.

Figure 1. Cable Consolidation Comparison

[1] The number of power cords required is based on *n*+2, if an *n*+1 configuration is desired; the power cord count is reduced by one for each modular server enclosure.

[2] The blade server supports an optional daughter card per blade. Available fabrics are Ethernet, Fibre Channel, or Infiniband.

[3] The number represented is the delta between the Blade Server Ethernet switch uplink ports and the 1U Server onboard network ports. Note: The Blade Server Ethernet switch has six uplink ports.

[4] Blade Modular Server Enclosure uses a keyboard/video/mouse (KVM) module to consolidate output from all the blades to a single connection.

	Blade Server (10 blade servers in one modular enclosure)	1U Server (single server)	Blade Server (60 blades in 42U rack)	1U Server (60 servers)	Blade Server Power/Cooling Reductions (60-server config.)
Base Configuration*					
Input power or heat output (watts)	4081	445	24486	26700	-2214 watts
Minimum system airflow requirement cubic feet per minute (CFM)	320	35	1920	2100	-180 CFM
AC current (amps)	19.6	2.1	117.6	126	-8.4 amps
Maximum Configuration*					
Input power or heat output (watts)	4934	560	29604	33600	-3996 watts
Current (amps)	20	2.7	120	162	-42 amps

* The following base configuration was used in this comparison (Dell PowerEdge 1855 Blade Server & Dell PowerEdge 1850 1U Server): two dual-core Intel® Xeon® processors with 2 MB L2 cache, 2 GB DDR2 memory; embedded single-channel Ultra320 SCSI drive controller; 2 one-inch Ultra320 hot-plug SCSI hard drives; maximum application load; and 208 VAC voltage; 25C (77F) or less air inlet temperature. Expansion capabilities: PowerEdge 1855 with no daughter card; PowerEdge 1850 with no PCI cards. The maximum configuration refers to the maximum configurations available for these servers.

Figure 2. Power and Cooling Comparison

I/O Module	External port speed	External ports	Fabric type	Media type
Ethernet Switch	10/100/1,000 Mbps	6	Ethernet	RJ-45
Ethernet pass-through	1,000 Mbps	10	Ethernet	RJ-45
Fibre Channel pass-through	1 or 2 Gbps	10	Fibre Channel	Small form-factor pluggable (SFP)
Fiber Channel Switch	1 or 2 Gbps	4+1*	Fibre Channel	SFP
Infiniband pass-through	4X Infiniband (10 Gbps)	10	Infiniband	Infiniband copper

*A single dedicated 10/100Mbps Ethernet management port

Figure 3. I/O Module Types and Associated Port, Fabric, and Media Specifications

eas. The exception is direct network connections, which only occur if the blade server enclosure Ethernet pass-through modules are chosen. In this case, each blade must be connected to a site's Ethernet fabric by physical cable attachments to the module. In contrast, if an Ethernet switch is used in the modular server enclosure, the network connections per rack are decreased, for this example from 120 to 72 for a savings of 12 network connections per rack. If the blade server enclosure does not require 6 Gbps of aggregated uplink speed or six network cable attachments per Ethernet switch, the number of network connections to the switch—and thus, the number of cables in the rack—can be further reduced. When using Ethernet switches in the blade server enclosure, the blades in an enclosure can normally communicate with each other at the fabric wire speed, in this example 1Gbps.

Figure 2 compares power and cooling between a blade server enclosure and a similarly designed 1U server in a 60-server configuration.[1] Sixty blade servers fit in six blade server enclosures in a single 42U rack. A similarly configured 60 1U-server installation requires slightly less than 11/2 42U racks.

The data in Figure 2 show that the blade-server configurations require less power and cooling than the 1U-server configurations.

Network Infrastructure

The blade server enclosure provides various I/O module options, which determine what media type is required. Figure 3 lists these I/O module options

---

[1] These power and cooling calculations are based on the Dell power calculator. For more information, see http://www1.us.dell.com/content/topics/topic.aspx/global/products/pedge/topics/en/config_calculator?.

provisioning

and associated ports, fabric, and media specifications.

Using the On-Blade Network

Each of the server blades in the earlier studies has two on-board 1-Gbps network controllers. Commonly referred to as LAN on motherboard (LOM), these controllers are routed to I/O modules in bays 1 and 2 located at the back of the enclosure. I/O module bays 1 and 2 support only Ethernet fabric types.

In addition to the I/O modules, the blade server enclosure includes ports for chassis manager(s) and keyboard, video, and mouse (KVM) switches. Figure 4 presents the specifications for these ports.

The blade enclosure houses several modules that provide graphical user and command-line interfaces for managing the Grid over the network. Chassis monitoring, out-of-band management, and KVM configuration can be performed through the chassis manager interface. The I/O module switches each provide an interface for switch configuration. Best practices recommend establishing a dedicated management subnet to access the chassis components for management purposes. The following tasks can help IT administrators define the management subnet:

- Identify a range of IP addresses and a subnet mask.
- Provide access to a Dynamic Host Configuration Protocol (DHCP)

> The blade solution is a practical choice for Grid computing where density, cable consolidation, operating cost, or cost per server is an issue.

server from the management network if dynamic IP addresses are used. In general, most chassis managers and I/O Module switches support DHCP-based IP addressing and static IP addressing.

- Provide access to a Dynamic Domain Name System (DDNS) server from the management network. In general most chassis managers support DDNS-based host name identification, and DDNS works with dynamic IP addresses assigned by DHCP servers.
- Provide access to a Trivial FTP (TFTP)

or FTP server from the management network. In general, most chassis manager and I/O modules support TFPT/FTP-based firmware update processes.

Cooling Blade Servers

Cooling a blade server enclosure normally involves several fan modules located in the enclosure, along with several power supplies. These fans, when running at their maximum cooling capacity, are designed to consume large amounts of air. In the case of the Dell study summarized in Figure 3, as much as 520 CFM of air can be consumed from the front of the enclosure. Data center administrators should help ensure that enough cool air is supplied to the front of the rack to support this airflow.[2]

Conclusion

Blade servers can provide an excellent environment for implementing a Grid solution. Following the considerations outlined in this article can help IT administrators to implement an optimized IT environment based on modular data center components. In addition, administrators should heed best practices for configuring power, networking, and cooling components to help ensure smooth server deployment and operations. The resulting blade-server environments can maximize data center space, while helping to streamline and centralize server management.

---

[2] For more information on airflow configuration, see the Dell white paper, "PowerEdge 1855: Best Practice Recommendations to Aid in Data Center Deployment," www.dell.com/downloads/global/products/pedge/en/PowerEdge%201855%20DC%20Whitepaper.pdf

© 2005 Dell Inc. All rights reserved.

Device	Network	Video	Other
Chassis Manager	10/100 Mbps RJ-45	n/a	9-pin serial
Digital KVM	10/100 Mbps RJ-45	DB15 VGA	6-pin PS2 keyboard
			6-pin PS2 mouse

Figure 4. Port Specifications for the Blade Modular Server Enclosure

Rewriting the Rules for Enterprise IT: Using Grid to Orchestrate Enterprise IT Resources

Enterprise IT in a World of Global Competition

In today's world of global competition, rapid business change, and narrowing margins, enterprises are under increasing pressure to simultaneously grow revenue and market share while reducing costs and simplifying infrastructure. As a result, technology has become more than simply a process enabler, but rather a key component in building sustainable competitive advantage.

Traditionally, IT has supported these demands through investments in ever more powerful computing resources and software. However, application silos, heterogeneous hardware environments, lack of technology integration, and increasingly complex system management challenges have slowed the realization of the expected return-on-investment (ROI) from these investments. IT is now expending more resources managing the infrastructure than supporting business imperatives, causing the enterprise to suffer.

The key is to align IT with the rest of the enterprise. By enabling enterprise IT agility, it can be used as a competitive weapon capable of immediately supporting the constantly changing business demands. In effect, heterogeneous technology infrastructures must be made to act as a single virtualized data center that can run any business application on any IT resource at any time, all while lowering capital and operating expenditures.

Songnian Zhou

PLATFORM COMPUTING

The Power of the Virtualized Data Center

With IT so critical to business processes, CIOs are focusing on reducing vulnerabilities and emphasizing more systematic investments in quality of service, which is often designed early in the life cycle of new applications and IT service architectures. By using the right type of systematic design for applications and infrastructure, a single virtualized data center could provide the ability to dynamically address service levels by shifting IT resources to IT services, based on predefined service-level agreements.

Clearly, the concept of a virtualized data center is gaining traction as a useful strategy for aligning enterprise IT with business objectives in today's competitive environment. However, traditional management and clustering software can't cope with these virtual distributed environments—it can't deal with virtualized resources, rapid resource allocation, or coordination of resources across the entire spectrum of application types and existing heterogeneous systems infrastructure.

What's needed is a software layer that can monitor the status of all available resources, track the demands of processes requiring those resources, allocate processes to appropriate resources based on policies, and then execute the resulting allocated processes. Today, this capability is available in high-performance computing (HPC) data centers through the use of using Grid computing solutions.

HPC environments have long used Grid computing to virtualize resources for improved utilization, increased efficiency, and lowering costs. It appears then, that to achieve a virtualized data center within the enterprise IT-run data center, Grid computing must be a core component of this architecture. While these HPC-only Grid silos offer individual instances of ROI and business value, enterprise-wide improvements remain elusive.

What's needed is an "enterprise Grid." An enterprise Grid is a large, virtualized pool of computing resources, serving multiple applications or user groups, which orchestrates on-demand and policy-based allocation of resources to applications. To put it simply, running all enterprise applications on a single virtual computer.

a much lower IT cost when compared to traditional HPC technologies such as mainframes and large symmetric multi-processing machines.

In addition, an enterprise Grid also enables superior overall utilization of your hardware infrastructure, allowing an organization to both reduce the total amount of hardware required while paradoxically increasing the performance level of applications. This is why Grid computing is often referred to as the technology that allows you to do more with less.

> An enterprise Grid enables an organization to reduce the total amount of hardware required while paradoxically increasing the performance level of applications.

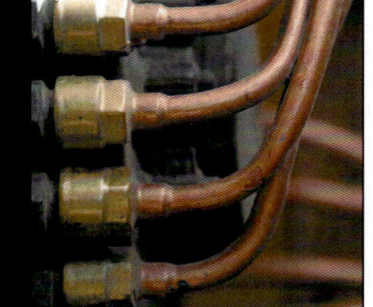

Grid Strategies Power Enterprise IT

An enterprise Grid provides the coordination and systems management necessary to efficiently automate, monitor, balance, and manage work, and address the issues that a client/server approach cannot. This is a key distinction and is the type of resource policy management that ensures resources are available wherever and whenever needed.

Grid strategies provide the ability to efficiently tap into the computational capability of a large pool of commodity-based hardware. This not only provides massive processing power but at

Building the Enterprise Grid and Virtualized Data Center

Platform Computing has addressed this need for an enterprise Grid platform with its Platform Enterprise Grid Orchestrator (EGO). Platform EGO delivers a software-based Grid layer that resides between the applications and the hardware on which they run. Platform EGO is the only Grid platform that can deliver the power of virtualization, automation, and the sharing of all IT resources to every application type. It is the core of an open enterprise Grid strategy that enables IT to allocate resources in real time for improved performance, organizational efficiency and accelerated results.

In fact, almost any type of application can be layered onto Platform EGO. So instead of having a series of application and administration silos based on monolithic programming practices, Platform EGO offers a modern object oriented building block approach where any number of applications and services can be deployed as needed, and without building silos.

This modular approach allows for growth and expansion at a pace that suits variable business needs. A single enterprise application can be deployed initially and new applications added as needed. The results dramatically improve ROI on enterprise IT investments, lower IT costs, improve resource utilization, and are a clear link to achieving strategic business objectives.

Technology Drives the Solution

Platform EGO uses information, allocation, and execution as key concepts in its enterprise Grid architecture. While many technologies effectively deal with information and execution activities associated with resource management, none take a comprehensive approach to the allocation component.

To accomplish this, Platform EGO uses a single common agent on each server to orchestrate the sharing of enterprise resources across application and organizational domains. Here's how these concepts are applied:

- Information about the state and utilization of the managed resources is centrally available to all applications.
- Allocation of all resources to the applications is made based on commercially proven scheduling techniques and user-defined policies.

> An enterprise Grid provides the coordination and systems management necessary to efficiently automate, monitor, balance, and manage work, and address the issues that a client/server approach cannot.

- Execution of application services is managed across the distributed, heterogeneous infrastructure to maximize workload throughput.

In effect, it is as if an automated game of Tetris is played on shape, size, type, and duration of resource requests, in the context of policy and resource availability in the data center. As a result, enterprise IT data centers are beginning to duplicate HPC Grid successes as they begin their migration to the virtualized data center.

Together, virtualization and enterprise Grid provide compelling value for enterprise IT. Using a Grid platform provides an agile, open, scalable way to service and manage all applications in a single virtual environment, in effect "orchestrating" resources and processes across the data center. Orchestration, using an enterprise Grid, is what ultimately allows for the creation and management of a true virtualized data center.

European Auto Manufacturer Needed to Reduce IT Complexity

PSA Peugeot Citroen, one of the largest European manufacturers of passenger cars and utility vehicles, was managing workload across their multi-site computing environment that contained a diverse mixture of hardware, including systems from Cray, HP, and IBM. In addition, the spread of multi-vendor hardware platforms across the company added to the increasing complexity of its computing environment.

Severe limitations with the existing workload manager were continually creating technical problems for IT staff, and impacting their ability to focus on their primary responsibilities. Christophe Prigent, IT Manager for PSA Peugeot Citroen, concluded that by selecting their Grid solution from Platform Computing, "All our team members, at every level of the organization and working from different geographic locations, now have access to a system that is transparent and, of necessity, reliable. This reliability is all the more appreciated since it minimizes operating costs."

The results are impressive:
- Consistent systems management, despite a variety of hardware types.
- Instant access to automobile design and simulation tools providing increased productivity.
- Elimination of technical problems allowing IT staff to focus on strategic IT initiatives.

Aerospace Supplier Accelerates Engine Design

In an effort to lower production costs and speed time to market, a leading aerospace engine supplier needed to reduce the amount of physical testing done on its products, and increase its computer-aided simulations during the design and development stages. In addition, resource utilization, overall computing performance, productivity, and efficiency were not at optimal levels, and costs were dramatically increasing.

They needed a flexible alternative to explore multiple design ideas before building a product. The ability to run simulations such as Computational Fluid Dynamics (CFD) and (structural) Finite Element Analysis (FEA) requires intensive compute power but does provide a method to reduce the exorbitant costs incurred by physical testing.

Following the initial deployment of Platform Computing's Grid solution to cluster their IT resources and orchestrate the workload, this manufacturer undertook an aircraft engine compressor project. This project formed the foundation of a new era in cost reductions because Platform's Grid solutions cut engineering time in half and this in turn reduced development costs by more than 50 percent. The reduction in engineering time enabled thousands of additional CFD and FEA simulations that substantially increased the engine's fuel efficiency, which then made the company more competitive.

Start Building Your Virtualized Data Center Today

A virtualized data center can be deployed incrementally across specific resources, lines-of-business or applications at whatever speed is comfortable. Each enterprise is unique, and as such, has the autonomy to decide just how fast and how best to deploy. Global markets will continue to become more competitive and squeeze margins, the demands for faster IT response and lower IT costs will grow, and increasingly complex business processes will demand more integration across enterprise IT. In the face of these challenges, Grid computing can help you enable your enterprise IT organization to become more agile and to allocate resources in real time at the speed of business change.

> Grid computing can help you enable your enterprise IT organization to become more agile and to allocate resources in real time at the speed of business change.

Preparing Grid for the Mainstream

Helping to drive Grid standardization efforts is a logical step for HP, which emphasizes open, standards-based technologies and supports heterogeneous environments. Along with scientific institutions and other major corporations, HP is an active participant in a leading standards body—the Global Grid Forum (GGF)—whose chair is HP Vice President Mark Linesch. The GGF has overseen creation of an Open Grid Services Architecture (OGSA), the service-oriented architecture for Grid computing.

HP has co-authored both the OGSA document and the Web Services Resource Framework (WSRF), a collection of specifications that defines a standard way to treat interactions among clients, services, and dynamic IT resources using Web Services. HP is also a founder and board member of the Enterprise Grid Alliance (EGA), which is addressing requirements and solutions for Grids in the enterprise.

AN INTERVIEW WITH HP'S MARK LINESCH

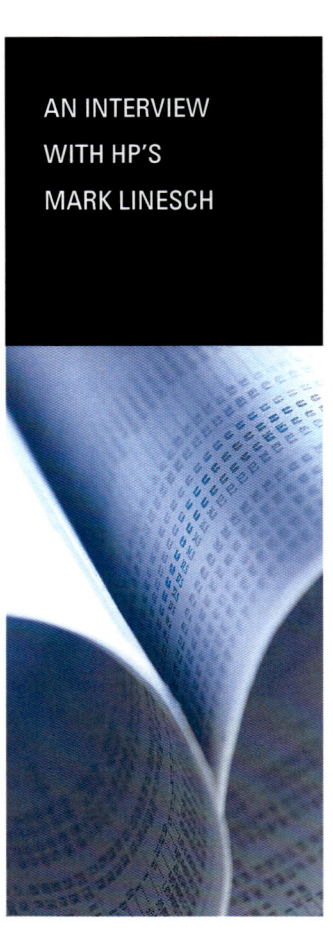

Industry experts have long touted Grid computing as the future of information technology. Today, Grids are the foundation for collaborative research and advanced scientific discovery worldwide. They also power compute- and data-intensive applications in fields as diverse as oil exploration, drug discovery, and financial services. But most mainstream companies are just beginning to explore the benefits of Grid technology and encountering the barriers that come with adopting any emerging technology.

Grid technology may well become a must-have on the list of every CIO—but first, enterprise customers must gain experience with the technology, and software providers must agree on standards that will allow Grids to interoperate. In this interview, Mark Linesch, chairman of the Global Grid Forum, and a vice president at HP, speaks about the progress of Grid computing standards and the benefits that Grid computing will bring to enterprise IT.

Mark Linesch, chairman of the Global Grid Forum, speaks about the progress of Grid computing standards and the benefits that Grid computing will bring to enterprise IT.

 Where did Grid computing first appear?

Grids gained an early following in the high-performance computing (HPC) area. The technology was adopted primarily by researchers who wanted to collaborate with other researchers, people who designed automobiles and businesses that crunched lots of numbers. In the business world, those companies are generally in the financial services, pharmaceutical, and manufacturing industries. Grids are now starting to move deeply into the enterprise—first in traditional HPC areas, and then to broader IT transaction and business intelligence areas.

 CIOs have heard about Grid computing for several years. Where are we now in the hype cycle?

Grids, like many emerging technologies, have been and will continue to be over-promoted. That's why research firms like Gartner have a hype cycle, which helps explain technology diffusion within our industry. The model starts out with wild exuberance when a new technology enters the field. Because the technology isn't very mature yet and doesn't have all of the components to make a practical solution for mainstream customers, customers become disillusioned. Then, just about the time everybody feels like the technology is nothing but hype, the technology starts to mature and build back some credibility. Lead users deploy it and get economic benefits, and that leads to an eventual understanding of the relevance of the technology.

These types of emerging-market models allow you to compare your understanding of a technology to what's happening in the popular press and the industry. By looking at past technologies that have been over-promoted, you can learn some lessons:

- First, organizations should not invest in technologies just because they're hyped.
- Second, companies should not disregard technologies just because those technologies aren't currently living up to expectations.

The same goes for Grid. Companies should invest in Grids when they deliver value in the form of significant cost savings and competitive advantage. Grids will help align IT with business objectives in a more dynamic, real-time way. There will be criticism along the way, but the caravan will continue because there's real value here.

 When can we expect Grids to take off in mainstream IT?

I think of the adoption model for Grid in three phases:

1. Early adoption.
2. Proven solutions.
3. Pervasive adoption.

The academic and research sector has progressed beyond the early adoption stage and is now in stage two with proven solutions in a variety of specific application areas. These provide real-world examples of the benefits and risks of Grid deployment and enable other people to leverage the successful experiences of the early pioneers.

In the enterprise space, the commercial industry is still in the early adoption phase, but we're moving toward proven solutions. Early adoption is primarily an exercise in handcrafting solutions. In the proven-solutions phase, you see Grid-enabled software from many vendors and Grid success stories in specific industries. In the pervasive-adoption phase, a majority of mainstream businesses can start to adopt Grids with packaged solutions and little risk. We're getting there, but it takes time.

 Grids will not be the right solution for every business in every industry in every application. How do CIOs know when Grid is right for them?

You start off with a business problem, and you decide that Grid might be an appropriate solution. For example, representatives from Bank of America recently spoke at Grid World and told a story: They had data centers in Chicago, New York, and London, and all three organizations wanted to build a Grid-like infrastructure to support their traders and risk analysts. Risk analysis is a CPU-intensive application, and Bank of America's goal was to shorten the amount of time needed to calculate risk. By building a Grid and sharing resources, they shortened one process from six hours to 40 minutes, and another process from four hours to 30 minutes.

After a success like that, Grid continues to progress. It's infectious. Somebody takes a risk on a technology and gets a good payback. Then people in the organization start to notice that something's faster or is saving money or increasing collaboration—and they wonder whether Grid can solve their problems, as well.

 What role do standards play in Grid adoption?

You can go through the first and second phases of adoption without much standardization. But in stage three, businesses will want to connect the Grids in their organizations with Grids in other organizations—and that's when we need standards. For those Grids to come together and interoperate, they need to speak the same language. That's why standards are imperative before we can reach pervasive adoption.

 Where are we in terms of standards development today?

The industry has made important strides with regard to some of the critical standards, but there is clearly more work ahead.

Standardization of Grid computing is being lead by the Global Grid Forum (GGF). GGF has developed the Open Grid Services Architecture (OGSA) and is working throughout the international community to champion this architectural blueprint and the associated specifications. OGSA provides guidance and acts as an integrating mechanism for public comment, more detailed specifications, standards recommendations, and broad industry adoption over time. OGSA is based on broadly adopted Internet standards and the Web Services specifications currently being adopted within the industry. This requires GGF to work extensively with other standards development organizations such as:

- Internet Engineering Task Force (IETF)
- World Wide Web Consortium (W3C)
- Organization for the Advancement of Structured Information Standards (OASIS)
- Distributed Management Task Force (DMTF)
- Storage Networking Industry Association (SNIA)

Together we are all working to knit together the standards required for pervasive adoption of Grid worldwide.

 What else do you want CIOs to know about Grid computing?

At the Global Grid Forum, we spend lot of time talking to CIOs and they tell us they want a shared-resources environment where they can dynamically bring in new resources and release unused resources. They want to manage that environment in an automated, efficient, utility-like manner. But they're not sure how to get there. I tell CIOs that Grids are a core part of the next stage of distributed computing, and it's important that they look for specific problems that they might solve with Grid. Then, start small. Let the infectious nature of Grids lead them to additional applications and solutions.

Another important point: this shouldn't be only about cost. CIOs have a significant opportunity to use Grid technology to change the rules of the game and drive competitive advantage. For example, companies in the automotive and aerospace industries are collaborating on next-generation designs, even though they are competitors. Companies that find themselves in this situation need to share computing and data resources while making sure their sensitive information and intellectual property is protected. Grids can help with this kind of problem—the need to collaboratively design or work across a supply chain. Those are benefits beyond the regular benefits of greater IT utilization and lower administration costs, and they help drive competitive advantage. CIOs should think about those kinds of exciting opportunities.

> CIOs have a significant opportunity to use Grid technology to change the rules of the game and drive competitive advantage.

efficiency

Understanding the Impact of Grid and Service-Oriented IT

AN INTERVIEW WITH MICROSOFT'S TONY HEY

It's no secret that Microsoft is a major player in the global IT market, but the software giant has not always been highly visible in the world of technical computing.

With some of the world's leading computing technology and systems companies moving aggressively to make their technical computing solutions attractive to the mainstream enterprise computing market, Microsoft has stepped out of the shadows and staked a claim in the emerging, yet lucrative, Grid and Service-Oriented IT markets.

Microsoft officially unveiled its strategy in this space during Microsoft's Chairman and Chief Software Architect Bill Gates' historic keynote speech at the Supercomputing 2005 (SC'05) conference in Seattle (November 2005). However, those with their ears pressed firmly against the IT ground saw Microsoft's strategy begin to take shape in May 2005, when the company announced it had hired Tony Hey, who at the time was the director of the cutting-edge United Kingdom e-Science Program, as Corporate Vice President for Technical Computing, Advanced Strategies and Policy.

Under Hey's directorship, the UK e-Science Program focused heavily on Grid computing, supporting numerous e-science applications in both the academic and industrial sectors, and establishing a National e-Science Centre, which a production National Grid Service. In addition, the UK e-Science Program is a participant in many Grid projects throughout Europe, including CERN's Large Hadron Collider Grid, the SIMDAT and NextGrid collaborative industrial Grid projects and Enabling Grids for E-scienceE (EGEE), a project dedicated to providing an always-on Grid infrastructure for European scientists. After hiring Hey, Microsoft brought aboard the then EGEE Project Director, Fabrizio Gagliardi, to further advance its Technical Computing Initiative. Any company would be hard pressed to find stronger technical leadership in building a Grid and Service-Oriented IT strategy.

Hey's résumé in high-performance computing also includes his instrumental role in the development of the MPI message-passing interface and his founding of the Southampton Parallel Applications Centre in 1991, among other contributions to the community. In 2005, Hey received a Commander of the Order of the British Empire honor for services to science. Clearly, Microsoft has plans to make a significant impact in the field of technical computing, including the emerging segments of Grid and Service-Oriented IT, and, clearly, it wanted someone with decades of leading-edge experience to lead the charge.

As an added benefit for the readers of *The Emergence of Grid and Service-Oriented IT*, *GRIDtoday* conducted an exclusive interview with Tony Hey to get his thoughts on the emergence of Grid

Tony Hey shares his thoughts on the emergence of Grid and service-oriented technologies in the commercial sector.

and service-oriented technologies in the commercial sector, as well as where Microsoft plays—and plans to play—in these markets.

Q: As enterprise IT decision makers evaluate technology, products, and approaches to implementation for their next-generation IT infrastructures, how can they best evaluate the potential impact of Grid and Service-Oriented IT?

I think the idea that businesses are just evaluating the technology is not quite right. Service-oriented technology has already been evaluated and is now being deployed in a number of major applications. I think industry has gotten past the evaluation phase of Service-Oriented IT and is now looking to build on their early experiences. Service-oriented architectures are here to stay and I see the Grid as a small piece of that space. In principal, it could be a larger piece, but at the moment, industry has mainly deployed computing Grids of various types, connecting clusters, using idle cycles, and generally attempting to use their IT resources more efficiently. As demonstrated in Bill Gates' keynote at SC'05, interoperability between Windows and Linux clusters located in different sites is now possible, although most of the early deployments of Grid technologies are actually still within a single enterprise. We are therefore talking about intra-enterprise Grids as opposed to inter-enterprise Grids.

I think inter-enterprise Grids will come, but at present we are mainly seeing intra-enterprise Grids being used in pharma, engineering, and other areas such as the financial sector. The evaluation of these early compute Grids has so far mostly been in these compute spaces. I believe there is much more to come when we get onto the data/information/knowledge management side of Grids. However, certainly Service-Oriented Architectures have been evaluated with a positive outcome and I think are now a fixture in the strategies of company IT directors.

Q: Why do you think Grid seems to have struggled in terms of gaining traction with commercial enterprise adoption?

There are examples of successful Grids in both academia and industry but they have not got enough generic appeal and functionality yet. This is because Grids are still work in progress-the ambitious Grid vision of fully virtualized resources and support for dynamic virtual organizations has not yet been realized. For example, we are still putting together all the pieces of the security puzzle—authentication, authorization, and so on. But some simple Grid services are out there and available and I think we could grow the market much more if we had some more clarity about what Grids are useful for. It would also help if there were some simple interoperable Grid service standards above the basic Web Services that could be agreed by the major players in the IT industry.

 Would it help if vendors touted the data management aspects of a Grid infrastructure, for example, versus the compute aspect, with which most people seem to be familiar?

Well, I can't speak for all vendors and Microsoft has not yet defined a Grid strategy in detail. Certainly, the emphasis for Microsoft would be much more about data, information, and knowledge management rather than just the computing aspects. In a sense, the compute aspect, making better use of compute cycles, is the easy thing. It is in actually integrating and federating data, finding powerful services, etc., where I suspect the real potential of Grids will pay off. So, Microsoft's Grid vision would certainly be more concerned with data, information, and knowledge management than just the compute part.

 What will fuel wider spread adoption of Grid in commercial enterprise environments?

I really believe that it was a good thing in 2001 that Grids took the decision to move toward Service-Oriented Architectures and Web Services protocols. Unfortunately, although IBM, Microsoft, and others had agreed to agree on Web Services, there was nonetheless a divergence between the IT vendors on Web Services as well as at least one false start. However, I think we now have the potential for a major reconciliation between the IBM/HP/Fujitsu WS Distributed Management/WSRF approach and the Microsoft/Intel/Sun approach with WS Management/WS Transfer approach. Once there is agreement on the basic Web Service protocols, I think the Grid community needs to get together and the leading companies and research groups agree on a simple set of base Grid standards very quickly. We could adopt a 'layered' approach, agreeing on the easy things and leaving the 'bells and whistles' for later. Whatever organization emerges from the discussions between GGF and EGA needs to fast-track these standards and demonstrate that it can constitute an effective standards body. We can then elaborate these base services into a full OGSA specification on a more leisurely timescale—but what we urgently need now is something fairly simple and soon. If the Grid community and the IT vendors can deliver on the above scenario, this will be the most effective way to build confidence in Grids and to grow the market for everyone. Through the existence of such Grid standards, not only would more people understand the Grid message but also customers could have confidence that if they bought a Grid solution from one supplier now, they would still retain the option of buying from another supplier in the future. I believe that this picture is not far away from realization—but I am an optimist, as you know.

 Do you feel that the proposed merger of the Global Grid Forum (GGF) and the Enterprise Grid Alliance (EGA) would help to expedite this process?

Well that is certainly what I would like to see. You have the companies in the EGA that are really concerned about business—here and now—with GGF addressing longer term concerns such as middleware services to support virtual organizations that have not yet been fully realized. So I think a merger could give us the best of both worlds. I actually think that it is vital for the Grid community that the GGF and the EGA combine to make sure that the scenario outlined above actually happens. Let's assume that there is reconciliation on the low-level Web Services protocols, which by and large are really too low level to be very interesting for Grid ap-

Industry has gotten past the evaluation phase of Service-Oriented IT and is now looking to build on their early experiences.

111

plication builders. All the major IT companies could surely agree on some very simple standards very rapidly. A new merged organization could then look in detail at elaborations of these basic Grid services as well as explore the higher level services more directly relevant to the applications. So I think that what we need now is an agreement on some non-controversial subset of the full OGSA Grid services. The GGF and EGA merger has the potential to achieve all these good things. The standards process could be driven by the IT companies with input from the leading Grid research groups—which is the way it should be. So with an agreed specification of part of the OGSA vision—'OGSA-lite', if you will—the community could elaborate on more complicated scenarios later. I think an EGA and GGF merger could make this opportunity a reality, and that's what I'd like to see.

Q Some companies seem to have leap-frogged right over discussions of Grid and are now focused on Service-Oriented IT. What is Microsoft's view of Service-Oriented IT, and what impact will it have on business computing?

Microsoft has for a long time championed the idea of a standards-based, Service-Oriented Architecture, and they have consistently been one of the driving forces for this view in the IT industry. In particular, Microsoft has fully signed up to the Web Services vision, and this has always been set in the context of Service-Oriented IT. So our vision is of interoperability for distributed IT systems through open standards and I think that these ser-

> Microsoft has demonstrated that it is wholly subscribed to an interoperable, Service-Oriented IT vision.

vice-oriented systems will be much more robust than previous distributed computing efforts. I believe that Microsoft has demonstrated that it is wholly subscribed to an interoperable, Service-Oriented IT vision and that this vision will deliver more robust distributed environments for the industry.

Grid services, embracing data integration and federation as much as compute services, with specific domain application functionalities will be built on the basis of these Web Service protocols. These will have an impact not only in the research sector but also in a range of industries—such as automotive, aerospace, oil and gas, pharma, etc. I suspect that in the longer term Grids will move into mainstream business sectors. Obviously I am not best qualified to be specific about the impact on mainstream business but certainly in the technical space, I think that Grid applications built on top of Service-Oriented Web Service protocols will have a big impact.

Q Could you briefly describe, to the best of your knowledge, how Grid and service-oriented technologies are related and how they are different?

In earlier attempts to build distributed applications one tended to define pointers to resources behind a firewall on the distributed site, where you had no control of the resource. This led to rather 'brittle' distributed applications. If anything changed on the remote site, the whole distributed application would tend to break. With Service-Oriented IT on the other hand, resources are exposed as services and interact using specified, agreed Web Service protocols. A service is specified in WSDL that is a simple protocol for exchanging information with XML and SOAP as the two key technologies. These protocols enable distributed systems to talk to each other and access WSDL specified services. These external interfaces are independent of changes to the way in which the service has been implemented behind the firewall. This is the basis for the general belief that Service-Orientation leads to more robust distributed system implementations. In the Grid space we want to use these Web Service protocols to build application domain-specific functionality for various vertical markets. Using these protocols we can plan Grid services that deliver compute capabilities and services for federating and integrating data.

Q **Will desktop, departmental, and enterprise computing resources ever be transparently shared in a truly on-demand environment with little or no human intervention? Is this the promise of Grid?**

As you know, I don't believe that optimizing computing resources is 'the be all and end all' for the Grid. I think this is a very partial view of the Grid, although at present it is probably the easiest sell for Grid technologies. Certainly, if one group within a company 'owns' a cluster that cannot be used by anybody else, even though they aren't themselves using it, that is a waste of resources. I think that virtualizing such resources so that cluster is actually available for the whole company will happen and will be an important driver for the IT strategy of a company. An alternative to dedicated clusters is the 'cycle-stealing' realization of the Grid that is cost-effective for applications in some industries—such as drug screening in pharma. This can also be a component of a Grid strategy for using IT resources more effectively. But, as I said, I believe that is only a partial view.

In the longer term, I believe that mining distributed data, extracting information and knowledge sharing—actually using the knowledge to build your business—will be a much more strategic use of the Grid. The importance for both research and industry of Grid technologies for sharing of data, combined with powerful data mining and visualization tools, seems to me to point to the fact that virtualization of data resources will in the end be more significant than a compute-dominated vision of Grids.

Q **What decisions should enterprise IT executives be making today in order to accommodate emerging Grid capabilities over the next year or two?**

At the moment, the most mature Grid offerings are the computing applications. IT executives can certainly go and talk with the major Grid technology vendors and see what sort of solutions they offer. But, as I have said just now, I also think they should also be looking down the road a bit for a time when the Grid vision will be not just focused on compute power but also on data. So I think they should be looking for companies moving in that direction.

Q **Finally, can you give some insight into what we might expect to see from Microsoft, in regard to the technologies we've been discussing, in the near future?**

Microsoft has many elements of Grid technologies in place—it has pioneered service-oriented architectures and has been a leader in the Web services space. We have not so far addressed the Grid application space, which is the reason why you haven't seen Microsoft very active in the Grid. However, we are now addressing technical computing—my role is vice president of technical computing—and we will be looking at the potential of using Microsoft's expertise in the underlying technologies to build activity in the technical application space. In the longer term, I believe these technologies will spill over into the business space. We have just now entered the cluster market with our compute cluster offering which is now in beta. As demonstrated in Bill's talk at SC05, our Windows cluster will interoperate with Linux and UNIX clusters. Of course, we need to ensure that our Windows compute cluster product performs competitively on the key scientific and engineering codes. We then need to extend our single cluster offering to multiple clusters spanning multiple administrative domains which will properly mark our entry into Grid computing. We will also be examining how to extend our Grid vision to encompass distributed data resources. Microsoft will be examining all of these options in the coming months.

> Mining distributed data, extracting information, and knowledge sharing—actually using the knowledge to build your business—will be a much more strategic use of the Grid.

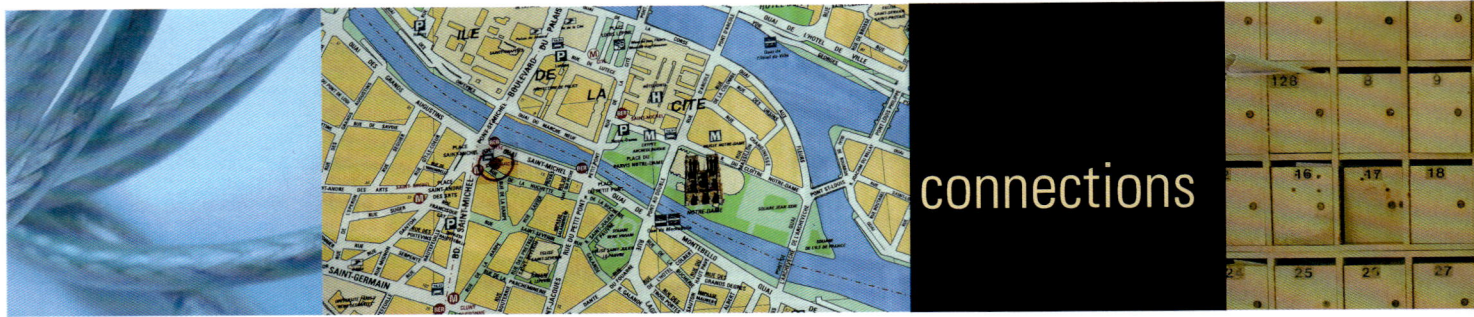

connections

Leveraging City Planning and other Social Metaphors to Guide SOA—Why Meta Matters

Annie Shum

BEA SYSTEMS

Service Oriented Architecture (SOA) has emerged recently as the centerpiece of a set of IT strategies and declarative design principles that promise to revolutionize the relationship between IT and real-world business. But is it "State of the Art" or simply "Same Old Architecture"?

Dating back more than two decades, the core model of SOA is not new to the IT industry. Instead, in the words of Victor Hugo, it is an idea whose time has come. Unlike its previous debut, however, SOA has undergone a remarkable metamorphosis with a decidedly different tenor and direction. While in the past SOA focused principally on software development, it now takes on a strategically compelling new mantra that focuses on business value chains by connecting IT to processes and people.

Although industry pundits and management consultants are virtually unanimous in their enthusiasm for this vision, software developers may, at times, find themselves wondering why all the hype. One reason is that software developers focus primarily on the way applications are written, rather than on the way applications are initially identified and specified. SOA does in fact have something to say about the process of coding applications, but that is only a small part of the SOA story.

Far more significant are the implications that SOA has for the way application software should be specified (modeled and designed) and the way that real-world businesses and application software should interact. The goal of this paper is to clarify these critically important issues using various metaphors while also briefly describing a new category of service infrastructure software required to allow SOA to achieve more of its full potential.

The Meta-morphosis of SOA: The Importance of Being "Meta"

"Every day, and in every way, we're getting meta and meta." —Philosopher John Wisdom[1]

SOA provides an architectural framework for addressing the fundamental problem of bridging the barrier between IT and business. A key insight that unlocks the solution is that SOA applies equally well to IT processes and business processes. But above all, the pivotal insight (albeit generally overlooked for now) is the *meta* foundation of SOA.[2] In particular, SOA is reflective—self-describing, metadata driven, and aspect oriented.[3]

By *externalizing* the process logic and the workflow interaction specifications, SOA promotes a clear separation (through the process of abstraction) from the code of the underlying IT implementation. In this way, after a set of real-world business processes has been explicitly characterized (modeled) in terms of SOA building blocks that adhere to the SOA core tenets and design principles, it is relatively straightforward to transform these externalized characterizations into a specification for software that explicitly mirrors the corresponding processes.

Externalized by design and reinforced by governance, the business logic and workflow interactions are now explicit, visible, and most significantly, modifiable in a declarative manner by myriad stakeholders beyond the traditional close circle of software developers. Likewise, it is straightforward to augment the business processes with new aspects (functionalities) by introducing new intermediary services to the existing business-process workflow. As it turns out, pervasive intermediation is a key strategy for high scalability. For more discussion, see the later section "SOA

Service-Oriented Architecture now takes on a strategically compelling new mantra that focuses on business value chains by connecting IT to processes and people.

and Post Office Operation: The Meta-Framework for Mail/Package Delivery."

More complex changes to business processes that call for modification of individual business services, such as changing business logic, can be represented by rewriting the code for individual autonomous (software) services. Although more technical effort is required for such code modification, the disruptive changes to consumers is minimal or nonexistent. Enabling modifications of such magnitude to be implemented quickly and easily is the essence of "agility" in real-world businesses and in the software applications that support these businesses.

Simply put, SOA is a meta and reflective architectural framework that enables broad-based interoperability and adaptive computing, giving IT the flexibility to deliver services when and where the business needs them. SOA enables composite applications to explicitly mirror business processes and adapt to changing business needs.

Hence, SOA begins with a set of prescriptive design principles and a metadata-driven transformation roadmap focused on the premise of aligning IT with business objectives.

SOA and City Planning: The Meta-Framework for Community Building

Perhaps the most instructive metaphor for SOA is the process of city planning, which has previously been cited, notably, by the CBDI Forum.[4]

---

[1] Nick Gall (an SOA visionary) cited this quote in his Weblog.

[2] The meta-foundation of SOA is what clearly sets it apart from the previous three computing paradigms—mainframe, client/server and Web *n*-tier. It is one of the most crucial ingredients of success in agility, and yet, for now, it is overlooked and undervalued by many software developers.

[3] Aspect—a new type of modularity. The concept of aspect orientation introduced a new unit of modularization (aspects) above components that crosscuts several components. The main rule for crosscutting concerns is that they are based on independent, semantically autonomous subject matters (such as bank, account, factory, purchase order, shipping, or travel reservation) (Davydov 2004).

[4] Previously, Gartner, IBM, and Yukio Namba (submitted as a Ph.D. thesis for the Tokyo Institute of Technology, January 2005) have cited city planning as a metaphor for Enterprise Architecture.

City planning does not concentrate on the design and construction of individual buildings. Rather, it is concerned with subjects such as the multi-aspect relationships of individual buildings to one another, to the areas of the city/community where they are constructed, and to access to common infrastructure services such as electricity, water, and sewage. In other words, city planning is not about discrete building architecture; it's about *meta-architecture* for communities of buildings with focus on subjects such as common infrastructure, governance, and cohesion. Filtered through a meta-framework prism, the similarity between city planning and SOA is remarkable. Just as city planning is the meta-architectural framework for building communities, SOA can be the meta-architectural framework for collaborative computing.

City planning is a separate field of work and study, and readily demarcated from fields of concentration such as architecture, electrical, and building. In the software development community, analysts who write specifications for applications might correspond to architects, and software developers might correspond to electrical engineers and builders. The initial hurdle with this metaphor is that, in most cases, the existing software development community has no *de facto* analog to the city planner. SOA is destined to resolve this problem by driving into the mainstream a comparatively new category of IT/business professional, the enterprise architect, whose range of responsibilities is similar to that of a city planner.

Like a city planner, the enterprise architect must have a "big picture" vision that transcends individual units (buildings, services) and focuses instead on the way collections of units (neighborhoods, communities) can fulfill a variety of different purposes. A manufacturing community might consist of a cluster of factories surrounded by homes for workers and connected by railroad links to suppliers of raw materials and component sub-assemblies, as well as to merchants who sell the manufactured products. The community has a need for schools, recreational facilities, police and fire stations, food markets, and so on. Each of these individual facilities could also be used for other purposes. For example, the worker housing could also be used by individuals who do not work at the manufacturing facility, the rail lines could be used to ship goods used for non-manufacturing purposes, and so on. The city planner needs to think about the full constellation of sharable resources that need to be assembled and coordinated.

These observations about city planning illustrate some highly relevant design principles that tomorrow's enterprise architects should heed when designing specifications for SOA-based IT services. Simply put, enterprise architects must shift their mind-set from today's stovepipe approach to a connected, virtualized, and federated ecosystem. Unlike the traditional software application architects, the enterprise architects' role extends well beyond software coding specifications. They must also act as the chief enablers of *borderless collaboration* by coordinating and prioritizing the input from disparate groups with different needs, interests, and views, including business stakeholders, software architects, developers, and database administrators, as well as external partners, suppliers, providers, customers, auditors, and so on.

One fundamentally important point for enterprise architects is that specifications must be flexible enough to allow for creativity, variability, and initiative in the design and implementation of individual units—whether these units are "bricks and mortar" buildings or individual IT services. However, this heterogeneity should be uniformly constrained by explicit boundaries and formal core tenets for each service in order to achieve the holistic cohesion that enables borderless collaboration and leverages IT asset reuse and the sharing of common infrastructure services.

In the case of IT services, the core tenets are defined in part by industry standards for messaging and externally visible descriptions of the capabilities of the service. Internal details related to the way capabilities are implemented are left to the designers and software specialists responsible for coding the individual services. In sharp contrast to specifying the detailed procedures that implementers must follow, enterprise architects should rigorously encapsulate any internal implementa-

> **By leveraging a network of pervasive intermediaries, the post office is able to provide an extraordinary degree of scalability.**

tion details and should *declare* only the outputs (as well as any policies for service invocations) that must be generated for each set of inputs. For this reason, this approach of service encapsulation can be characterized as *declarative*, rather than *procedural*, design.

In addition to fostering loose coupling and separation of concerns, declarative design also facilitates reusability by inhibiting the temptation to tailor the implementation of a service to meet the specialized requirements of the particular application that is currently under development. Indeed, one of the most compelling promises of SOA is the business benefit of highly *polymorphic* service interfaces, namely the broad-based access of a service simply by means of declaration of intent. But one of the key challenges for enterprise architects in designing polymorphic service interfaces is to create specifications for services that are broad enough to support multiple (including unintended) users and allow flexibility in the choice of design and implementation strategies, while still providing the functionality needed to meet the requirements of the current application.

Another important lesson from city planning is the co-existence of the old and the new. Many reasons exist for preserving structures that were implemented before current standards were in force. These structures might be historic buildings constructed as stand-alone entities without city water and electric power, akin to legacy applications that were constructed as stand-alone monolithic applications without messaging support and industry-standards-based (such as XML) interface descriptions.

In both examples, a complete overhaul (demolish-and-replace approach) is unrealistic and rarely cost-effective. Instead, legacy structures can be preserved by retrofitting them with stan-

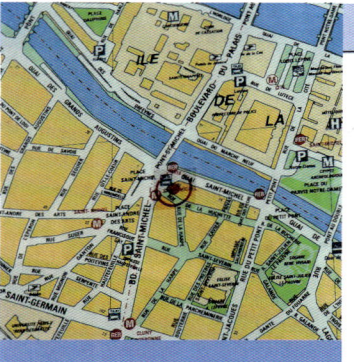

SOA provides an architectural framework for addressing the fundamental problem of bridging the barrier between IT and business.

dards-based interfaces that enable them to connect to the shared infrastructure of the city (for example, retrofitting Notre Dame in Paris with facilities such as electricity, water, and plumbing) or the SOA ecosystem (for example, exposing a legacy backend process via SOAP, XML, and WSDL to encapsulate coarse-grained CICS business transactions executing on zSeries).

Managing growth by clustering neighborhoods into communities, communities into cities, and cities into regions is another lesson of city (and regional) planning that has far-reaching implications for enterprise architects designing scalable SOA ecosystems. The fractal-like nature of services allows them to be composed into composite services, which can then be composed into higher-level composite services, and so on. This hierarchy of composite services operates like a nested set of spheres within spheres and makes it possible for each service to retain local autonomy over its own internal opera-

tions while also containing complexity and maximizing global interoperability and connectivity through standards-based shared common interfaces. Emerging concepts such as "networks of networks" and "Grids of Grids" exemplify these principles and give new meaning to the old political maxim of "Think globally but act locally."

SOA and Post Office Operation: The Meta-Framework for Mail/Package Delivery

The worldwide postal system provides additional design examples for enterprise architects to emulate. Every post office operates on the same meta-framework of dynamic binding for delivery: namely, the recipient address is treated as self-describing (reflective) metadata, while the mail is *en route* to the recipient by traversing through a series of sorting offices. The binding takes place only when it reaches the final sorting office prior to actual delivery to the destination address.

Each post office and sorting station has a well-defined set of input and output requirements, but the internal operating procedures used within any one of these offices or stations could be modified without affecting the overall operation of the system. Moreover, the entire system is remarkably scalable. If a particular sorting station becomes overloaded and creates a performance bottleneck, that bottleneck can be eliminated by building a new sorting sub-station and rerouting some of the workload to it. New sorting sub-stations can be positioned geographically in a way that optimizes their performance benefit.

Each sorting station serves as an intermediary in the process of delivering a letter from a sender to a receiver. The number of intermediaries, and their relationship to one another, can be completely transparent to both the sender and the receiver, and are not part of the post office's service contract for senders and receivers of mail. Once again, this service contract is an example of a declarative, rather than procedural, specification.

By leveraging a network of pervasive intermediaries,[5] the post office is able to provide an extraordinary degree of scalability. Enterprise architects might find inspiration for the design of highly scalable IT services by studying this example carefully. In particular, robust pervasive intermediation exemplifies the strategic culmination of *modularity, delegation, and federation*.[6] Nick Gall (2005) of Gartner observed that intermediation enables simultaneous operations and accelerates the innovation from edge to core. Clearly, the Internet or more precisely the World Wide Web is one of the most successful showcases for pervasive intermediation.

SOA and Business Protocols/ Boilerplate: The Meta-framework for Human Commerce

The fact that many SOA design principles follow time-tested business protocols was noted earlier in this paper. Similar to the analogy between city planning and SOA, the resonance between the boilerplate for business protocols and SOA is most apparent when filtered through the prism of the meta-framework. Throughout history, human commerce has been built on the meta-framework that consists of the boilerplate for business protocols.

Business partners typically do not share application and workflow implementation technologies, nor do they allow unrestricted external control over the use of their backend applications. Instead, "loose coupling based on precise external protocols is required. Such protocols are by necessity message-centric; they specify the flow of messages representing business actions among

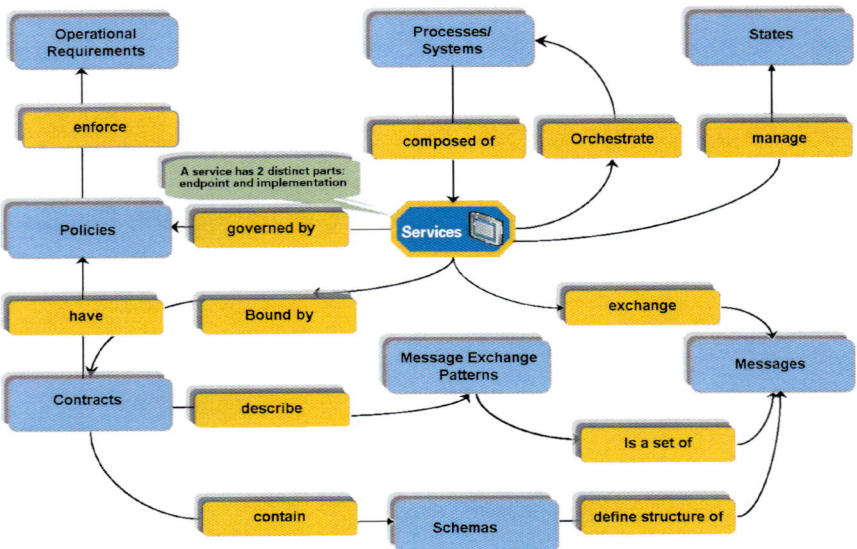

Figure 1. Schematic Diagram Depicting the Core Concepts of a Service
Figure 1 is adapted from Microsoft

trading partners, without requiring any specific implementation mechanism" (Thatte 2001). Figure 1 depicts the relationships between the core concepts that characterize the services in an SOA ecosystem. Following some of the arrows, note how SOA emulates the business boilerplate. For example, services are bound by contracts, contracts have policies, and policies enforce operational requirements.

The notion of a formal business contract, refined throughout many centuries of human commerce, provides numerous important lessons for the enterprise architect. Essentially, contracts enable heterogeneous and autonomous enterprises to cooperate according to well-defined rules. In addition, external facing contracts adhere to the document-centric paradigm and embed strategic business collaboration principles, including separation of concerns, polymorphism via declaration of intent, and reflectiveness. This structured document-centric cooperation, reflecting the social order, can be highly cost-effective by producing objects of value that individual enterprises would be unable to produce entirely on their own.

In a nutshell, transitioning to a "contract first" model based on exchanging reflective (such as XML) documents via messaging mirrors the way people interact/collaborate in human commerce. When a service provider prepares a contract specifying the nature (namely the "what" and the invocation policies) of a reusable/sharable service, any service consumer that can satisfy the terms of contract should be able to access the service simply by declaring intent, without any knowledge of how the service will be provided.

Furthermore, the service provider should be able to subcontract portions of the job to other service providers

---

[5] Pervasive Intermediation is a term coined by Jon Udell (2004) of *InfoWorld*.

[6] Michael Curry (IBM/Ascential) cited three characteristics as absolutely necessary to fully realize the potential of SOA: modularity, delegation, and federation (Curry 2004).

who agree to a set of subcontracts. Enterprises that concentrate on creating well-focused service contracts and actively seeking "best of breed" suppliers for each component are well positioned to succeed in a competitive environment. The success of Toyota Motors in the global marketplace represents one highly publicized example of this business philosophy.[7]

Herein lies one of the important design lessons for enterprise architects working in IT: decouple the service providers from the service consumers, and remain as open as possible in the concrete binding between service consumer and service provider. A design goal is to anticipate that service providers are likely to change over time while service consumers can be extended to include an unintended or non-targeted audience.

These lessons are the hallmark of the much-touted "loosely coupled" design principle of SOA that underscores agility and flexibility. Kelly Williams, CIO of First Franklin, who embraced SOA with the aim of maintaining a leading edge in mortgage lending, concluded that "no matter what the component model, if the services or applications talk point-to-point, you'll end up with spaghetti" (Manasco 2005). Interestingly, this design principle manifests "Software Reflection" and coincides with the rise of reflective coding (self describing, metadata driven and aspect oriented). Proper use of Software Reflection can produce flexible, adaptable applications. Steve Vinoski (2004) of Iona observed that reflective applications, like reflective people, are capable of dynamic self-improvement and offer significant flexible advantages towards flexible IT software.

Orthogonal to the traditional software development pattern, (that is, static binding constrained by compile-time checking), enterprise architects should strive for loosely coupled designs that enable dynamic binding (including dynamic brokering via brokers) by embracing and promoting the use of reflective metadata.

The Rise of Reflective Metadata to Enable Loose Coupling and Agility

Using reflective metadata encoded in the message documents to specify the requirements for constructing dynamic invocations (interactions) at runtime is perhaps one of the more compelling approaches to achieving delay binding and loose coupling.[8] The maturing open industry standard WSDL is gathering momentum as the de facto standard for enabling delay in concrete binding when implementing service end points.[9] Figure 2 illustrates the schematic diagram of a WSDL document construct that depicts the separation of the abstract metadata from the concrete binding.

With the reflective metadata approach, there is a small amount of IT overhead, and it may be less efficient than tightly coupling the identity of the service provider into the service consumer (a common practice in client-server architectures). However, from the perspective of the service consumer, this slight loss

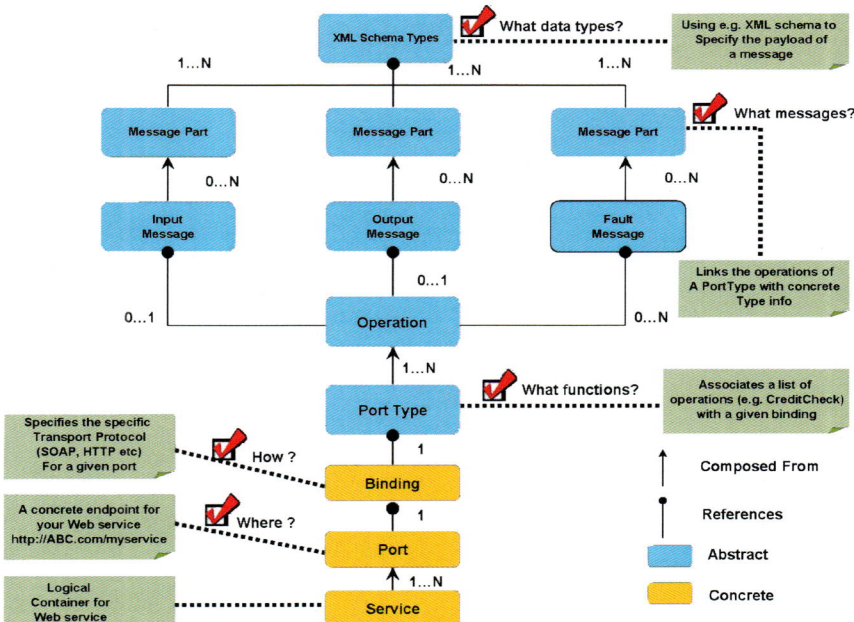

Figure 2. Schematic Diagram of a WSDL Document

---

[7] John Hagel and John Seely Brown highlighted this example in their most recent book, *The Only Sustainable Edge: Why Business Strategy Depends on Productive Friction and Dynamic Specialization*, Harvard Business School Press; May, 2005.

[8] The "metadata might specify a controlled form of process, such as an orchestration that specifies a well-ordered series of steps, or it might specify a looser form of process flow that designates only the preconditions and post-conditions for each service interaction (often called a choreography). In either case, the metadata only specify the requirements for service invocation, and not specifically how the underlying software components must control or execute the process (Bloomberg 2005).

[9] For now, as a contract language, however, WSDL is still rather restrictive and in some cases can constrain the underlying service implementations, resulting not so much in a robust SOA but in tightly coupled and "RPC style" innovations (Webber 2005).

of efficiency is more than outweighed by the benefits of using best of breed service providers and tapping into an infrastructure that provides a wealth of pre-assembled services. The resulting freedom of choice and the ability to customize flexibly the orchestration of services are essential to the success of the real time sense-and-respond enterprise. From the perspective of the service provider, the decoupling of service consumers through delayed binding facilitates pervasive intermediation and the ability to support broad-based unintended consumers. There is a net gain not only of operating efficiency but also, more importantly, scalability and business growth.

In other words, while today's *vertical* stovepipe-oriented IT focuses on internal command, control, and efficiency, tomorrow's on-demand-driven IT is all about interoperability, connection, and domain-specific collaboration. This collaboration supports *horizontal* value chains that connect a federated and virtualized network of business partners, including customers, suppliers, providers, retailers, manufacturers, auditors, financial institutions, and so on.[10] Michael Hammer forecasted in a 2001 *Harvard Business Review* article that "the victors will be those companies that are able to take a new approach to business, working closely with partners to design and manage processes that extend across traditional corporate boundaries. They will be the ones that make the leap from efficiency to superefficiency."

The Roads to Different SOA Styles

Making the transition from today's IT stovepipe environment to the service-oriented IT world of the future presents its own set of formidable challenges. Most companies already have an extensive portfolio of established business processes and legacy IT applications. One approach is to begin with a blank slate and identify systematically all core services within the enterprise in a central directory. The core services are then implemented within an enterprise-wide Web services management system and deployed systematically while stand-alone legacy applications are carefully phased out.

This top down deployment strategy, which has been characterized as the "big bang" approach, is being followed successfully by Motorola. According to Motorola CIO Toby Redshaw, 180 core services have been exposed thus far, and the project is proceeding well (Udell 2005).

Not all enterprises have Motorola's degree of centralized control and the financial resources required for this type of deployment strategy. However, individual core services can still be exposed on a step-by-step basis so that interoperability is achieved gradually over a period of time. This strategy is especially appropriate when services belonging to independent organizations should be integrated to improve service to common customers or to elevate the standards of service provided by all cooperating organizations. John Halamka, MD, CIO of Harvard Medical School, and architect of the New England Healthcare EDI Network (NEHEN), described a successful deployment strategy that has been structured in this manner (Udell 2005).

The main lesson from these two examples is that there is no single "correct" way to make the transition to SOA.[11] Such transitions always involve up-front costs, but these investments can be expected to be repaid over time through service reuse, lower operating costs, and improved levels of service by responding to accelerated changing business requirements.

Meta Service Infrastructure and the Rise of Visual/Declarative Modeling

As SOA continues to gain momentum, major software vendors have begun to recognize opportunities for new categories of products that support the SOA ecosystem. In particular, successful SOA implementations depend on a meta-infrastructure that provides shared services for management functions spanning metadata, registry, messaging, security/identity, service life cycle, policies, workflow, and performance management. The meta-infrastructure must also provide shared databases/repositories/registries for service descriptions, metadata, and so on.

The most promising innovation will likely come from a new crop of *visual, declarative, and reflective* tools for modeling basic business (process) capabilities, service interactions, and more importantly, service composition (assembly)—orchestrations, choreographies, and co-ordinations—at *run time*. By explicitly externalizing the process logic and the workflow-interaction specifications, SOA promotes a clear separation from the underlying code. But the realization of the potential of process-centric SOA hinges on the maturation and successful adoption of the nascent modeling tools. This dove-

---

[10] For more detailed discussions, see Thomas Friedman's book, *The World is Flat*, (Friedman 2005).

[11] Always start with a prudent SOA pilot. But beware of the all-too-common SOA trap in which an SOA pilot falls short and is reduced to a skeletal Web services pilot. Jason Bloomberg (2005) of Zapthink cautioned: "Implementing a Web Services pilot is a near-trivial exercise in exposing standards-based interfaces with little need for a consideration of architecture. SOA pilots, however, are mostly exercises in architectural planning, modeling, and organization."

tails with what Ronald Schmelzer (2005) of Zapthink described as a bi-directional runtime business process model, "one in which a change to the model will in turn change the way that the business and its systems operate, and vice versa, where a change to the business will automatically appear in the business process model."

In 2003, Forrester Research introduced the concept of Applistructure,[12] which refers to a business application framework that is designed to provide such composable "service infrastructure." Think of it as a meta-container for business logic that abstracts the complexities of underlying IT technologies, and a composition framework for service assembly. For now, the Applistructure concept has remained under the radar, but is not likely to stay there for long. Major software vendors are responding earnestly by ushering in broad-based middleware product suites for "SOA Applistructure." For example BEA recently (June 2005) launched their AquaLogic product line for SOA Service Infrastructure.

Applistructure reflects the growing convergence[13] of infrastructure middleware and business-process-centric applications that is driven by the need for IT–business alignment, IT-complexity containment, and IT flexibility. The concept of Applistructure provides the underpinning of the composite application platform. Unlike traditional application platforms, it is declarative via configuration/composition and represents a true application development paradigm shift towards IT agility for the emerging "User Organized Enterprise."[14] "The bigger picture here is about . . . redefining business processes and workflows—and providing the capabilities that enable these elements of work to be continually rethought, redesigned, and improved" (Manasco 2005).

Simply put, traditional commercial off-the-shelf (COTS) and Web-based applications are static and WYSIWYG (What You See Is What You Get), while SOA-based Applistructure can be uniformly assembled and composed, and can interoperate adaptively on demand to meet changing business needs. The traditional approach is generally procedural and is all about conventional technical software coding by developers and scheduled roll-out. The SOA approach, on the other hand, is *meta* and *declarative*. It is based on policy-driven configuration and composition, and on visual methods to describe (orchestrate, choreograph, coordinate), by myriad IT stakeholders, business process flows, and value-chain connections/coordination.

Industry analysts applaud this compelling vision of IT agility. For example, Gartner was unequivocal in the May 2005 report, "Gartner's Positions on the Five Hottest IT Topics and Trends in 2005": "SOA shifts developer focus from software to business functions, thereby transforming installed software from an *inhibitor to a facilitator* of rapid business change."

Conclusion: Meta Matters in a Connected, Virtualized, Federated SOA Ecosystem

Service-Oriented Architecture seems certain to transform the software industry and revolutionize the relationship between IT and real-world business. As in city planning, SOA promises to provide an elegant meta-framework for IT strategy that enables collaboration among business stakeholders, enter-

Enterprise architects must rigorously and continuously enforce overarching governance and service life-cycle management.

prise architects, and software developers so they can build cross-business-boundary value chains for the new digital business era. To all parties involved, SOA provides a unified meta approach as follows:

1. *Business Stakeholders:* connecting an extended and virtualized enterprise that includes employees (information workers), lines of business/departments, customers, auditors, consultants, partners, and suppliers

---

[12] Applistructure supports "the increased usage of pre-built business processes... resulting in a blurring of the boundary between application software and infrastructure middleware and creating a new class of software that could be referred to as 'Applistructure' software" (Vollmer 2003).

[13] This convergence should not be confused with the traditional MVC patterns of tight-coupling business logic (frozen in monolithic applications) and code implementation. SOA Applistructure mandates a clear separation of business logic and processes.

[14] Attachmate coined the term *User Organized Enterprise*.

to form collaborative value chains.
2. *Enterprise Architects:* connecting technical IT resources while delivering on cross-cutting concerns including security, identity, SLAs, policies, management, and governance.
3. *Developers:* connecting reusable (sharable) service/component logic to support the mirroring of business processes.

However, the true success of SOA depends on the cohesive metadata-driven blueprints that are carefully designed (as well as incrementally updated and constantly reinforced by overarching governance) by skilled enterprise architects who understand and adhere to SOA design principles and the nature of the business processes on which their enterprises are based. A high performing, cross-business-boundary (sometimes referred to as *borderless*) SOA ecosystem must begin with a collaborative (cross-discipline) modeling exercise along with meta-schema and metadata (business capability modeling, service interactions, and aspects modeling), prioritized by input from multiple stakeholders prior to technology implementations.

Just as important, enterprise architects must rigorously and continuously enforce overarching governance and service life-cycle management. Currently, such multi-faceted individuals are difficult to find, and there is a critical need for training in this area. In a recent piece on IT trend analysis, Forrester Research highlighted that "...Enterprise Architects, project managers, and business analyst roles are, in fact, in heightened demand and well-paid as a result. These jobs depend on communication skills, business process knowledge, and project management expertise, all of which depend on education and training"[15] (Barlas 2005). The metaphors and examples presented in this paper illustrate many of the design principles that enterprise architects will be required to master.

New innovative software products that provide a meta-framework of "service infrastructure" for SOA composite applications will also be a critical component in the successful transition to process-centric SOA. In this regard, there is a growing consensus among industry observers and analysts alike. J.J. Dubray (2005) of Attachmate succinctly summarized this, "The software industry must come up with a Composite Application Model that lets us build new solutions for the 'connected world' from existing IT assets that require little or no integration, based on data, process and UI (user interface) federation." Such a model would fit comfortably within Forrester Research's concept of Applistructure, and products in this category are just beginning to emerge. Applistructure will become a critical toolbox for enterprise architects, and the next 12 months are likely to represent a crucial juncture for this class of products.

---

[15] For example, Forrester suggests that one of the strategies universities can utilize to help businesses enhance their IT skilled personnel is by creating a hybrid business process, project management, and technology M.B.A. Program. (Barlas 2005)

References

Bloomberg, Jason. 2005. The SOA Pilot Pitfall. ZapFlash 13 July. <http://www.zapthink.com/report.html?id=ZAPFLASH-2005713>.

Barlas, Demir. 2005. State of IT. <http://www.portalsmag.com/articles/default.asp?ArticleID=6702&TopicID=10>

Curry, Michael. 2004. Modularity, Delegation, and Federation. 5 August. <http://blogs.ascential.com/soa/archives/2004/08/index.html>.

Davydov, Mark. 2004. Exposing EJB Components as Business Services: An Architect's View. <http://www.oracle.com/technology/pub/articles/davydov_ejb.html>.

Dubray, J.J. 2005. Composite Applications: Value Proposition and Architecture. <http://www.ebpml.org/capp.ppt>.

Friedman, Thomas. 2005. The World is Flat: A Brief History of the 21st Century. New York: Farrar, Straus and Giroux.

Gall, Nick. 2005. Breakthrough Business Performance: Driving Pervasive Integration through IT Innovation. METAmorphosis.

Hammer, Michael. 2001. The Superefficient Company. Harvard Business Review. September.

Manasco, Britton. 2005. Meta-Spaghetti. <http://blogs.zdnet.com/service-oriented/?p=226>.

Schmelzer, Ronald. 2005. Business Process: Sweetness & Light or Evil Hellspawn? <http://zapthink.com/report.html?id=ZAPFLASH-2005630>.

Thatte, Satish. 2001. XLANG: Web Service for Business Process Design. <http://www.gotdotnet.com/team/xml_wsspecs/xlang-c/default.htm>.

Udell, Jon. 2004. Pervasive Intermediation. <http://weblog.infoworld.com/udell/2004/10/18.html>.

Udell, Jon. 2005. SOA Styles. <http://www.infoworld.com/article/05/05/25/22OPstrategic_1.html>.

Vinoski, Steve. 2005. A Time for Reflection. <http://iona.com/hyplan/vinoski/pdfs/IEEE-A_Time_for_Reflection.pdf>.

Vollmer, Ken. 2003. The Emergence of 'Applistructure.' 18 March. Forrester Research.

Webber, Jim. 2005. The Tail Does Not Wag the Dog: A Cautionary Tale for Contract First Development. <http://webservices.org/index.php/ws/content/view/full/62161>.

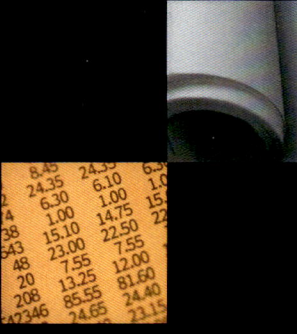

Grids and
SOA in Action:
Lessons Learned

introduction

Looking at Deployment Levels Among Investment Banks

The Impact of SOA and the Six-level Lifecycle Model

A Service-Oriented Architecture (SOA) defines how two computing entities interact in such a way as to enable one entity to perform a unit of work on behalf of the other entity. The unit of work is referred to as a service, and the service interactions are defined using a description language, usually based on Web Services.

When The 451 Group looks at the financial services sector, we see banks pursuing Grid computing not as an endgame in itself, but typically as an underpinning for other strategic corporate objectives, with basic cost savings at one end of the arc and the establishment of SOAs at the other. Indeed, the SOA concept now appears to be gaining real traction within the investment banking sector, and Grid vendors will benefit from aligning themselves with Independent Software Vendors (ISVs) supplying SOA infrastructure software.

At the same time, other investment banks are concerned that tools for supporting SOAs are too immature, and they are not using Grids to directly support initiatives in this space. Their view is that Web Services, in the componentization sense, will certainly occur before enterprise IT as a 'service' is realized—if indeed it happens at all. However, even if the approaches don't yet overlap for some, we expect they will, and sooner rather than later.

CONTRIBUTED BY WILLIAM FELLOWS AND STEVE WALLAGE, THE 451 GROUP

Bank of America and UBS typify those that recognize first and foremost the computing potential of Grids. Wachovia, Barclays Capital and CSFB have a much stronger services orientation. TD Securities and Merrill Lynch are examples of banks that expect to transition their focus from one through to the other. JPMorgan Chase, a well-publicized early adopter of Grids, is now looking at SOA as a way of improving interaction with clients and partners. Its goal is to try to deepen these interactions by providing online tools, reporting functions, and transactional functions as 'services.' One goal for a services-based approach is simply to get fund managers to move from dial-up to broadband interactions.

The key lesson is that Grids are not the goal for financial services companies, and vendors should ensure they can be accommodated as a pluggable layer in the SOA stack.

Six-level Lifecycle Model

The 451 Group has created a six-level lifecycle model that it uses to classify the evolution of Grid deployments at enterprise IT organizations. In this model, level one denotes the lowest entry level of deployment, whereas level six indicates the most sophisticated, mature level of deployment. In the financial services sector, the vast majority of investment banks have at least one Grid deployment. A few are holding out because they believe they have already made significant hardware investments elsewhere, or they worry about costs—and particularly the human costs—of Grids. Yet even these investment banks are likely to have tried out and seriously evaluated single Grid applications.

As rated on the lifecycle model, most investment banks are now at level 3 or 4. Interestingly, the majority of level 2 deployments were done almost 'under the radar' of the central IT group. They were all about particular departments—typically credit, risk, or derivatives groups—wanting to use Grid computing to not just enhance utilization on their applications, but to run simulations that could not be run before. This also depends on the organizational structure at the investment banks. At some banks, the line-of-business CIO/CTO has such power that s/he reports directly to the board. At other banks, the line of business' IT department is very much under the thumb of the central IT group.

The evolution from level 3 has two interesting implications for vendors:

- New suppliers—those that did not win contracts in the initial line-of-business deployments—have an opportunity to become part of new deployments (level 4 and beyond) through the central IT department.
- The existing suppliers that have developed strong relationships with line-of-business managers cannot afford to be at all complacent. They need to develop an equally strong relationship with the central IT department.

As deployments move to levels 3 and 4, the central IT group becomes more involved and enterprise Grid computing starts to fit more naturally into the wider company's IT goals, particularly the SOA strategy. The depth and clarity of thinking around SOAs varies widely between the investment banks. It is becoming the norm for investment banks to view Grid computing as one element in a longer-term vision to move toward the SOA model.

IT vendors need to step up to meet the changing needs of investment banks. Vendors also need to address issues such as I/O (rather than just raw compute power), workflow (moving beyond sequential problems), tuning and troubleshooting, infrastructure planning, predictive response, and SLA and policy management.

A key lesson for the vendors is that they must emphasize selling directly to the central IT department and CIO at investment banks, and can no longer rely on their relationships at the departmental level to further Grid adoption. As for retail banks and insurers, they are typically two to four years behind the investment banks. Although they are likely to use Grid computing to run single, specific applications, this will still tend to be under the auspices of the central IT group.

It is worth pointing out that it is by no means certain that all investment banks will follow the Grid adoption curve through the six levels. The 451 Group has heard of at least three investment banks that are seriously reconsidering their Grid deployments because the implementation has not met expectations, and they also see major problems in trying to extend the deployments. At least one bank has found that Grid computing is not as cost-effective as a mainframe solution. Suppliers cannot expect investment banks to continue being cheerleaders for the Grid industry. They must work hard to overcome all the challenges early adopters face.

Join us now for a closer look at the drivers behind enterprise adoption of Grids as well as the barriers that stand in the way.

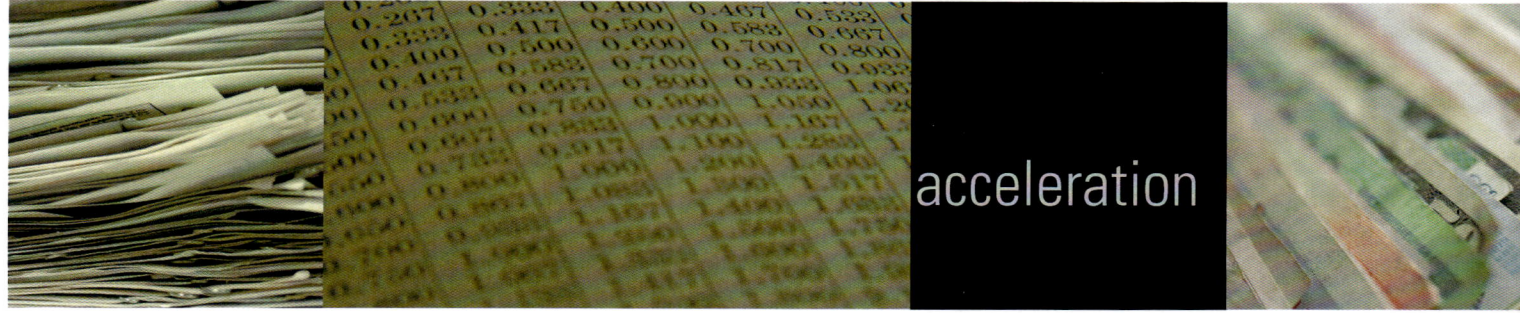

acceleration

Grid Computing Drives Business Agility: Enterprise Case Studies

Kelly Vizzini

DATASYNAPSE

Homegrown distributed-computing solutions can no longer solve the problems they were once designed to address, giving rise to the next-generation IT infrastructure based on advanced virtualization and Grid computing solutions. Those tightly coupled environments restricted to hard-coded legacy technologies and unable to react immediately to changing business demands have been replaced by an agile and responsive infrastructure where multiple applications can run on a shared environment and application demand can be fulfilled in real-time.

The "traditional approach" typically includes segmenting and partitioning for both users and application workloads, creating "distributed" but fixed processing silos, across which users and workload are "sprayed". This infrastructure is complex, is costly to maintain, and it cannot adapt to usage patterns or service-oriented business requirements.

Instead of applications being configured and provisioned on specific computers, applications can now be configured to run on the Grid without the need to identify the exact set of computers on which they will run. This capability creates a highly adaptive environment for running applications on a shared set of computers or Grid. Additionally, with demand-based allocation, applications requiring more compute resources can now scale dynamically at runtime to accommodate volatile application workloads.

Applied to computational and transactional applications alike, Grid is clearly the next step in the evolution of the IT environment. The price and performance gains of a Grid-enabled infrastructure are exponential. Grid is the key to accelerating Service-Oriented Architectures (SOAs) without having to undergo exhaustive and costly application rewrites or system re-architecture.

This article will explore the factors that contributed to the Grid deployment at Hewitt Associates, Genworth Financial, and Wachovia Securities, including the decision to buy vs. build; the advantages and business results achieved from implementing DataSynapse's infrastructure software, GridServer® Virtual Enterprise Edition; and next steps for expanding Grid initiatives across multiple lines of business for these companies.

Use-Case 1: Hewitt Associates

Hewitt Associates is a global human resources outsourcing and consulting firm delivering a complete range of human capital management services. The firm manages HR benefits for one in every 20 Americans, processing more than 70 million online transactions a week for companies such as Sony Electronics, Inc. and Johnson and Johnson. The company has operations in 38 countries, supported by 87 offices and 15,000 associates worldwide.

Applied to computational and transactional applications alike, Grid is clearly the next step in the evolution of the IT environment.

Hewitt's core service offering, representing nearly two-thirds of the company's overall revenues, consists of HR outsourcing service including everything from managing health insurance benefits to cutting payroll checks for companies with 10,000 or more employees. With the rise of the Internet, HR managers began to demand immediate access to employee data via the Web, forcing Hewitt to develop new and effective means of sharing large volumes of data with customers on demand.

Hewitt's pension calculation engine offers customers a quick and easy tool to calculate "what if" scenarios concerning individual pension benefits. As a result of mergers and acquisitions as well as new client acquisition, Hewitt experienced a dramatic surge in pension calculation requests. External drivers prompted client employees to visit the Hewitt site in order to evaluate retirement options using its self-service pension calculation feature. Jumping from 50,000 to more than 200,000 requests daily, Hewitt's portal environment running on the mainframe could not guarantee timely response to end-user requests. The unpredictable load and widely skewed requirements hindered the mainframe's ability to process requests in a timely manner. Moreover the high volume of requests caused a significant increase in transaction costs and impeded customer service levels, making the Hewitt calculation engine unprofitable to service.

Hewitt needed to deploy more computing capacity and processing power to the mainframe environment without enduring the high cost of purchasing new hardware and software—or internally rewriting applications. Secondly, the HR outsourcer looks to speed performance and reduced turnaround time of its core document generation applications. Hewitt sought a means to improve application runtimes and high-volume print requests for print communications such as account balances, service reports, policy forms, and billing statements, which could generate as much as 100,000 output pages per job. The goal was to arm customers with data-intensive reports in days vs. weeks, furthering Hewitt's commitment to superior client service.

To maximize its hardware investments, including IBM zSeries mainframes and xSeries Linux blades, and to achieve scale without increasing overhead or complexity, Hewitt implemented DataSynapse's GridServer software. Running pension calculations on the Grid, Hewitt was able to improve service levels and application resiliency by migrating application workloads to the most appropriate platform based on application requirements and resource availability at runtime. The end result was a highly scalable IT infrastructure that could quickly and effectively respond to changing business requirements in real time.

Due to the successful initial deployment of GridServer, Hewitt then extended the Grid environment to address its complex print composition applications (Sefas Document Factory Solution), expanding the company's capabilities for business growth and competitive advantage.

By offloading pension calculation requests to lower cost blade servers, while maintaining the active data on the mainframe, the company reduced transaction costs by 90 percent. Rather than waiting for mainframe batches to run, Hewitt customers exploit the large-scale parallelism of Grid and can now access reports in hours—instead of days or weeks. By Grid-enabling Sefas on GridServer, Hewitt has improved performance levels and transaction processing by as much as 50 times its previous run rate. Larger runs, which would previously take weeks, are now completed in hours without compromising any processing features that made the Sefas product so compelling.

"Everything we have done on the Grid comes up the same or substantially faster than on the mainframe alone," said Dan Kaberon, director of computing resource management at Hewitt Associates. "All the protocols we're using are Grid protocols. They are different from cluster approaches in that we can easily add many different machines to this configuration. We could throw 100 blades into the Grid without reconfiguring substantially. There's no cluster you can do that with."

Use-Case 2: Genworth Financial

Genworth is a leading insurance holding company serving the lifestyle protection, retirement income, investment, and mortgage insurance needs of more than 15 million customers. Built on GE heritage, the company has more than 5,000 skilled professionals overseeing $103 billion in assets throughout its global operations in 20 countries.

During the last decade the insurance industry experienced a paradigm shift led by new compliance and regulatory issues and a realization that legacy technologies were ill equipped to handle the speed and capacity require-

"I think it would be very difficult for a CIO to find a technology and an application that has the payback that Grid does."
—Kevin Gordon, Genworth

ments needed to improve analytic capabilities and bring products to market faster.

These regulatory pressures gave rise to more stringent requirements for internal capital assessment and risk profile calculations. Genworth needed to increase the accuracy of its calculations and drive down unmanaged risk while satisfying the industry's growing appetite for speed and capacity—ensuring that customer retention remained high.

With demand for compute-intensive workloads such as actuarial analysis surpassing existing IT resources, Genworth sought new ways to guarantee workload execution and improve the run-time rates of its actuarial applications for financial projects.

To keep up with the exponential demand for computing power, control costs, and maintain its competitive advantage, the company adopted a Grid computing strategy. Rather than enduring the high costs to build a homegrown distributed-computing solution, Genworth deployed the flexible and highly scalable GridServer Virtual Enterprise Edition software from DataSynapse. The standards-based infrastructure software virtualizes data components and business logic found in mission-critical applications and distributes these services across available systems resources as needed.

"The cost to deploy application processing across a Grid was nominal compared to the expenses associated with building out a clustered configuration, or adding new server boxes," said Scott McKay, global CIO of Genworth.

With GridServer, Genworth was able to leverage available and underutilized compute capacity within its existing IT infrastructure to reduce cycle times of its actuarial projection software (MG-Alfa, MoSes, PolySystems) from days to minutes, giving the actuarial team improved performance and control in determining premiums and optimizing cash flow while minimizing risk.

Replacing a farm of 10 dedicated servers with 35 desktop machines linked by GridServer allowed Genworth to accelerate time to results and increase the number of modeling iterations achieved within a given timeframe.

"The amount of additional computing power we're getting from the Grid is tremendous," said McKay. "With GridServer, we're seeing anywhere from 10 times or more improvement to cycle time, just by retiring dedicated hardware and leveraging assets that we already had."

The success achieved by placing actuarial software on the Grid inspired Genworth to evaluate Grid enabling other business-critical applications including life insurance application, Genius; annuity administration software, Transcend; and asset liability application, Profit. To identify and transition into production appropriate applications,

Genworth used DataSynapse's GRIDesign Lifecycle, a patent pending, best-practices methodology that helps companies identify and Grid-enable the applications that yield the highest business benefit when integrating into a virtual application infrastructure.

After completing the GRIDesign proof-of-concept, Transcend was targeted as the next Grid-worthy application capable of reaping tremendous performance advantages operating in a Grid environment. A variable annuity administration system managing accounts in the $700,000 range, the application suffered from long-running batch cycles, draining computing resources and negatively impacting Genworth's ability to deliver enviable service. To improve performance against service level agreements (SLAs) and drive better risk management, Transcend was added to the Grid. Once in production, policy valuation jobs taking 28 hours were processed in only 90 minutes.

Now, to achieve repeated success across the enterprise and to scale without the purchase of additional hardware, Genworth has migrated from a departmental to enterprise-wide Grid strategy.

DataSynapse's GridServer solution armed Genworth with an affordable and resilient IT environment for fast, in-depth analysis and improved decision support. Genworth was able to conduct stateful, iterative analysis using temporary resources to meet both the time windows and depth of analysis necessary to maximize return and minimize exposure. As such, the company is able to perform additional, more sophisticated stochastic analysis to drive better risk management, reduce cycle time for close processes and support regulatory requirements with ease. Once capable of running actuarial models on an annual basis, today Genworth has the compute capacity to run the same workloads multiple times per quarter at no additional cost.

"With GridServer we are able to do a better job managing risk," said McKay. "As a life insurance business, you're winning on the backend because the policies you're selling are better underwritten and therefore more profitable."

In contrast to running 35 engines on the Grid for one actuarial application and achieving 38 percent faster cycle times, today Genworth has 100 engines on the Grid supporting multiple applications and all modeling efforts. The company has significantly reduced IT expenses by retiring costly hardware. With dramatically improved application performance and response time, the company is able to introduce new competitive offerings and revenue-generating services.

"I think it would be very difficult for a CIO to find a technology and an application that has the payback that Grid does. The cost is so low and the benefits are so high that it can't be ignored," said Kevin Gordon, CIO of Insurance and Investment Systems at Genworth.

Use-Case 3: Wachovia Corporate Investment Bank

Based on client assets, Wachovia Corporation (NYSE: WB) is the third-largest, full-service brokerage firm in the U.S. and a leading provider of financial services to retail, brokerage, and corporate customers.

Of its core businesses and part of the Wachovia Securities entity, the Corporate and Investment Bank division provides capital raising, market making, financial advisory, and transaction processing services to meet the needs of corporate and institutional clients worldwide. The group is comprised of several business units, including Investment Banking, Fixed Income, Treasury Services, Credit Capital Markets, Equity Linked Products, International and Principal Investing, Equity Capital Markets, and Capital Finance. The Corporate and Investment Bank division is headquartered in Charlotte, North Carolina, with offices in Baltimore, Philadelphia, New York, San Francisco, Atlanta, Boston, Chicago, and London.

After migrating to a new trading platform, Wachovia's Corporate and Investment Bank encountered performance problems when trying to leverage the system's enhanced analytic capabilities. The solution lacked scalability and processing speed, and could not reliably guarantee failover capabilities in the event of hardware, software, or network failures. In addition, it was not able to prioritize computing jobs; dynamically match jobs with available, appropriate resources; or automatically reschedule jobs in the event of an interruption.

Users also faced unacceptable report turnaround times. For example, over-

> "In some cases we went from running a 15-hour application down to 15 minutes, using the workstations we already had as a single collective."
> —Robert Ortega, Wachovia

night risk reports with enhanced analytics took up to 15 hours, preventing traders from knowing their limits at the start of each day and affecting their decision-making abilities. Furthermore, certain complex but highly profitable products could not be priced accurately within necessary time constraints.

After assessing all of these challenges, Wachovia determined it needed a better infrastructure to support the significant increases in trading volume and reduce time to results of risk reports. To meet the traders' and risk managers' requirements, the bank decided it needed to either purchase additional hardware or implement a distributed computing solution.

Seeking to improve application performance and reliability while extending the value of its existing hardware, Wachovia focused on ways to leverage its underutilized resources. After exploring its options, the Corporate and Investment Bank found a partner in DataSynapse and its GridServer offering.

Wachovia's Corporate and Investment Bank first deployed DataSynapse's GridServer in April 2001 to support the bank's production system. The standards-based solution quickly proved successful, harnessing idle computing resources to generate unparalleled levels of application performance, scalability, and reliability. Wachovia has gone on to implement GridServer within its Credit, Global Risk, Equity, and Mortgage-backed Securities areas.

"We have more than 700 nodes on our Grid," says Robert Ortega, vice president of architecture and engineering for Wachovia. "Grid is our virtual application server that includes Windows, Linux, and Solaris/Sun applications. We do have (dedicated) application servers, but our basic plan is to use Grid to provide a very viable alternative to expensive Sun platform boxes."

Upon implementation, the Corporate Investment Bank realized GridServer drove significant application performance gains from time to build and deploy to improvements in scalability and resiliency. It was clear to see the steps toward a SOA saved money and improved computing efficiency.

"DataSynapse's ability to Grid-enable a wide range of resources including transactional and service-based applications makes it a compelling solution," said Mark Cates, chief technology officer for Wachovia's Corporate and Investment Bank. "We rely on GridServer to scale the business, control infrastructure costs, migrate to SOA, and maintain a high quality of service for our clients."

> "The cost to deploy processing across a Grid was nominal compared to the expenses associated with building out a clustered configuration, or adding new server boxes." —Scott McKay, Genworth

Some of the benefits Wachovia has experienced using GridServer include:

- ***Performance Gains:*** The solution enables four times more volume and 25 times more modeling simulations, supporting the trade of complex financial products.
- ***Improved Report Turnaround Time:*** Overnight risk reports have transformed from a 15-hour process to a 15-minute intraday cycle, enabling traders to make better decisions based on the timeliest data available.
- ***Increased Trading Volume:*** Trading volume for exotic instruments tripled, generating profits per deal of up to $1 million.
- ***Increased Simulations:*** The bank can run up to 100,000 simulations per deal as compared to 4,000 prior to GridServer.

In 2004, Wachovia's Corporate and Investment Bank's architecture team and DataSynapse conducted an assessment and design process to determine how to extend the bank's use of GridServer. The evaluation was conducted utilizing DataSynapse's GRIDesign methodology.

Not only did the joint discovery process uncover specific areas of opportunity where GridServer could be applied to drive significant improvements, it led to DataSynapse's GridServer becoming Wachovia's enterprise standard.

"Originally, the Grid was only used for compute-intensive applications, but now we're positioning it as a general-purpose transactional environment," said Ortega. "As a service execution platform for enterprise-wide SOA, GridServer has significantly improved productivity and performance levels at Wachovia, enabling a high degree of computing efficiency, speed, flexibility, and environment management. In some cases we went from running a 15-hour application down to 15 minutes, using the workstations we already had as a single collective."

versatility

Stripped-down Grid: A Lightweight Grid for Developing Countries

CONTRIBUTED BY HP

Grid computing has the potential to transform everything from drug discovery to aerospace design to analyzing stock portfolios but, until recently, its benefits were confined to regions where computing infrastructure is plentiful.

HP is working with researchers in Brazil to change that—exploring new technologies that could bring the advantages of Grid computing to some developing countries.

By hooking together individual computers around the world, scientists have created virtual supercomputers or Grids that can quickly process vast amounts of information, helping to produce breakthroughs in meteorology, physics, medicine, and other fields.

The Brazilian effort, relying on a software program called OurGrid, represents a lightweight approach to Grid computing. Most Grids today are composed of large organizations and new users must negotiate entry. To join the new network, users need only download the open source software (the latest release is OurGrid 3.0.2). By installing and using this software, users can make their own resources available to others and also become able to access resources from peers.

Standard Grid Computing: Far from Reality for Most

Unlike a classic Grid approach, the Brazilian effort's uses are limited to applications that can be divided into smaller tasks running independently of each other such as data mining, massive searches, computer imaging, and computational biology.

Regardless, scientists have found OurGrid to be plenty useful: The software has possible applications to projects ranging from drought forecasting to medical research.

"Despite the great progress made in the last years, Grid computing is still far from reality to most users," says Walfredo Cirne of Universidade Federal de Campina Grande (UFCG), which initiated the effort. "OurGrid is an attempt to change this, delivering Grid power to whoever needs it."

Simple, Decentralized, and Open

HP began funding the UFCG effort in 2003, and researchers from HP Brazil and HP Labs Bristol (UK) then also began contributing to the collaborative effort. The collaboration is one of numerous Grid projects at HP.

"There's a well-known slogan about Grid that says it'll do for computing resources what the Web did for data," says Miranda Mowbray, a researcher at HP Labs Bristol who worked on the system's resource-allocation mechanism and advised on ways to strengthen the system's online community.

"Grids use the same insight—that a simple, decentralized, open system may be more effective than a proprietary one," she adds. "Our implementation goes a step further than the standard approach in its simplicity and the autonomy of its distributed parts."

Along the way to developing the new technology, researchers faced (and continue to face) a series of challenges, including skepticism from the broader Grid community about their unorthodox approach. In addition, key characteristics of the technology—that it is lightweight and decentralized—pose further problems. Without centralized information on the state of the network, there's no way of knowing whether a specific machine is available, or to provide a global audit trail or shared cryptographic infrastructure. As a result, researchers have to find new ways to do scheduling, resource allocation, and security while using limited information.

Facilitating Research to Save Lives and Prevent Suffering

Members of the new Grid community are already producing results in medical and scientific research.

A medical research project in Rio de Janeiro used the system's computing power to successfully screen drugs for effectiveness with an HIV variant that is more common in Brazil and parts of Africa but rare in US and the EU—the two markets that sway new drug development.

"The results of this type of project could have a huge impact on the availability of the proper medications in Brazil and Africa," says Darlei Abreu of HP Brazil R&D.

Other scientists are experimenting with system resources to create a better model for predicting drought cycles in the Sertão area of Northeast Brazil. This vast region is the poorest in Brazil and suffers from severe and recurring drought. More accurate predictions could lead to better water allocation and more effective relief programs.

"This kind of research could save lives and prevent unnecessary suffering," says UFCG's Cirne.

A key feature of the new technology is that it enables users to exchange resources, a simple peer-to-peer protocol known as network of favors.

Peer-to-peer Network

A key feature of the new technology is that it enables users to exchange resources, a simple peer-to-peer protocol known as network of favors. Users are encouraged to donate their idle resources to execute applications for peers (doing them a "favor") because doing so increases their chances of receiving an equivalent favor back from the community.

"In some sense, users 'store' their idle resources—which would otherwise be wasted—on the community for later use," says Roque Scheer, an HP Brazil R&D manager.

Instead of requiring negotiation as a standard Grid does, the new Grid technology enables a much simpler automatic entry.

"Network of Favors ensures that, on average, you get back from the community the same amount of resources (CPU time) you donated," Cirne adds.

Next Steps

Some of HP's technical contributions to the collaborative effort are finding their way back into HP research projects. In Bristol, researchers are testing to determine whether the Grid's resource allocation mechanism can be used in a trial of a service utility for film animators. At the same time, researchers at HP, UFCG, and other institutions are working to make the technology more versatile and more useful, exploring ways to use Grid technology in commercial settings, creating large-scale community Grids and looking into Grid scheduling and dynamic resource allocation.

They also hope to make it possible for the system to run more types of applications, and they are working to apply Grid standards set by the Global Grid Forum so that the new system can interoperate with other Grids around the world.

Mowbray, who hopes to return to UFCG this summer to explore whether OurGrid can be extended to support sharing of data as well as sharing of computing power, says the work is both exciting and rewarding.

"It's just great to work on a project that supports applications like screening pharmaceuticals to treat a Brazilian variant of HIV/AIDS, and planning for water security in drought-prone Northeast Brazil," she says. "I find that very motivating."

Network of favors ensures that, on average, you get back from the community the same amount of resources (CPU time) you donated.

A Broad New Role for Grid in Commercial Applications: A Financial Services Case Study

One of the largest financial services companies in the world, working with Sun Microsystems, has demonstrated Grid hosting for near real-time transaction processing. Our work points to wider use of Grids in commerce.

Responding to growth in some of the heaviest transaction loads anywhere, Sun's customer implemented a high-performance Grid. Designed with proven, open, service-oriented technologies, this Grid takes application performance to the next level.

Business Drivers

The rapid growth of the Sun customer, here called FSCo as in "Financial Services Company," was pushing its flagship risk management application up against the performance ceiling of its centralized, batch architecture. To continue to grow and roll out new products and services, FSCo needed a solution that would move batch transaction processing inline and eliminate performance bottlenecks. Sun teamed with FSCo to develop that solution.

The solution architects realized that transactions related to different customers were independent of one another. Such independence allows peer transactions to be processed in parallel and pointed toward a distributed, service-oriented design.

Victoria Livschitz

SUN MICROSYSTEMS, INC.

The architects also noted a link between transactions and application data. Even though this application operates on 330 gigabytes of active records, any individual transaction is evaluated based on a small, identifiable subset of the data.

The affinity of transactions to specific data subsets suggested a performance-boosting service distribution approach. A Grid may be turned into a *memory Grid* by caching portions of a database in the memory of the service hosts. Incoming transactions are directed toward the copy of the service that has local access to the right data. As processing volumes rise and fall, a management service can provision data and services over a larger or smaller number of servers.

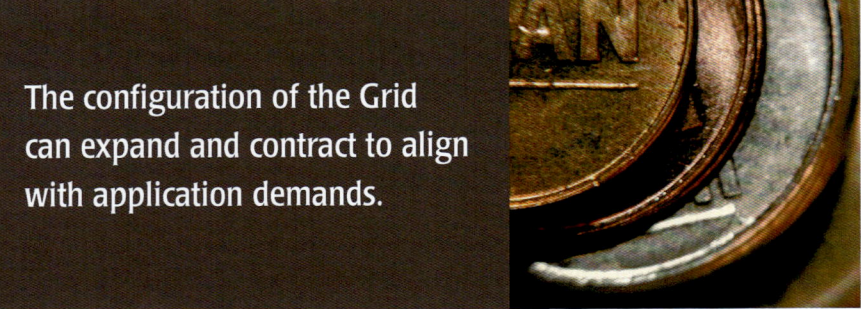

The configuration of the Grid can expand and contract to align with application demands.

Transaction independence and transaction-data affinity permitted FSCo to build the scalable, near real-time application hosting model it was looking for.

Solution

FSCo built a high-performance Grid that processes thousands of transactions per second. The transactions arrive from external client systems as messages. Results are calculated on the Grid and forwarded to external destinations. The configuration of the Grid can expand and contract to align with application demands.

The solution's service-oriented application architecture features three subsystems:

- *Functional*, for processing business transactions.
- *Service management*, for distributing services across the Grid.
- *Data management*, for distributing data across the Grid.

The implementation of each application subsystem can evolve independently, to keep up with requirements and technology.

Physical Architecture

FSCo's deployment configuration is based on 29 identical quad-processor Sun Fire™ V40z servers equipped with 2.2 GHz AMD Opteron™-based model 875 processors and 16 GB of memory.

Each server runs the Solaris™ 10 Operating System (OS), targeting x64 (x86, 64-bit) processors. Servers and storage are networked with gigabit Ethernet.

Service-Oriented Application

A *functional subsystem* groups three coarse-grained, distributed services:

- Business processing.
- Transaction dispatching.
- Result forwarding.

Business Processing Service

The business processing service is responsible for rating the desirability of transactions. Many copies of this service are deployed on the Grid at any time. As the load increases, additional copies start up on more servers. FSCo has tested the application with up to 112 copies. Each copy of the business service encapsulates a private copy of FSCo's scoring algorithm.

Transaction-dispatching Service

The transaction-dispatching service handles the delivery of incoming transactions to the business-processing service. This service examines the transaction, locates the data for which the transaction has affinity, and forwards the transaction to the corresponding business processing service in a message.

Result-forwarding Service

The result-forwarding service receives the processed transactions and their ratings from the business processing services across the Grid. Before forwarding the results to appropriate external parties, this service may further analyze ratings to determine proper actions, such as issuing an alarm. The result-forwarding service also handles maintenance functions such as logging.

These functional services are written using the Java™ 2 Platform, Standard Edition 5.0 with the exception of the scoring algorithm, which is as originally written, in C++, and accessed using the Java™ Native Interface.

A *service management subsystem* looks after the health of functional services across the Grid. This subsystem's services:

- Decide what services to deploy on which servers.
- Provision services to designated servers, during startup and failover.
- Monitor availability and the usage levels of the Grid's servers.

scalability

- Monitor the health and performance of application services.
- Initiate failover.

The service management subsystem uses Project Rio, an open source service management framework. Rio is based on open source Jini™ network technology that enables self-organizing, service-oriented networks. The Rio and Jini technologies were developed at Sun and contributed to the open source community.

A *data management subsystem*:
- Breaks the application master database into *data buckets*, the units of data distribution.
- Copies data buckets efficiently across the network into each Grid server's memory.
- Synchronizes data in each Grid server's local memory with the remote master database.

FSCo's application distributes 330 GB of application data into the memory of the Grid's 28 servers at startup. Three-quarters of the 16 GB in each server is reserved for the data buckets. Testing showed 112 data buckets with 3 GB of data in each bucket to be optimal. Each data bucket supports one copy of the business processing service.

Every time the contents of a data bucket change, the data management subsystem propagates the changes to the remote master database. Should a server fail, the service management subsystem detects the failure and automatically initiates a recovery process. For each copy of the business processing service that had been running on the failed server, the service management subsystem identifies a new host, provisions a new copy of this service onto the new host (along with a replacement for the lost data bucket), and starts the new service.

A Grid may be turned into a memory Grid by caching portions of a database in the memory of the service hosts.

Results

Our Grid-hosted application exceeded customer expectations. FSCo wanted 95% of the transactions completed within 50 milliseconds (ms.) when transactions arrive at 6,400 transactions-per-second (tps). To test the resulting system, nearly 24 million transactions were pushed through at five rates. Table 1 highlights performance outcomes.

At 6,400 tps, 99.9% of the transactions finished within 40 milliseconds. Even at 12,000 transactions per second, 99.6% finished within 40 milliseconds. Mean transaction duration for the 6,400 tps feed was 10.4 milliseconds including dispatching, network, and queuing time. The business processing service, which performs the numerically intensive calculations, accounted for about half of the mean duration in all five tests.

These measurements demonstrate that it is possible for FSCo to transition from batch to near real-time transaction processing, in spite of a demanding transaction volume.

Compared to the centralized-batch

Metric	4,000 tps	6,400 tps	8,000 tps	10,000 tps	12,000 tps
Average transaction duration in ms.	9.5	10.4	11.3	12.9	16.3
Percent of transactions longer than 40 ms.	0.080%	0.086%	0.087%	0.149%	0.376%
Transaction count	23,515,590	23,423,679	23,322,306	23,199,289	23,079,026

Table 1: Results for Simulator Transactions at Five Submission Rates

starting point, the new distributed Grid system nearly triples throughput in a tested configuration. Testing indicated nearly linear scaling as a number of servers were added to the Grid.

Lessons Learned

The lessons learned on this project suggest to us a few design principles of general interest. Stripped of application specifics, these principles may be suitable for many IT organizations running mainstream business applications:

- Applications with independent payloads such as transactions, messages, queries, sessions, jobs, and batches may be a natural fit for Grid hosting.
- Applications with Grid-friendly characteristics such as those mentioned here may encourage business logic designed as coarse-grained distributed services.
- For some applications, a Grid may look like a pool of CPUs. For other applications, a Grid may look like a pool of memory. Both views may be important at once.
- Even for Grid-hosted applications, scalability is a function of design.

The Future of Grid-hosted Commercial Applications

This case study updates IT expectations for transactional throughput in business Grids. Our solution moves the frontier of Grid computing beyond science and engineering. Today's feasible objective is robust, adaptive, transaction processing using service-oriented application design and mature, open, deployment technologies. FSCo's Grid marks the leading edge of Grid hosting for high-performance, mission-critical business applications.

The proof points suggesting a wider role for Grids in commerce reside in this case study of one Sun customer's achievements in financial services. FSCo's service-oriented approach to hosting business applications improves throughput beyond FSCo's needs today. No ceiling on scaling is in sight. Sun Grid technologies embodied in service-oriented application design have demonstrated robust, dynamic scalability for near real-time performance in FSCo's business-critical commercial applications.

©2005 Sun Microsystems, Inc. All rights reserved.

Compared to the centralized-batch starting point, the new distributed Grid system nearly triples throughput.

Bibliography

Livschitz, V., S. Farias, and S. Polansky (May 13 – 15, 2005) "Building Next Generation Grid-Enabled Business Applications with Today's Technologies," Sun SUPerG Conference (Washington D.C.).

Sun (2005) "A Broad New Role for Grid in Commercial Applications," to appear, http://www.sun.com.

Sun (2005) "Java 2 Platform, Standard Edition (J2SE), 5.0" http://java.sun.com/j2se/index.jsp.

Sun (2005) "Rio Project home," http://rio.jini.org/.

Sun (2005) "Solaris 10 OS," http://www.sun.com/software/solaris/.

Sun (2005) "Sun Fire V40z Server," http://www.sun.com/servers/entry/v40z/index.jsp.

Sun (2005) "Welcome to Jini.org," http://www.jini.org/.

perspective

Delivering Results with Grid: An Industry Perspective

Patricia Chavez

IBM

There's no doubt that Grid computing has countless business benefits—from productivity enhancement to informational insights to cost savings. Benefits gained are just as varied as the companies that are implementing Grids. Within some industries, competitive advantage comes from wringing efficiencies from operations, while in others the emphasis is on closer connections to customers.

In the financial services sector, for example, there is pressure to speed up the delivery of products and services to customers, and at the same time, develop a better understanding of those customers. A Grid solution improved Japan-based Higo Bank's efficiency by approximately 30 percent.

Manufacturers tend to be once removed from customers, and may be more concerned with being able to turn around product designs and testing within tight deadlines. In this case, Grid cut an application's processing speed from several days to just hours for Altair® Engineering, Inc., a provider of product design and development software for the advanced manufacturing industry.

Complex service organizations, such as government agencies, may be more focused on back-end cost efficiencies to better serve constituents within tight funding constraints. Again, Grid is delivering results—the U.S. Navy has access to more reliable and timely weather forecasts.

Organizations from these various industry sectors have leveraged the power of Grid computing to meet these varied goals and achieve impressive business results.

Banking on Grid

Consumers have a huge array of choices among institutions and products within the highly competitive financial services industry. Around the world, customers can go to any number of banks and financial service companies for loans, general banking, and investment guidance. The most important competitive differentiator in this market is the speed at which an institution can deliver quality products and follow-up service.

Higo Bank, a major Japanese regional bank, recognized the importance of fast turnaround time for customer loan applications. However, the bank's ability to deliver these products was often slowed by incompatible systems developed over the years on an ad-hoc basis.

As a result, bank employees had to access separate databases through separate computer terminals, print out data from each system, and then manually re-key data into the loan application. This system was time consuming, wasteful, error prone, and slow. The bank needed a single, more powerful system that could pull all the data from disparate systems and present it in one place, and process financing information quickly, and at a higher level of quality.

Instead of scrapping and building a new system that fulfills the bank's needs, executives decided to implement a data Grid that could provide a unified view of data spread across these systems to appear to the end user as one single set of data while protecting existing customer investments. The bank deployed Grid architecture across all its data sources, which included legacy databases, as well as a data warehouse. The data Grid solution, built on IBM eServer running WebSphere Information Integrator, provided information on demand by enabling the management of various loan and financing information on multiple platforms, allowing for real-time information integration.

"We can expect efficient and upgraded loan operations and human resource development through control of various customer data under a centralized management system," says Yuji Segawa, manager with Higo's New Total Financing System Project Office.

The new process provides new business insight by allowing the sales department and loan departments to share data, thus allowing the bank to offer new promotions or programs based on timely data. The new system also enabled Higo Bank to cut its loan-processing times nearly in half, to less than two days. Overall, the new system improved efficiency by approximately 30 percent, and freed personnel who used to spend their time transferring information between systems to concentrate on sales activities.

Additionally, since Higo Bank personnel can now access all customer data in real time from a centralized interface, the new system has eliminated the need to print out customer data in hard copy—a practice that previously used 1.5 million sheets of paper annually.

Grid for the Defense

The U.S. Navy, like most other organizations, needs to closely monitor its spending. Yet, the Navy has a big job to do in support of many far-flung operations across the globe. The challenge is to be able to constantly improve the delivery of timely information to battle groups stationed in all the oceans, while staying within budget.

The Navy moves vital information around the globe, but few things are more important to sailors and pilots than up-to-date weather forecasts. The weather can make or break operational plans, with cloud cover, for example, forcing a change in flyover locations or targeting, or poor sea conditions altering the timing or type of naval maneuvers. The Navy needed to be able to upgrade its weather forecasting systems capabilities without making expensive new system purchases.

The workloads that the Navy's Fleet Numerical Meteorology and Oceanography Center (FNMOC) required are very cyclical, explains Chuck Kleinschmidt, FNMOC's director of Enterprise High-Performance Computing (HPC).

> A company's ability to quickly turn out quality products often requires a deft balancing act.

"Twice a day there's a major peak where we just run models intensely, because we're putting out a weather forecast. There's a real crunch in terms of putting out our forecast within a space of three to four hours—there's a big surge. But if we can't do the forecasting in time, then it's not really useful."

FNMOC could not cost-justify buying a high-performance system to handle the two daily workload spikes.

To increase its computing power during these daily spikes, the FNMOC implemented a Grid arrangement between its own data center and that of another supercomputing center. The total capacity of this HPC environment is around 4.4 TFLOPS peak, though this need will grow to more than 20 TFLOPS within the next five years. When FNMOC needs more computing horsepower, the organization can easily add additional servers or share resources with other Department of Defense data centers.

Thanks in large part to this Grid deployment, FNMOC is better able to help the U.S. Navy and others receive reliable and timely weather forecasts. And because it's building a scalable HPC environment, it is better prepared for the future, supporting current military needs, as well as those planned as part of the Navy's Sea Power 21 doctrine, which calls for rapidly deployable and flexible sea bases near adversaries. Weather conditions are a key consideration in the ability to deploy these sea bases.

Speed by Design

For many manufacturers, time-to-market can make or break the success of a new product. A company's ability to quickly turn out quality products often requires a deft balancing act. Companies involved in product design and development, for example, are under tremendous pressure to achieve both quality and speed concepts that are generally diametrically opposed.

No one understands this natural tension more than Altair Engineering, who delivers innovative consulting and advanced engineering technology for high-end product design and development. To improve job execution and speed, and to increase the overall quality and accuracy of its designs, the 20-year-old company needed to automate certain cumbersome procedures in its design process. Previously, employees spent days meshing design data and converting geometric information from computer-aided design (CAD) diagrams into mathematical models suitable for use in further analysis. The meshing process was largely manual and labor-intensive. Altair started examining new ways to mesh and transform data into an automated job that could be completed overnight.

The new solution needed incredibly powerful hardware, capable of processing staggering amounts of geometric data in very short periods of time. Rather than purchase an expensive new system, the company rewrote their source codes to utilize across Grid technology. The Grid solution, provided by IBM, provides the high-performance computing resources necessary to support automated batch meshing across a massive Grid of servers throughout the Altair global enterprise.

By enabling the batch meshing solution to run on IBM Grid technology, Altair's meshing times are cut from several days to hours. The dramatic reduction in time and resources will allow the company to save costs and reallocate employees to more crucial tasks in the design process. In turn, the solution will enable more products to reach the market faster. In the future, Altair can use the IBM Grid to test more scenarios and consider additional variables, resulting in an overall improvement of product quality. Altair Engineering also plans to offer this same packaged Grid solution to its customers.

The most important competitive differentiator in this market is the speed at which an institution can deliver quality products and follow-up service.

Conclusion

In conclusion, the key advantage each of these organizations had is the benefit of an experienced partner to guide them through the Grid computing process. IBM has worked with numerous organizations to develop Grid computing solutions that make businesses more competitive with unique solutions based on their individual IT and business needs.

complexity

Reconstructing the Big Bang!
What the Business of Particle Physics
Has in Common with Business IT

An Introduction to the CERN Laboratory

The European Organization for Nuclear Research, "Conseil Europeen pour la Recherche Nucleaire" (also known as CERN), laboratory is located on the Franco-Swiss boarder near Geneva, Switzerland, and was founded in 1954 as one of Europe's first joint ventures. Today it boasts participation of 20 Member States and employs nearly 2,500 physicists, engineers, technicians, craftsmen, and administrators. Now the world's largest particle physics centre, CERN exists primarily to provide scientists with the necessary tools to conduct particle physics experiments involving high-energy particle accelerators. Some 6,500 visiting scientists, half of the world's particle physicists, come to CERN for their research into the nature of matter as it first existed immediately following the Big Bang and what forces hold it together. They represent approximately 500 laboratories and universities from more than 80 countries.

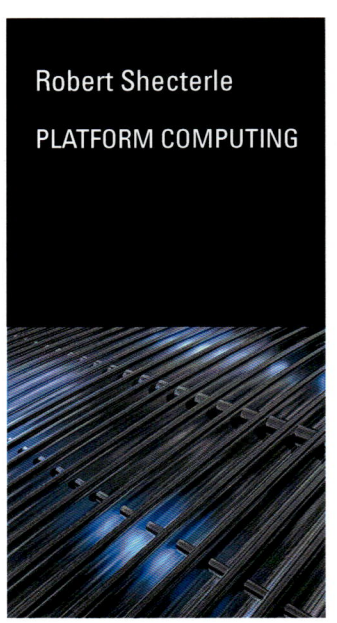

Robert Shecterle

PLATFORM COMPUTING

The Business of Particle Physics

Scientists have found that everything in the universe is made from a small number of basic building blocks, called elementary particles, which are governed by a few fundamental forces. Some of these particles are stable and form normal matter, while other, less-stable particles live only for fractions of a second before they decay into the stable ones. All of these particles—both stable and unstable—coexisted for a few instants after the Big Bang.

Now, it is only by smashing certain types of particles together, using the enormous concentration of energy that can only be achieved in an accelerator at facilities such as CERN, that the unstable particles can be brought back to life, recreating conditions immediately following the Big Bang. CERN's largest accelerator, which is being installed in a tunnel 100 meters underground and shaped in a circle 27 kilometers around, accelerates particles close to the speed of light—a speed equivalent to circling the full 27 kilometers more than 11,000 times every second—before causing them to collide with other particles.

At points where the collisions occur, very sophisticated detectors built by scientists from around the world enable physicists to study the collisions and observe such tiny and short-lived particles. By accelerating and smashing particles, physicists can identify their components or create new particles, revealing the nature of the interactions between them and the forces that hold them together. Studying particle collisions is like looking back in time, recreating the environment present at the origin of our universe.

The Challenges of Massive Data Analysis and Storage

Smashing beams of particles into each other generates staggering amounts of data. That data is captured and stored in CERN's custom-built data storage system, where physicists at CERN, or in locations throughout the world, can then use CERN's prodigious processing capacity to analyze the data for information that will help them prove or disprove their theories on particles and their interactions. This analysis, and the many simulations that typically accompany it, results in vast numbers of compute- and data-intensive jobs submitted to CERN's data center each day.

In the past, CERN has supported these growing IT demands by investing in ever more powerful computing and storage resources. As in many organizations, CERN's data center and its IT infrastructure evolved over the past ten plus years from a legacy mainframe environment—DEC VAX/VMX and IBM 3090-VM/CMS—to a distributed client/server topology. As additional compute and storage resources were needed, the IT infrastructure gained a mixture of HP, Sun, IBM, and SGI systems running a variety of Unix- and Windows-based operating systems that were purchased primarily to lower computing costs.

However, the resulting heterogeneous hardware environment drove up costs, while the increasingly complex system management challenges created barriers to effectively meeting the needs of the scientists and researchers using the facility. As a result, CERN has implemented a single, Linux-based cluster, which stands today at 2,500 Linux servers, all located in CERN's data center.

On the data management side, to handle their unique data storage requirements, capturing vast amounts of data very quickly from the particle detector equipment, CERN developed its own hierarchical data storage management system called CASTOR. Tape robots provide the platform for the CASTOR system, which also includes a large spooling disk based on a dedicated array of file servers.

> Enterprise Grid technology addresses common IT challenges independent of application type, offering a scalable Grid infrastructure regardless of industry and compute load.

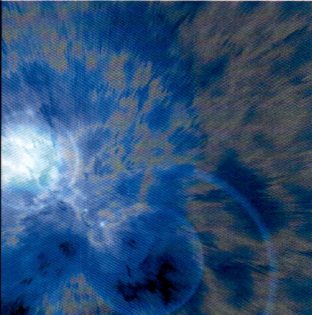

The Solution—Meeting the Challenges Head On

Realizing that its legacy workload queuing system could not keep up with this changing environment or scale to meet its rapidly growing needs, CERN implemented Platform Computing's LSF workload manager software to schedule and prioritize application workload across its Linux-based Grid.

Platform LSF matches the jobs submitted with the available computing resources and keeps these resources running at maximum capacity. Platform LSF also balances job priorities and handles the different user requests—some want jobs to run quickly vs. overnight, while other may run simulations for weeks. In addition, workload for CASTOR is also managed by Platform LSF in order to give physicists quick and easy access to experimental data.

Ultimate Grid Value

"With as many as 200,000 jobs being submitted every week, Platform LSF ensures that our computing cluster delivers results to our physicist users when they want them" says Dr. Tony Cass, Leader of the Computing Fabric, Infrastructure, and Operations Group at CERN. He continues by saying "We've had a very fruitful collaboration with Platform. We've both benefited from this in terms of improvements in areas such as queuing techniques and failover, and in the interesting new ways of using the Platform LSF product, such as for Grid-level scheduling."

What CERN's Grid Strategy Means to Commercial IT

What does a high-tech research facility like CERN have in common with commercial IT data centers? Both face complex heterogeneous IT infrastructures. Both are looking to virtualization to optimize unused compute capacity. Both are moving to lower cost, scale-out technology using commodity clusters. Both must manage large amounts of data across multiple application types while reacting to changing compute demands. In fact, it is only the character of the applications themselves that is materially different. In the past, these differences made it difficult to adapt commercial applications to take advantage of a Grid infrastructure. Today, enterprise Grid technology addresses these common IT challenges independent of application type, offering a scalable Grid infrastructure regardless of industry and compute load.

Platform Computing's range of Grid products deliver the power of virtualization, automation, and sharing of all IT resources to every application type. It is the core of an open enterprise Grid strategy that enables IT to allocate resources in real time for improved performance, organizational efficiency, and accelerated results. Furthermore, Platform Computing offers a flexible, modular approach to allow for growth and expansion at a pace that suits both high-tech and commercial business needs, so a single application can be deployed initially, and new applications can added when needed. The result is dramatically improved ROI on IT data center investments, lower IT costs, improved resource utilization, and a clear link to achieving strategic business objectives.

The result is dramatically improved ROI on IT data center investments, lower IT costs, improved resource utilization, and a clear link to achieving strategic business objectives.

What Comes Next for CERN?

For CERN, the future arrives in 2007 when the new and much-anticipated Large Hadron Collider (LHC) is expected to go operational, bringing unprecedented new levels of energy to the task of smashing particles. Physicists expect that the LHC will be able to confirm or disprove the existence of Higgs boson particles predicted to exist by the standard model particle physics. The bosons are a component of the Higgs Field, which is thought to permeate the universe and to give mass to other particles. No experiment to date has definitively detected or disproved the existence of the Higgs bosons.

The size and complexity of LHC experiments will result in huge volumes of data that will be exponentially greater than before. These experiments are expected to push CERN's detector and storage technology beyond its existing ability. One planned experiment involves a detector device that has 150 million detection channels compared with existing devices that have only 150 thousand channels. The speed of detection and the yield complexity would be a 1,000-fold increase in the volume of data needed to be captured and stored.

Analyzing all this data will require vast increases in computing power, and CERN's Platform LSF powered Grid computing solution is expected to grow to between 10 and 16 thousand Linux-based servers in 2007. Even at that level, the CERN Grid will only represent about 1/6 of the total worldwide computing resources needed to analyze data from the LHC experiments. Who knows, we may even learn more about the Big Bang.

reliability

Building and Scaling Out a Database Grid Using Industry-standard Grid Components

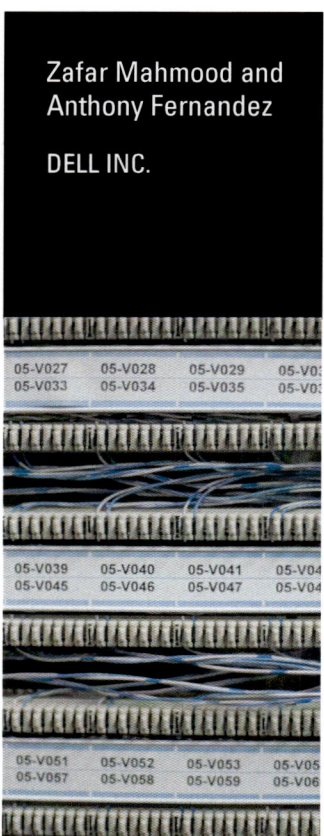

Zafar Mahmood and
Anthony Fernandez

DELL INC.

Database Grids allocate services across multiple, standards-based nodes to provide high performance and high availability—if a node fails or the workload fluctuates, the Grid can automatically adapt to address that need. Oracle® 10*g* Real Application Clusters (RAC) software running on industry standards-based servers and storage can provide a flexible, reliable platform for a database Grid. In particular, Oracle 10*g* RAC databases on standards-based hardware can easily be scaled out to provide the redundancy or additional capacity required by the Grid environment.

In the past, IT professionals typically added computing resources to database servers by scaling up vertically—that is, when database application response time degraded because of additional users, more complex queries, or database growth, administrators would add hardware or upgrade to larger, faster components. Scaling up often involves proprietary hardware and large symmetric multiprocessing (SMP) systems, which must be replaced once they reach capacity limits. This approach can ultimately lead to significant losses in hardware resources, performance, and availability. After reaching maximum capacity, further scaling up can become prohibitively expensive or even impossible until vendors release the next generation of hardware.

Scaling up can also be problematic for software because database servers have internal mechanisms that handle locking and other multi-user issues. For example, the 3-GB limit on the maximum user-space memory available to a process on a 32-bit OS can limit the amount of data that a relational database management system can cache on a single server. Software limitations become the primary impediment to continued scaling up. For this reason, SMP performance usually fails to demonstrate linear upward scalability as more processor power or memory is added. Typically, if this performance were graphed, after the curve started to flatten, the SMP system would require expensive hardware upgrades to gain miniscule performance improvements.

A Scale-out Database Environment

A cost-efficient growth strategy is to implement a database system that can scale out horizontally. Using open standards-based hardware, the scale-out environment can provide redundant servers, storage systems, and components—resulting in a high-performance, highly available architecture with low total cost of ownership (TCO).

Implementing a Scalable Oracle Database Environment Using Industry-standard Servers

Oracle 10g RAC software running on standards-based components can be used to build a scalable database environment. Each node in the cluster with equal access to the shared storage has its own set of Oracle background processes and memory structures, which are synchronized over a high-speed interconnect. Oracle 10g RAC uses Cache Fusion technology for global cache synchronization across nodes. Figure 1 depicts a typical four-node Oracle 10g RAC database cluster on high-availability industry-standard hardware. This

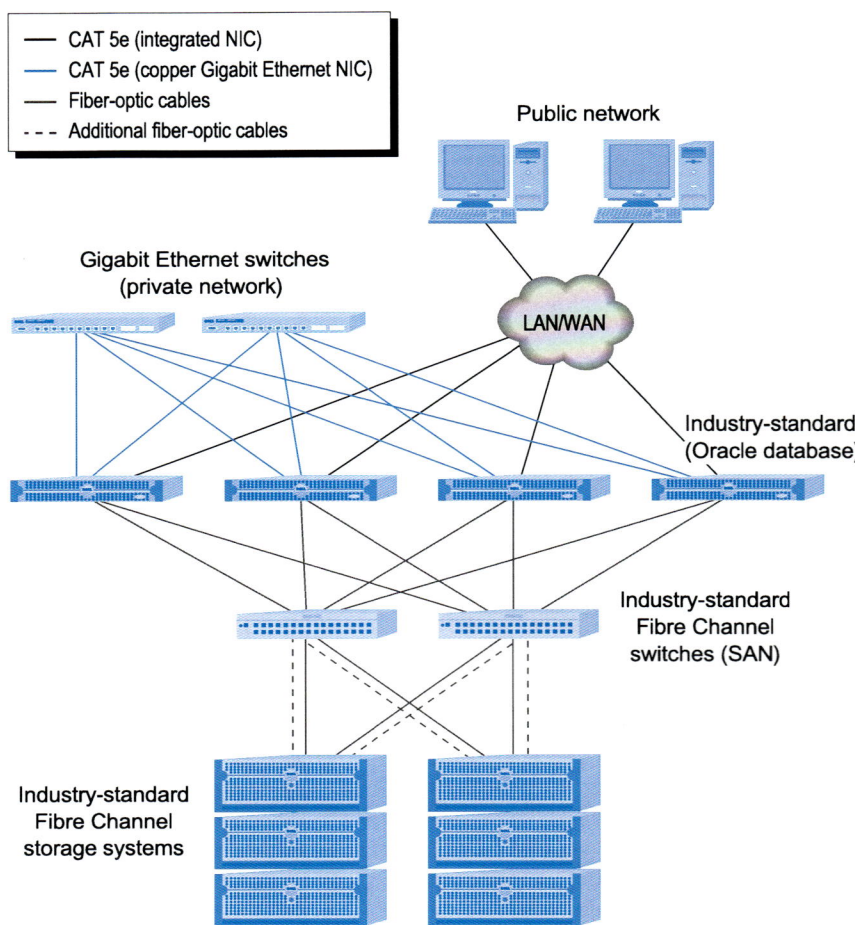

Figure 1. Typical Four-node Oracle 10g RAC Database Cluster on Industry-standard Hardware

architecture is designed to provide redundancy down to the component level.

Scale-out Tasks for Oracle 10g Database Grid

An Oracle 10g RAC database is designed with the inherent capability to scale out. RAC software includes built-in tools to scale out the database from the Clusterware level to the database instance. However, basic prerequisites must be met before the RAC application can be scaled out. Additional nodes must be:

- Installed in the exact manner as existing nodes, using the same OS mount points and configuration parameters.
- Made part of the cluster at the network layer.
- Made part of the storage area network (SAN).
- Prepared for a Cluster File System or Oracle Automatic Storage Management (ASM) database storage before they are made part of the database.

After meeting these prerequisites, Oracle tools can help integrate an additional node into the existing cluster. The following steps can be taken to scale out the Oracle 10g RAC environment at the Clusterware, database, and instance layers:

1. Scaling out the Clusterware layer: In this step, the Oracle Universal Installer modifies the existing cluster layer and makes existing nodes aware of the newly added node. The required Oracle Clusterware files and binaries are automatically copied to the added node from the existing cluster nodes, and the Oracle Notification Services are set up.
2. Scaling out the database layer: This process extends the Oracle database home from the existing nodes to the newly added node. Using the Oracle Universal Installer, the required Oracle binaries are copied from the existing nodes to the newly added node and the virtual IP address and private interconnects are defined within the Oracle Cluster Repository location.
3. Scaling out the database instance layer: This step extends the existing Oracle database instances to create and add the new database instance that will run on the new node. The Oracle Database Configuration Assistant is used to perform the necessary tasks such as ASM instance creation, node application setup, Oracle high availability component configuration, and Oracle Net configuration set to enable database users to perform database operations on the newly added node.

Automating the Scale-out Tasks

Although Oracle provides tools to scale out the Clusterware and database, these tools cannot perform bare-metal OS deployments. Consequently, third-party configuration tools are needed to help meet prerequisites before the Oracle scale-out tasks can be fully automated. Several third party tools that integrate with server management solutions can facilitate bare-metal OS deployments and enable newly added nodes to be quickly integrated into the Oracle cluster.

Testing Scalability

In June 2005, Dell engineers tested the scalability of Oracle 10*g* RAC software on Dell hardware. Figure 2 shows the configuration used in the test environment. The test started with one node and scaled up to four nodes. A typical online transaction processing workload was run on one-, two-, three-, and four-node RAC configurations. All other variables remained constant. The number of transactions per second was captured for each RAC configuration. Each node simulated 200 concurrent users performing database transactions. As

> The ability to scale out is the basic component of Grid computing.

	Hardware	**Software**
Cluster nodes	Dell PowerEdge 2850 servers, each with: • Two Intel® Pentium® 4 processors at 3.6 GHz • 4 GB RAM • 800 MHz frontside bus • 1 Gbps Intel NIC for the public LAN • Two 1 Gbps LAN on Motherboards (LOMs) teamed for the private interconnect • Two QLogic QLA2340 HBAs • Dell Remote Access Controller	• Red Hat Enterprise Linux AS 4 QU1 • EMC® PowerPath® 4.4 • EMC Navisphere® agent • Oracle 10g R1 10.1.0.4 • Oracle ASM 10.1.0.4 • Oracle CRS 10.1.0.4 • Linux bonding driver for the private interconnect • Dell OpenManage
Storage	• Dell/EMC CX700 storage array • Dell/EMC Disk Array Enclosure (DAE) with 30 disks (73 GB 15,000 rpm) • Two 16-port Brocade SilkWorm 3800 Fibre Channel switches • Eight paths configured to each logical volume	• EMC FLARE™ Code Release 16
Network	• 24-port Dell PowerConnect™ 5224 Gigabit Ethernet switch for the private interconnect • 24-port Dell PowerConnect 5224 Gigabit Ethernet switch for the public LAN	• Linux binding driver used to team dual on-board NICs for the private interconnect

Figure 2. Hardware and Software Configuration for the Oracle 10*g* RAC Cluster

Figure 3 shows, near-linear scalability was achieved from one to four nodes in the number of transactions per second on each node.

It is recommended that all Grid components have the same hardware and software configuration so that scaling may be as linear as possible. To compare test results when the hardware configuration is not identical, the test team ran a second test with the same scenario as the first test, with one exception. Each of the first three nodes had two host bus adapters (HBAs) and used NIC teaming on the private interconnect, but the fourth node had only one HBA and no NIC teaming. Because this node lacked I/O load balancing and NIC teaming features, its transaction numbers were reduced to almost half that of the other nodes (see Figure 3).

Oracle 10*g* RAC Services Framework

The ability to scale out is the basic component of Grid computing. In a Grid environment where many nodes are part of an Oracle 10*g* RAC database, applications connect to the database Grid using RAC Services. RAC Services is a recent feature that tightly integrates with Oracle Cluster Ready Services (CRS) to provide these capabilities:

- Applications connect to services, which are defined within the database Grid.
- Services can span multiple instances, with additional instances made available in response to failures or workload demands.
- Services are available continuously, and the load is shared across one or more instances.
- When a database Grid is configured, the nodes that will host the services can be one of two types: preferred instances, which start the service and are the primary nodes; and available instances, which are used to replace failed preferred instances or to meet increasing workload demands.
- Services are available in the database Grid as long as one surviving node exists.

Figure 4 depicts a four-node database Grid with four services configured. Each service is configured with two primary instance nodes; the other two nodes serve as the available instances. These RAC services can span over to additional nodes in response to increased workloads on the preferred nodes or failures in the database Grid.

> Today's data center demands an infrastructure that is highly available and scalable.

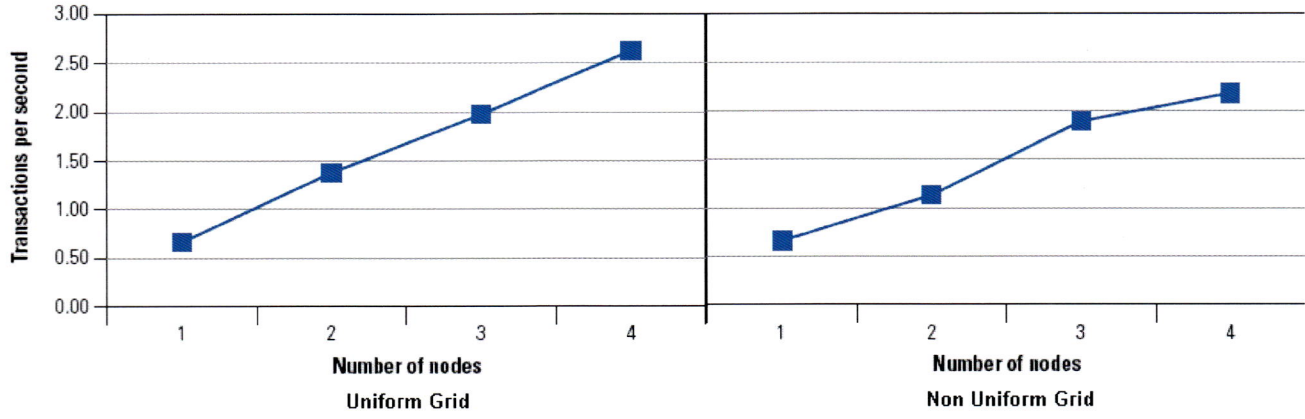

Note: The results shown in Figure 3 are not actual numbers and have been normalized. These results represent the relative scalability of an Oracle RAC database with minimal database and OS tuning. Actual transactions per second will vary based on hardware configuration as well as OS and Oracle tuning parameters.

Figure 3. Transactions per Second as Nodes are Added

reliability

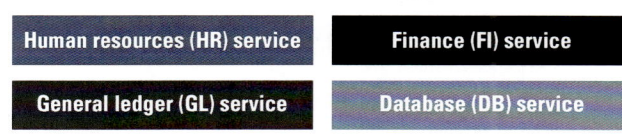
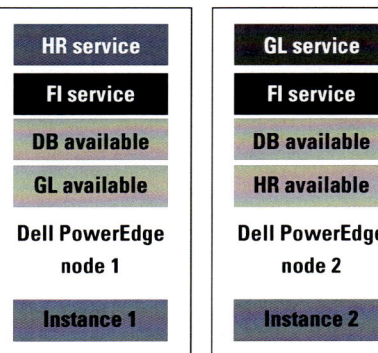
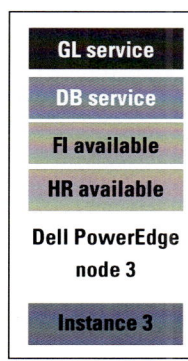
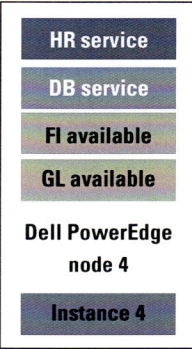

Figure 4. RAC Database Grid Comprising Four Nodes and Four Services

Testing Failover and Load Balancing in Oracle 10g RAC Services

In this study, Dell engineers also tested the failover and load-balancing capabilities of an Oracle 10g RAC database Grid. Using the same hardware and software setup, the team configured a two-node RAC database with a service called *orasrv*. The two nodes—*oradb1* and *oradb2*—both served as preferred instances. An order-entry client application performed various data definition language and data manipulation language operations on the RAC database using the *orasrv* service. The service was used to make 250 connections to both nodes. At a steady state, the user count was almost evenly distributed across both nodes, processing a total of 538 transactions per minute. When instance, *oradb1*, was powered down, its existing user connections failed over to the surviving node, *oradb2*, using the Oracle Transparent Application Failover feature. This feature also enabled the new connections to automatically connect to instance *oradb2* and allowed the database to continue executing transactions. Because only one node was available for transaction processing, the transactions declined to 314 TPM and CPU utilization on the surviving node almost doubled.

When the failed node was brought back online, Oracle CRS automatically restarted the database instance and *orasrv* service on instance *oradb1*, and notified *oradb2* of the other node's availability. It was observed that the client connections automatically load balanced over time across both nodes using the server-side load balancing feature of Oracle10g RAC. Performance returned to almost 538 TPM.

Building a Scalable, Highly Available Database Grid

Today's data center demands an infrastructure that is highly available and scalable. Oracle 10g RAC database software running on industry-standard architecture components is designed to provide high levels of redundancy and scalability, and to overcome the CPU, memory, I/O bandwidth, and interconnect limitations faced by proprietary, monolithic, single-node environments. Using tools provided by Oracle and third-party OS deployment vendors, administrators can easily deploy and scale out this database environment. Oracle 10g RAC software running on industry-standard servers are also helping define Grid computing technology through its robust services framework designed to fail over, relocate, and expand services transparently in response to failures and workload demands.

© 2005 Dell Inc. All rights reserved.

The scale-out environment can provide redundant servers, storage systems, and components—resulting in a high-performance, highly available architecture with low TCO.

149

From Industry Vision to Business Success

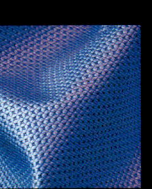

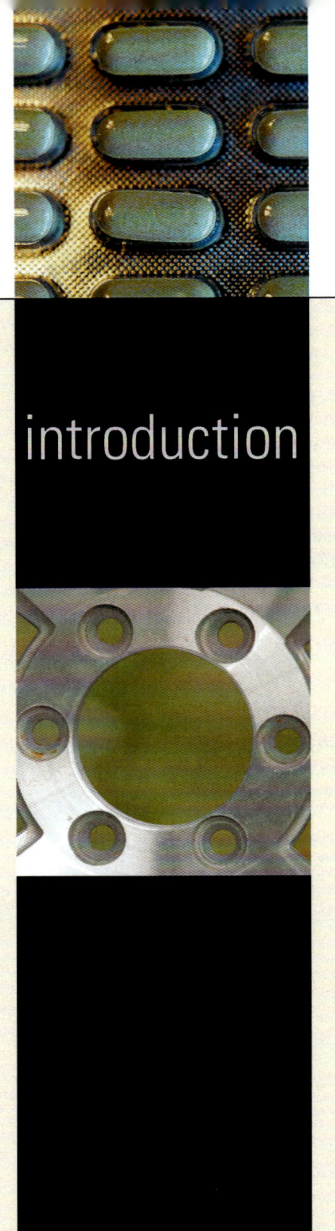

introduction

Enterprise Grid Adoption to Accelerate, Driven by 'Agility'

The 451 Group believes the acceleration in Grid adoption in the coming 12 months will be accompanied by a shakeout among the vendors and a rush by those keen to embrace the notion of enterprise Grids. The increased penetration of Grids in commercial areas, and early adopters' desire to run an increasingly wide variety of applications on them, will force many Independent Software Vendors (ISVs) to rethink Grid enablement and support, as well as software licensing. The term 'Grids' will not always be at the forefront of such moves, because ISVs couch their strategies more in terms of utility computing and Service-Oriented Architecture (SOA).

Many ISVs have paid lip service to the notion of Grid support, with 'Grid enablement' often limited to one or two applications. Take Adobe, for example. Working with GridIron, it Grid-enables After-Effects for the digital media industry but does not support it elsewhere. A deeper approach to Grid enablement has been seen from SAS, commonly requested by Grid users. It has enabled its data mining and data integration applications, together with the SAS Grid Manager, which includes Grid middleware licensed from Platform Computing. By the end of the year, other large ISVs will have gone further than SAS, which itself is likely to make further strides in Grid support over the year.

CONTRIBUTED BY WILLIAM FELLOWS AND STEVE WALLAGE, THE 451 GROUP

Inextricably linked to this is the issue of software licensing. It is not just about Grids; other drivers such as open source and multicore are provoking a wider rethink. However, Grid users will drive change in the year that will vary between verticals. Although broader changes will need a significant change from the likes of IBM and Oracle, particular verticals (and key Grid users) often have a reliance on just a few ISVs. Take pharmaceuticals—drug discovery software from Schrodinger, Tripos and Accelrys—or EDA users—Cadence, Synopsys and Mentor Graphics. It requires just one of these companies to make a break and some are very aware of the Grid opportunity to cause a sea change in the licensing environment. This will happen over the year.

As the Grid market matures and evolves, vendors will also seek to develop broader and more open approaches. Among the Grid middleware vendors, there will be pressure to support competitors' software, both from enterprise IT organizations (particularly the banks) and from the need to operate in other verticals.

Grid mergers and acquisitions have so far been limited, and many startups are now preferring to position themselves as something different, whether 'next generation' or 'SOA' or something else. The key driver over the next 12 months will be the necessity for larger vendors to broaden their portfolios, and, in particular, to meet the needs of users in data management. There was limited movement in 2005 on this issue, but activity will be much stronger in 2006.

Adoption Scenarios

Doing new things and responding more quickly to changing requirements and conditions—call it 'agility'—is becoming a key driver for the Grid plans of enterprise early adopters.

What has become clear is that virtualization is paving the way for enterprise Grid adoption, and that it is not simply Grids, per se, that users are concerned with. It is how Grid technologies (virtualization, resource reallocation, automation, flexibility and management), plus the business and delivery models they support, can underpin strategic enterprise IT goals. Grids, however, will continue to gain ground as an infrastructure technology for SOA, datacenter automation/management, business/IT alignment and shared utility models.

The first conversations inside enterprise IT organizations around the benefits delivered by Grid implementations are driven by resource reallocation, total cost of ownership, better performance consolidation and better utilization. But findings within the 451 Grid Adoption Research Service indicate this conversation turns very quickly—after initial benefits are realized—to one that revolves around using Grids to improve response to customer and internal requirements, to improve time to market and competitive position, and to do new things and do them more quickly. Again, agility. We expect this conversation and these benefits to move to the center of the industry's dialog around Grids as users move beyond initial Grid application beachheads.

So what about reducing costs? The reality about saving money using Grids, as HSBC observes in an interview with The 451 Group, is that while "a reduction in total cost of ownership would be nice, you won't save money, but (using Grids) you will be able to make more money." For vendors, the challenge is to drive Grids from being used in tactical deployments into more strategic enterprise-wide roles. The key issue is whether users have, or will want to buy or build, applications that can take advantage of Grids outside the initial beachheads—downstream from high-performance computing applications.

The chasm is behind us—the forward direction is clear. Enterprises want to have greater agility.

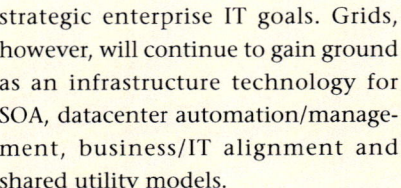

Doing new things and responding more quickly to changing requirements and conditions—call it 'agility'—is becoming a key driver for the Grid plans of enterprise early adopters.

Where is Enterprise Grid Computing Going, and How Do We Get There?

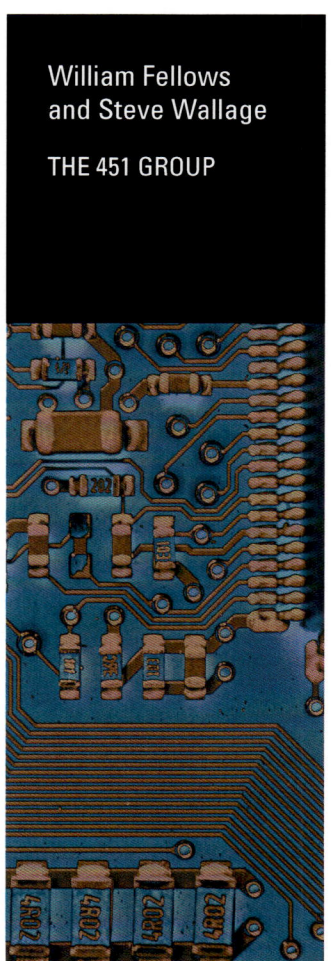

William Fellows
and Steve Wallage

THE 451 GROUP

The year 2005 brought on an increasing awareness of Grid computing within enterprise organizations. The term itself now has more value and prevalence than ever. We saw the major IT vendors spend heavily to market the concept of Grid computing, with the smaller vendors benefiting from the ride at their expense. Grid computing technology even made it into TV ads. Expectations for the growth of enterprise Grids have never been so high, and soon we will see whether it was money well spent.

Grid computing is no longer only about high-performance computing (HPC) or implementing commodity servers. Grid computing has developed into a means to support Service-Oriented Architecture (SOA) application infrastructure, utility computing delivery infrastructure, and the automated datacenter. With integrators and Independent Software Vendors (ISVs) coming to Grid computing and SOA and utility IT models coming into view, the expectation is that this will be the year that Grid technologies start to cross the chasm into the enterprise. In vertical markets we are already seeing that Grids are becoming better established at doing the grunt work—i.e., complex modeling and design tasks. And a few companies are making strides in Grid adoption, moving quickly from small clusters, usually based around homogenous servers, to hundreds or thousands of devices. But where are we with Grid computing in a broader enterprise role? What is driving enterprise adoption, and what are the barriers that stand in its way?

The Drivers of Enterprise Adoption

The 451 Group's Grid Adoption Research Service (GARS) has focused on understanding the needs of enterprise early adopters of Grid computing. 451 analysts have interviewed more than 200 early adopters and have an extensive database tracking their adoption. Initial conversations with early adopters, for the most part, have revolved around improving utilization and lowering costs. But as some firms are benefiting from initial Grid deployments, the conversation is shifting to Grid technology's ability to respond more quickly to changing customer and internal requirements, the ability to improve time to market and the ability to do more new things more quickly. These are increasingly the key drivers of accelerated adoption.

The 451 Group has identified several major business and IT drivers of Grid adoption at many companies:

Cost savings and improved utilization
Saving money by moving to commodity hardware and increasing utilization have been key drivers, particularly with early investments in clusters. There are clear cost benefits in connecting clusters and consolidating hardware on an enterprise basis. One company in the manufacturing sector believes its previously installed Unix systems provided similar performance at ten times the price. Another company gets better performance from its new clusters for the cost of just maintaining its old Unix servers.

Better utilization of expensive software licenses is another benefit of Grid deployment. Some early adopters expect to easily meet ROI criteria simply by improving license utilization.

Improved performance
While cost savings are often the initial driver for Grids, it is improved performance and the ability to do new things

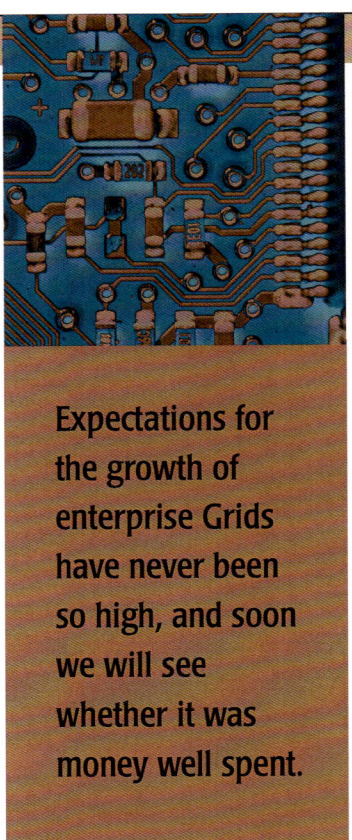

Expectations for the growth of enterprise Grids have never been so high, and soon we will see whether it was money well spent.

that lead to greater penetration and use of Grids. Within some companies, various departments are seeing the performance benefits enjoyed by other groups and are deploying clusters on their own, often without being formally sanctioned or without needing to be coordinated by the central IT department. For others, the investment in clusters was based on consolidation and better utilization of resources, but the move to Grids has been led by the ability to innovate in response to customer requirements.

Doing new things
Many enterprise Grid early adopters claim not only the ability to do things more quickly, but also the ability to do more complex analyses. Indeed, some companies might not be capable of certain projects without clustering of commodity hardware.

Centralized data
To both enable collaboration and meet regulatory requirements, the centralization and sharing of data are important issues for many companies. There are also legal reasons for strong data management. In the automotive space, government regulations require that companies record all crash testing results in one place, an often difficult proposition when the research has been carried out across multiple locations.

IBM believes that a specific advantage of Grids is that they remove some of the human element, and therefore enhance the speed and accuracy of processing large amounts of data. There are clearly security issues with sharing data and resources, which has led to some resistance from users.

Improved time to market
Improving time to market is often an important business driver for many companies. In the manufacturing sector, more detailed simulations let engineers increase product reliability and fuel efficiency before building a physical model. By decreasing turnaround time for product design, companies are able to speed analysis of design alternatives and achieve faster time to market.

Collaboration
Collaboration is about more than simply providing a centralized data resource. For companies that have grown through acquisition and, as a result, are scattered across various cities, countries, and continents, improving communication and interaction between these divisions is a major challenge. In some cases, facilities are located away from major metro areas, and therefore away from the main communications hubs. Many companies are looking to move to a shared infrastructure, with Grids being the obvious underpinning, to link its operations.

The Barriers to Enterprise Adoption

Now that the compute element is reasonably well understood, the next challenges in Grid computing are essentially those that are 'beyond the compute Grid.' The 451 Group has learned that early adopters from different vertical markets share many of the same key challenges and concerns. These concerns correspond with what many early adopters and 451 analysts have identified as the main challenges—and barriers—to adoption.

Software licensing

Software licensing is definitely the key concern for an increasing number of early adopters. For all of the potential benefits of Grids, early adopters cannot afford to buy software licenses for every device in the Grid—which is a necessity, since the Grid, by its nature, dynamically consumes resources. 451 analysts believe that as early adopters evolve into using Grids as a more mainstream technology, the restrictions of current software licensing will become an even greater obstacle.

Many of the Grid vendors talk about supporting the ability to proactively manage the use of software licenses based on business objectives. But early adopters have their doubts about this and are asking for real and tangible changes. Because of this, we could start to see early adopters collectively exerting pressure, within vertical markets, on suppliers for change.

Alternative purchase models, as well as new technologies, such as multi-core and virtualization, suggest a change is under way that will have a cumulative and disruptive impact on vendor licensing policies and practices. For that reason, software licensing for Grids must be seen within the context of the changes taking place throughout the industry, since there is a lot of money at stake.

Data management

Aggregating compute resources without aggregating data to support it does not make much sense in commercial environments. However, much less time has been devoted to figuring out how data can get to where it needs to be, when it needs to be there, and to how this process is managed, than to the compute element.

As momentum for enterprise Grid adoption builds, the ability to put data in the most suitable places—so that it can be shared with other applications when required—is increasingly coming into the spotlight. The 451 Group has identified elements such as data streaming, caching, synchronization, replication, namespace, movement, and transfer as important for this goal. Yet none of the major IT vendors are able to offer all the elements of this data management stack, and many users have either developed strategies to get around these problems (such as only

Vendors need to start taking steps to migrate existing applications to Grids, whether developed as new for Grids or supplied using software-as-a-service models.

using their Grids for applications where latency is not a major issue) or built their own in-house software, as in the case of some investment banks. A combination of technologies—and suppliers—is the most typical solution.

Cultural and organizational barriers

Most early adopters have long-term and far-reaching plans to extend their Grid activities, but reaching beyond departmental deployments brings issues like trust, control, sharing and ownership into play.

Standards

The world of standards has contributed very little to commercial, enterprise Grid computing. The proliferation of Grid industry bodies only means more confusion, not less, and has slowed the momentum of Grids. The standards that do exist today are not relevant, and there is no evidence that standards are being used in implementations or that any product is being built using them. If Grids can find a place in one of the open source stacks, such as LAMP, it would undoubtedly help further adoption.

The 451 Group believes that there needs to be a convergence of standards efforts. The Global Grid Forum (GGF) announced that it would try to find synergies with other standards groups in order to avoid duplicating efforts. GGF and the Enterprise Grid Alliance (EGA) have already mentioned that they plan to combine their organizations. This is a start. The hard part will be how to reconcile short-term enterprise goals with longer-term global ambitions.

Design models, development approaches

Only a few applications have been written specifically for Grid computing, and only a small number of today's applications have been deployed on Grids. The tools, models, and infrastructure technology for developing Grid applications and services have been mostly focused on HPC to date.

But as enterprise momentum for Grid computing increases, new design points, development models, and tools for creating and enabling commercial applications for Grids will be required.

A Look Forward

IT vendors have gambled that Grids will be used more widely in the enterprise, to support a range of activities that include SOA, datacenter automation and utility delivery down to development, disaster recovery, ERP and supply chain—not just for HPC applications or consolidation purposes. The limited availability of commercial applications for Grids, as well as utilities and design points, presents a real and present barrier to this happening.

To date, only a few applications have been written specifically for Grids, and only a small number of today's applications that appear suitable have been deployed on Grids. In order to encourage the use of Grids downstream from HPC, vendors need applications that can take advantage of Grid adoption. Vendors need to take steps to migrate existing applications to Grids, whether developed as new for Grids or supplied using software-as-a-service models.

The Grid industry—IT vendors, Grid middleware providers, system integrators and ISVs—are laying foundations that will see the Grid-enablement of applications accelerate significantly. HP's planned Application Provisioning Service is a good example of the latter. Sun and IBM both have application ISV partner programs. Middleware providers—generally known for job scheduling and reporting—are also eager for customers to move Grids downstream of HPC. Platform Computing, DataSynapse, United Devices, and Univa hope to create sustainable, scalable businesses by facilitating and managing downstream enterprise Grids.

The 451 Group expects companies like Accenture, CSC, EDS, and IBM to move from proof-of-concept Grid engagements to production references. Second-tier systems integrators and offshore companies, including Satyam, Tata Consultancy Services, Infosys Technologies, and Wipro Technologies, are also establishing enterprise Grid practices. Collectively, systems integrators (SIs) can leverage huge communities of partners to build momentum around the use of Grids in the enterprise.

Early adopter interest in deploying Grids across the enterprise hinges entirely on business need, with applications as the essential driver. Where it makes sense, vertical-market ISVs have already embraced Grids, and more are coming every quarter. The 451 Group expects that what happens in the market will depend on what the major IT vendors do. Companies to watch will be SAP, Oracle, and business intelligence vendors, among others.

A Final Thought

Eventually, Grid technologies will become more invisible as they are pushed down into systems and systems/network management software stacks. Changes in the way companies buy software and IT services—such as pay as you go, subscription and outsourcing—suggest there is a long-term and cumulative disruption under way in the economic model for enterprise IT.

Despite all the hype, it will take a lot of time and effort to turn everything into a service. The use of Grids to support utility models and SOAs within enterprises will be the key market initially, with companies testing outsourced Grid services for additional capacity and loads. Grids can underpin SOA, the 21st century datacenter and utility computing models, but the extent to which they can be integrated with legacy event-driven services, messaging, database systems, and networking systems will be crucial to their success. IT as a shared utility underpinned by Grid technologies, and the business models this supports, will become increasingly important.

451 analysts expect that enterprise early adopters will still be plagued by the barriers mentioned—but that IT vendors will begin to address them. Grid is a means to an end. The destination, not the journey, should be the focus.

Coming up . . .

Over the coming months, The 451 Group will continue to analyze enterprise early adopters' progress toward implementation of Grid computing, as well as the issues they face along the way. Look for 451 analysts to revisit the Grid computing opportunity within the financial services market. Also look for reports covering Grid enablement and the 'killer app,' and another that compares usage and experiences across all vertical segments.

> Early adopter interest in deploying Grids across the enterprise hinges entirely on business need, with applications as the essential driver.

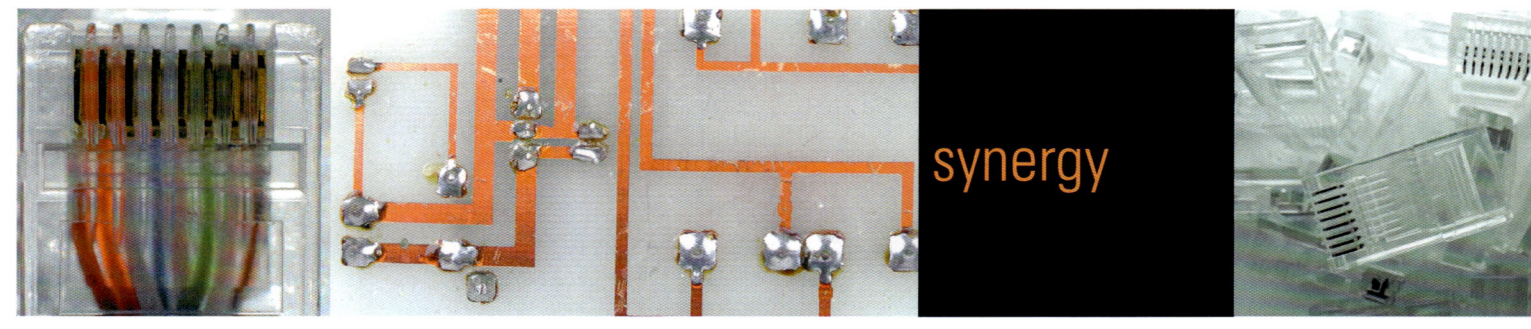

synergy

Taking a Fresh Look at Grid Computing

IDC's worldwide market studies have repeatedly indicated that organizations are focusing on ways to lower their costs while making their investments in information technology (IT) provide short-term, real, measurable business value. As in the past, this has lead IT decision makers to a focus on how to deploy distributed computing solutions based upon low cost, industry standard systems and sophisticated virtualization software rather than relying only on single-vendor midrange or mainframe systems. Today, these configurations are called "Grids." These configurations are often at the very heart of Web-based application architectures.

This, of course, is not really a new trend. Organizations have been deploying distributed computing solutions, including Grids, since the late 1960s. Unfortunately, each time a vendor offers an incremental improvement in technology, it often also declares a new catch phrase or buzzword in the attempt to gain some competitive advantage over others offering similar technology. Although the concepts of Grid computing are relatively easy to understand on a conceptual level, there are a dizzying array of phrases being used to describe what is essentially the same thing—a computing solution in which each application or application component is hosted on the platform considered by the IT decision maker to be the one most suited to that task.

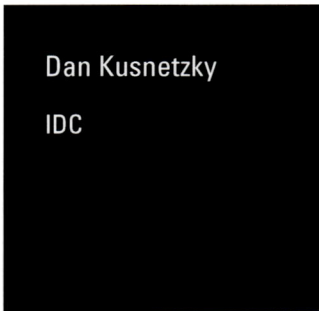

Dan Kusnetzky

IDC

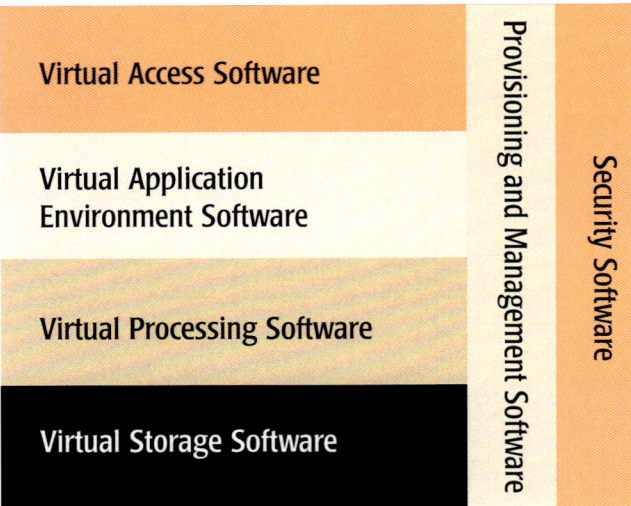

Figure 1: IDC's Virtual Environment Software Model Source: IDC, 2005

Some of the catch phrases vendors have used since the late 1960s include: on-demand computing, adaptive infrastructure, autonomic computing, distributed computing, client/server computing, clusters, compute farms, computational Grids, blade computing, server-centric computing, thin-client computing, matrix computing, and even fabric computing. I'm sure that if we all think about it, we'd be able to come up with many more phrases.

In IDC's view, this complex distributed approach can be summarized using IDC's virtual environment software (VES) model. Each layer of this model consists of many different types of software. Each type of software in a given layer focuses on abstracting a given function away from the underlying hardware in the hopes of providing an environment that is infinitively powerful, scalable, reliable, and manageable. The word "infinitely," in this case, is defined as the answer to the question "How large of an investment does the organization wish to make in this function?"

Virtual environment software creates an image of a single computing resource to the end user even though the actual computing environment might be made up of either centralized resources in a single datacenter or distributed systems housed in datacenters all over the globe (see Figure 1).

Virtual environment software can break the link between a given function and the underlying systems. This means that functions may survive the loss of their original host system. In case of a failure or slowdown, some forms of virtual environment software will either start the function on another system or pass the request to another instance of that application or function. The newest generation of virtual environment software allows organizations to increasingly see their systems as a pool of shared resources that appear to be both self-healing and self-managing.

In the end, this approach allows organizations to not only protect their investment in hardware and software but also to optimize this investment. A completely virtual environment allows established applications or functions to access features of newer systems and to be more reliable, more powerful, more scalable, or enhanced in some other way. To take part in a virtualized environment, it is critical that organizations carefully consider all these factors and then deploy support for each of these layers of software. It's important to note that suppliers often combine several of these layers into a single product.

The segments of the model can be described as follows:

- *Virtual Access Software.* This software allows applications to be accessed from nearly any intelligent access point device over just about any network without the application having to have been architected to support that device or network.

- *Virtual Application Environment Software.* This software creates an application development and deployment environment that allows properly developed applications to be more robust and reliable and also allows them to be unaware of the underlying operating environment and hardware platform. These benefits are *only* available to applications written for this environment.

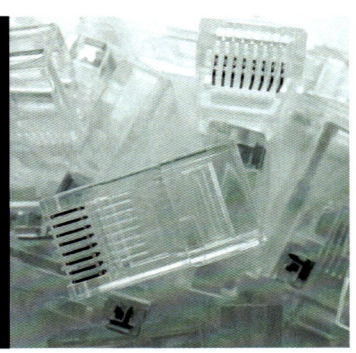

Organizations have been deploying distributed computing solutions, including Grids, since the late 1960s.

- **Virtual Processing Software.** This category of software ranges from virtual machine software making a single system appear to be many systems, each supporting its own operating environment, to single-system image clustering software, which makes many systems appear to be a single computing resource, running a single operating environment. This category also includes parallel processing software, load balancing software, and data and application availability software. This layer is the primary support for Grid computing, blade computing and configurations described as "compute farms."
- **Virtual Storage Software.** This software allows applications to be unaware of where and how application and data files are actually stored. This software supports both storage area network (SAN) and network attached software (NAS) hardware configurations.
- **Provisioning and Management Software.** This software makes it possible for operators and administrators to load, manage, and operate multi-system configurations regardless if any of the other virtual environment software categories are present. This is a primary component of "on-demand" or "adaptive environment" approaches to application deployment.
- **Security Software.** As applications are decomposed into components (sometimes called services), identity management and access control become increasingly important. Without a strong security layer, "black hats" could pick apart the distributed architecture and commandeer application components or functions to the organization's detriment.

Most uses of Grid computing fall into one of four categories: computational

Organizations are increasingly deploying applications using Service-Oriented Architectures to reduce the costs of development and support.

Grids, application Grids, storage Grids, and optimization Grids.

- **Computational Grids.** Computational Grids are configurations designed to offer organizations very high computational performance though the use of a number of inexpensive industry standard systems rather than relying on a single super computer. These configurations typically deploy virtual processing software, virtual storage software, and provisioning and management software.
- **Application Grids.** Application Grids are configurations designed to offer organizations a high level of performance, reliability and scalability for their transactional and content management applications. These configurations typically deploy virtual application environment software, virtual storage software, provisioning and management software, and security software.

synergy

- **Storage Grids.** Storage Grids are configurations designed to offer organizations a very large storage system that is fast, responsive, scalable and reliable. These configurations typically deploy virtual storage software and provisioning and management software.
- **Optimization Grids.** Optimization Grids are only now emerging. This type of configuration treats a number of industry standard systems as a pool of resources that can be assigned to a task and reassigned to another task when either that first task completes or when a higher priority task is presented for processing. These configurations often deploy all of the layers of IDC's virtual environment software model.

"Why are organizations using this approach?" is an obvious question to ask at this point. The answer is relatively simple. The organization usually wants to be able to deploy IT solutions using the lowest cost systems that can still fulfill the basic requirements of having one or more of the following characteristics: high performance, high levels of scalability, data and application availability, or the ability to create a self-optimizing pool of computing resources. Furthermore, organizations are increasingly deploying applications using Service-Oriented Architectures to reduce the costs of development and support, which is likely to rely on one or more layers of the virtual environment software model.

It's clear from IDC's research on the subject that many organizations feel that virtual environment software is big. By the end of 2004, virtual environment software produced $19.2 billion in revenue worldwide. By 2008, IDC expects virtual environment software to have grown to be an impressive $30 billion in revenue worldwide.

adoption

Grid Solutions for the Enterprise

Parviz Peiravi and
Enrique Castro-Leon

INTEL CORPORATION

Grid technology initially emerged from the academic and scientific communities as a way to aggregate computing facilities from multiple locations to work on really large technical problems. However, the challenges addressed by Grid technology, namely dynamically allocating and managing diverse distributed resources, are the same issues faced by corporations seeking to take their IT infrastructure to the next level of agility and responsiveness. This article discusses how the latest generation of standard, high-volume commercial computing platforms supports the Grid paradigm, with some advice on how to specify Grid architecture to ensure optimal performance. We also show how an enterprise Grid can be built on an existing IT infrastructure to support a wide range of usage models including high-performance computing (HPC), integrated enterprise applications, and "real-time enterprise" applications with distributed sensors, RFID readers, and other autonomous data sources.

Hardware Advances Enable Grid Adoption

While much of the infrastructure that enables Grid technology consists of multiple layers of standards-based software, there are also a number of hardware technology transitions taking place that will accelerate the adoption of Grid. The new technologies not only provide more raw processing power, but also expand the speed and flexibility of interconnections, and increase the ability to remotely manage hardware resources. These improvements allow computing and storage platforms to be configured and managed in ways that provide the most utility for a given set of requirements. Some of the most important hardware developments include:

- **Multi-core CPUs:** For the past 20 years, single-chip CPUs have been the *de facto* building blocks for computers. However, it is now possible to place two or more CPU cores on a chip, with higher aggregate performance than if the same number of transistors were placed in a single, more complex core. In the future, multi-core processors and chipsets will essentially comprise another distributed processing layer at the level of the physical device. That is one reason why the Intel® Itanium® processor was designed with three levels of cache memory—to ensure that the data bandwidth is efficiently matched to both processor and inter-processor data movement requirements. The multi-core level of the Grid will add significant performance gains while being essentially invisible to the layers above. The pervasive presence of multi-core CPUs will become a major motivator for building software applications so they can execute efficiently on many CPUs running in parallel.

- **On-chip Virtualization Support:** The latest processors and chipsets now have special operating modes and facilities that enhance the performance, stability, and security of Virtual Machine Manager (VMM) software that provides a standardized interface for using and managing hardware resources. The VMM layer is a critical enabler for the full realization of Grid.

- **High-bandwidth, Low-latency Memory Architectures:** Reductions in cost per byte have made it possible to build mainstream systems with more than 4GB of physical memory per CPU. This makes it possible to economically build large Grid arrays with enough dedicated memory for each processor to be highly efficient.

- **PCI-Express-enabled Chipsets:** The new PCI-Express standard is a serial, point-to-point data transfer protocol that can be aggregated (i.e., multiple lines can be used together) to achieve virtually any target bandwidth. Even implementations for transferring data from one chip to another on a single circuit board are feasible and highly efficient and economical.

- **InfiniBand:** InfiniBand is a point-to-point protocol that moves data between devices located a few feet from each other at extremely high rates, overcoming the limitation of the traditional "backplane" bus when connecting together multiple computing and storage elements. InfiniBand increases the flexibility of distributed systems by enabling processing components to be physically separate from storage facilities. Compute nodes can then be installed or removed almost at will, making maintenance extremely easy. Even if a node has a local boot drive, it can be pulled out and replaced by another node that gets "re-imaged" from a common data store on the fly.

- **Backplane interconnects:** Size reductions in platform form factor now make it practical to build large-scale "blade server" systems. Small but completely functional computers can be arranged like books in a bookcase, an improvement over the "pancake" form factor used in previous systems. Blades are simply inserted into a metal enclosure or cage and get power and transfer data via a *backplane connector*. I/O can be accomplished with any of a number of technologies, including Ethernet, FibreChannel, or InfiniBand.

Grid can enable compute-intensive applications to take advantage of unused processor cycles and memory on desktop computers.

Achieving Maximum Performance: The Rule of 10

One of the greatest advantages of Grid is that performance of any application can be managed dynamically and automatically, with Grid management software allocating more resources as needed to maintain an acceptable service level. However, there are still performance issues for the IT manager to consider when using Grid technology.

A typical Grid system has multiple CPUs in a node (i.e., a "box"), multiple nodes in a cluster, and multiple clusters forming the Grid. The equipment used to build a Grid does not have to be physically different from other equipment in a datacenter—the difference is in how the layers are integrated to enable a large number of computers to run a single application.

A key determinant of the performance of a Grid is the data movement capability in each one of the layers. For instance, moving data across two nodes in a LAN involves spanning a significantly longer physical distance than moving data to a CPU from its associated RAM memory. The longer distance causes latency to increase and bandwidth to decrease. The reduction of effective bandwidth between any two levels in the Grid data hierarchy must be controlled if the system is be balanced for optimal performance. Experience has shown that the degradation (or difference in data throughput) should not be more than an order of magnitude between levels, a guideline conveniently referred to as "The Rule of 10."

Let's compute the ratios for a configuration of clusters joined through Gigabit Ethernet, a very common Grid structure. Looking at the node-cluster boundary, the speed ratio is defined by the ratio of memory bandwidth to network bandwidth. 3.2 to 6.4 GB/s is typical in commodity servers, while the effective bandwidth for Gigabit Ethernet is about 100 MB/s. Hence the speed discontinuity ratio (the difference in bandwidth between the two levels) is between 32 and 64. This spread is quite large, and such a system typically won't run jobs spanning more than 8–16 nodes very well. This might be just fine in a shop that never needs to allocate more than a small number of nodes to a specific job.

An unbalanced system tends to be communication bound. As a data set grows, it can't be moved among processors fast enough, resulting in a scalability limit that defines the largest problem (application) that can be effectively run on a given configuration. Beyond this application size, adding more processors won't make the job run much faster. Because implementations are less than perfect, practical limits are usually reached well before the theoretical limit. Of course, the ultimate performance of the system is determined by the absolute speed of each level, as well as the balance between levels. But to get the most performance out of a given grade of equipment, it proves economically beneficial to pay careful attention to the balance between levels of the Grid architecture. It also becomes progressively harder to tune a specific algorithm to run in a distributed fashion as the differential between levels gets larger than 10.

The Rule of 10 is a rough heuristic—a system with a difference in data bandwidth between layers that is larger than 10 is not necessarily useless. It generally means that the range of problems for which it is relatively efficient is narrower. The 10X ratio works well for "middle of the road" applications, such as those based on dense linear algebra. Some application classes, such as Monte Carlo simulations used in computational finance, are more tolerant of limited data transfer speeds and can be run successfully in Grids where wider ratios exist between levels. On the other hand, some scientific algorithms—like those used to design weapons systems at national labs—are less tolerant, and need to run on a system with close ratios.

The architecture of Grids exhibits a distinct hierarchy in terms of compute components, data communication and storage, e.g. performance hierarchy in Table 1. The Rule of 10, introduced above, gives an indication of the architectural balance of a Grid. This architectural balance ultimately determines the type and size of the problem that can be run on Grid.

Using Grid in the Enterprise

Now that we have powerful, virtualized platforms that can be connected by very high-bandwidth connections in a great variety of configurations, what is the best way to move from a traditional IT infrastructure to a flexible, enterprise-wide Grid architecture? First, we have to recognize that, for the foreseeable future, we will actually have a mixture of three different types of computing resources that we will need to accommodate within an enterprise Grid:

- Conventional standalone resources (i.e., platforms—hardware and soft-

Compute Engine	Storage
CPU Core	Cache
CPU	Main memory, video memory, ROM
Node	In-box storage (spinning, solid state)
Cluster	SAN, Federated
Grid	SAN, iSCSI, Federated

Table 1. Performance Hierarchy for Grids

ware—dedicated to a specific application.

- Dedicated clusters (i.e., a set of tightly-coupled compute platforms used for a single application...this might include HPC clusters).
- Virtual servers and server farms (i.e., platforms that have been "virtualized" with appropriate VMM and management software which are dynamically allocated to applications as the need arises).

Grid technology can immediately provide two beneficial new usage models while utilizing the existing infrastructure. The first is to enable consolidation of applications onto virtualized servers. Instead of each application being permanently "married" to specific physical computers, multiple applications can run on virtual server farms consisting of many servers that have been virtualized using VMM software. The average utilization of resources configured in this way can be much higher since the individual workloads of many applications spread across many servers in a virtual server farm tends to smooth the overall workload. The result is utilization rates in the 80% range rather than the typical 10–15% of "siloed" applications on dedicated resources. Existing clusters can be incorporated as one of the resources within the virtual server farm, or they can be dedicated to specific applications when this is more advantageous.

Grid can also enable compute-intensive applications to take advantage of unused processor cycles and memory on desktop computers. By placing a Grid management agent on each PC, its resources can be made available to an enterprise application that needs more compute power. This could be restricted to night hours or other times when the PC is not normally in use, with no impact on the PC user. This is a cost-

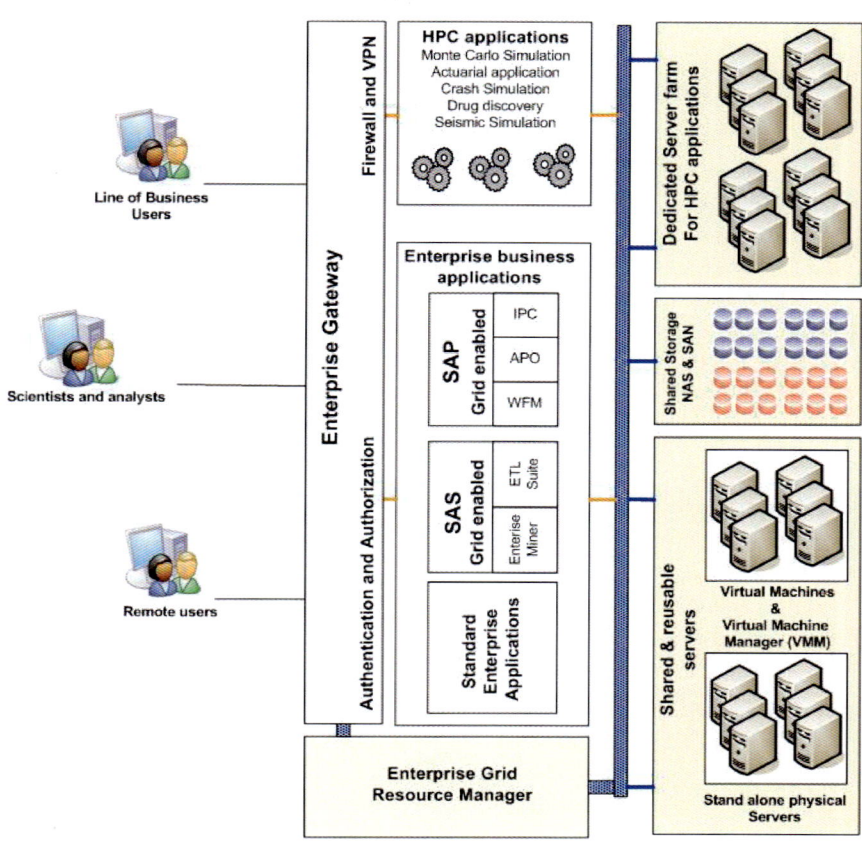

Figure 1. The Enterprise Utility Computing Data Center

effective way to expand high-performance computing (HPC) capability for a specific application without buying additional dedicated compute center resources.

IT can also start moving to a utility computing model by incorporating selected Grid components into the infrastructure. As the following example demonstrates, this does not require a "rip and replace" conversion to Grid. Figure 1 illustrates a Grid framework for a so-called Enterprise Utility Computing (EUC) datacenter built from commercially available components. In this scenario, Grid technology takes on a new role beyond its traditional HPC workload by managing the use of all enterprise compute resources. The Enterprise Grid Resources Manager (EGRM) is responsible for dynamically allocating compute resources to common compute-intensive enterprise applications such as Enterprise Resource Planning (ERP), Business Intelligence (BI), financial reporting, Customer Relationship Management (CRM), and so on. Computing resources consist of a combination of dedicated (clustered and non-clustered) datacenter servers, as well as standalone and virtual servers distributed across geographically disperse locations. Virtual servers are based on currently available server virtualization technologies such as VMWare, Microsoft Virtual Server, and the open source Xen virtual machine (VM) software. A Virtual Machine Manger is responsible for registering, commissioning, decommissioning, and updating the virtual server farm.

Figure 2 shows a typical EUC Business Intelligence use case. Business users, developers, and remote and mobile clients access business intelligence services through the Enterprise Gateway. For example:

- Business analysts can prepare up-to-date business reports on the company financial status for the CxO.
- Customer service representatives can access real-time and historical records to offer relevant products and services based on the customer's buying behavior.
- Brokers can ask for real-time stock quotes.
- Enterprise developers can run a batch-oriented job that accesses multiple data sources using the ETL suite to perform Extraction, Transformation, and Loading operations at regular intervals.

In traditional IT datacenters, the above operations would happen in an isolated fashion, with each client request routed to a specific "silo application" running on its own server or cluster, and managing its own database. However, in the Grid scenario each request is routed through the enterprise gateway that calls on the security/authorization services to authenticate the user and validates the request. If the user is verified and authorized to access the requested business services, the request is relayed to the Enterprise Grid Resources Manger (EGRM). EGRM is the heart of enterprise IT, managing all compute and storage resources. EGRM provides a resource registry, resource scheduling, request routing, policy management, and communications with other monitoring and analysis services that enforce the shared resources policy. EGRM orchestrates resources by communicating with conventional network, storage, virtualization manager, and data management entities to route the client's request to the appropriate resources.

For example, when the business analyst queries the BI server, the request is validated through the Security/Authorization services and then passed on to the EGRM. EGRM checks the availability of the BI server, and if it is available the request is routed to the BI server for processing. In another instance, a corporate developer may want to run a batch job. Again, the request is handled by the EGRM and, in this case, routed to the ETL server. The ETL server initiates a request to EGRM to schedule an ETL job spanning multiple nodes on dedicated server farm. If needed, EGRM can allocate even more resources from the corporate-wide pool of virtual server farms. Provisioning of specific virtual servers can be done on behalf of EGRM by existing server management products already in place in the enterprise. The ETL job is completed by extracting, transforming and loading the resulting data into the Operational Data Store where it is available for use by all applications. EGRM also communicates with Resource Monitoring and Charge-back applications to ensure proper IT cost allocation, and also to support analysis of resource usage. This usage analysis is used to update the EGRM policy engine heuristics to make better resource planning decisions with refined knowledge of peak load times and other empirical operational data.

The capabilities described above are already being integrated into leading Grid middleware products from commercial software vendors.

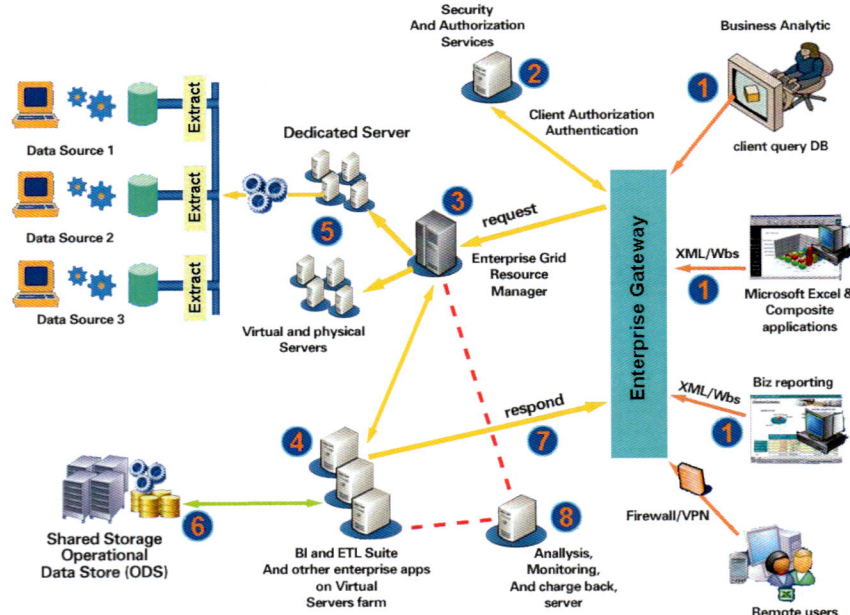

Figure 2. Enterprise Utility Computing Business Intelligence Use Case

Transitions in Business Practices and Infrastructure

As we move into the era of "pervasive computing" when there will be not one, but hundreds of computers operating on behalf of each person, the notion of a Grid can be extended out toward simpler devices at the edge of the Internet and in the home, such as:

- Smart connected appliances.
- Portable Digital Assistants.
- Cell phones.
- Electronic "motes" (wireless sensors).
- Active and passive RFID devices.

For example, Grids can be used to implement wireless sensor networks, where data is collected from real physical processes and events, and made available to services existing in "cyberspace" (i.e., on the Internet). Data entry, or perhaps more important, data re-entry, becomes unnecessary in such an environment because once data is available in cyberspace, it can be used by any information services that need it.

A typical scenario might be a package-delivery company using embedded RFID tags on packages to register them with a logistics system at pickup time. The objective is for the tag (and the package it represents) to remain "in sight"' of the computing system until it is actually delivered. As soon as the sender hands the package to the carrier, it is detected by a wireless device worn by the driver, which relays the data to the truck. The truck in turn relays the data to the Internet-based logistics Grid, triggering several database updates, including retrieving the sender's account and making a credit-card charge. As the package subsequently moves to a local warehouse, the regional hub, a local warehouse at the delivery end, and finally the receiver's destination, different Grid nodes are automatically activated and participate in the tracking function along the way.

The truck driver wears a specialized combined PDA/VoIP mobile phone with an RFID detector. The truck is fitted with a router equipped with WiFi, WiMax, and satellite links which it uses to communicate with the company's datacenter. The logistics database itself could be distributed, with different pieces of business logic provided by a number of service providers, and the whole infrastructure integrated using Web services interfaces. In this scenario, the availability of open standards allows the delivery company to outsource nearly any component of the system, including trucks, aircraft, and information services. Yet the high level of the system interoperability ensures that the package goes through a series of smooth handoffs as it moves along, no matter who has possession of it at any point in time.

In these scenarios, the batch-oriented ETL cycle morphs into a continuous process where true data integration is needed to ensure immediate sharing of critical business process information. At this stage, Grid refers not just to the integration of distributed processing elements, but also to a distributed, but fully integrated, data environment as well. This is where the so-called compute Grid and data Grid meet to create true real-time business processes supported by global information systems.

Start the Evolution Now

While Grid presents some new technologies to master and some changes in the approach to IT architecture planning, the payoff is huge in terms of efficiency and agility of the overall IT infrastructure. As enterprise information services continue to become more and more integrated across the corporation, and among multiple companies, the move to Grid will become essential for IT organizations to deliver the level of services required. Most of the needed technology components are available off the shelf now, including virtualization software that can adapt their current platforms to work in a Grid environment. If customers choose products based on open standards, they can start evolving toward a gird architecture using high-volume commodity equipment, and also leverage their existing resources.

> While Grid presents some new technologies to master and some changes in the approach to IT architecture planning, the payoff is huge in terms of efficiency and agility of the overall IT infrastructure.

Accelerating Analytics in the SOA

Lothar Schubert

SAP

Service-Oriented Architectures (SOAs) stand to deliver significant benefits to enterprises. They will give businesses new levels of ease and flexibility in designing and modifying business processes. They will promote reuse of software functionality to keep costs low. They will even enable organizations to transact more routine business matters without, or with minimal, human interaction. They will free up resources, in terms of revenues and human intelligence, which can be transferred from supporting existing business processes to innovating new ones.

But to work effectively, the SOA—what SAP calls the Enterprise Services Architecture, or ESA—will require some resources of its own. It will need a hardware/software infrastructure that features high performance and high scalability—necessary because of the expected surge in new services and new users that will come from the ease of service creation. And, importantly, the SOA will require an extremely robust analytics infrastructure.

Analytics will be used in several ways. For one, they will increasingly be used to drive smarter decision making, and more effective process execution. Adoption of analytics is expected to grow significantly, as SOA allows analytics to be seamlessly interwoven deeper into business applications, middleware, and user productivity tools. Analytic applications will report results and forecasts, and even take actions to optimize decisions and processes "on the fly."

For another, analytics will be used with information governance in general. This is critical because of the many-to-many sharing that will be part of services operations. Analytic applications will monitor the performance of the services themselves, and increasingly will be used to support rapid prototyping and rapid deployment of new services. Here, analytics can test and measure the effects of new services on the business processes they support, and so speed up overall development and deployment.

The Need for Robust Analytics

But why do services need a "robust" analytics infrastructure? The answer is simple: more data, less time.

Now, to elaborate, let's define "robust" as meaning high performance, high capacity, and high scalability. The analytics infrastructure will need all of these things for the two reasons stated above.

More Data

Anyone who's worked with conventional analytics/business intelligence systems knows that even ordinary applications produce reams of potentially valuable data, and it is a significant challenge to comb through that data to uncover the actual intelligence, or insight, that's hidden within. As applications become more complex—serving multiple users, for instance, in multiple locations—the raw data can grow exponentially.

Now look at the composite applications that will coordinate and invoke enterprise services. These will be composed of functions that will be not just infinitely reusable, but re-deployable in infinite combinations. One business-process function might be used in 100 different application specific services, for instance, and in each use it would be combined with a different set of other functions, and those functions would be changing, as well. Moreover, services will be open-ended in terms of where they go—from company to company and continent to continent—to what external databases or other resources they draw on, and what other users and applications they touch along the way.

No wonder industry experts are predicting that analytics data volumes will grow by as much as 50 percent per year, and analytics users will likely double each year, into the foreseeable future.

Less Time

It's a classic tradeoff in analytics, but the "time versus data" paradox will be particularly challenging in the new world of enterprise services. The reason is that the concept of real time, or even near real time, will have real meaning for services performance. Services will go fast, they'll interact with other services, they'll deliver results, and then trigger actions. Analytics will be effective only if they can keep up with and even anticipate the zigs and zags of such services.

Also, because services will frequently move across geographical distances to connect, say, supply-chain vendors and suppliers, the analytic infrastructure will have even less time to do its work, since added time will be consumed by the necessities of the physical networks.

What's in a Blade?

Business intelligence (BI) accelerators are often based on high-performing "blade" hardware with 64-bit state-of-the-art processors. Blades are easily upgradeable, since they include self-configuration and self-management functionality. Such qualities make the BI accelerator "linearly scalable," so it can be expanded in economical increments as processing needs increase.

> Why do services need a "robust" analytics infrastructure? The answer is simple: more data, less time.

Performance Options: Hardware, Software, Both

The CIO and IT managers can cope with the new need for analytics performance in several ways, depending upon the nature and scope of their analytics infrastructure.

If the software architecture is in place and operating effectively, the most viable option may be to increase the performance of the underlying hardware. Typically, this means upgrading database servers or application servers, adding memory or other storage, and perhaps implementing a server-farm architecture, where load-balancing intelligence can divide up the jobs and parcel out assignments in ways that make the most efficient use of the various servers. Once in place, the server farm makes upgrading—by adding still more processing hardware—relatively simple.

A second option involves tuning the analytics software. This can involve a number of different approaches. For example, IT may bring information partitioning to bear earlier in the analytics-gathering process, in order to save time later in the processes, when reports are prepared and distributed. IT could do this by staging all source data in an operational data store (ODS), as a preliminary step before bringing it into the data warehouse. In the ODS, low-level partitioning could sort out information into several basic subgroups – into sales regions, for instance, or different company divisions. Then, when the data goes to the data warehouse, it will require fewer iterations, and so will turn into actionable insight that much faster.

Other types of software enhancements are possible, too. One example uses special "delta" loading techniques for bringing source data into the ODS (or the data warehouse) from the operational systems, reducing the data volumes to be transferred significantly. Another example involves tuning of data aggregation processes. Based on forecasts for system access patterns, data are pre-aggregates into smaller chunks, which in turn are faster to process—pending that those access forecasts were right.

Combining Hardware and Software: The Business Intelligence Accelerator

Yet another option is to take a "black box" approach. An appliance made up of pre-integrated, bundled hardware and software is added onto the existing analytics infrastructure. This device, which could be called a business intelligence (BI) accelerator, takes advantage of the advent of powerful new server hardware (see sidebar: "What's

> SOAs . . . will let organizations transact routine business matters without, or with minimal, human interaction.

in a Blade?"), and combines it with specialized software that uses state-of-the-art techniques for compressing data, managing memory, and boosting search-engine performance, for example. The result: in effect, an analytics turbocharger.

In operation, such a BI accelerator can plug into the existing analytics infrastructure via a cable connection to the BI server. It's then up to the IT administrator to determine, via a browser interface, exactly which analytics data cubes will now move through the accelerator. For example, the IT administrator might decide to employ the accelerator to speed up a CRM project by identifying the dozen-or-so cubes involved in the project.

The BI accelerator then creates a highly compressed index of the available information that can be loaded into memory whenever required to respond to user requests. When activated, the accelerator processes queries entirely in memory, using high-performance aggregation techniques, and delivers the results to the user.

With such an accelerator in place, the IT administrator, the CIO, and the line-of-business manager often can expect some significant results. Overall performance may improve by factors of 10 to 100 times; loading new data will be as much as 80 percent faster; and scaling up to cover more users, or more data cubes, will be a simple matter of plugging in additional blades into the accelerators.

Transparent to Users, Invaluable for SOA

Because it is packaged as an appliance, the accelerator is simple for the IT administrator to hook up and configure. To the end user, it's literally transparent, which is how it should be. But its strength can be felt in the responsiveness of the analytic applications that use it.

For example, an analytics dashboard for a CRM credit evaluation application is able to deliver results in real-time, recalculated at the push of a button—with information scanned from billions of records in a matter of sub-seconds.

At a higher level, the accelerator turns enterprise analytics into SOA-ready analytics. Because of the boost in performance, the enterprise now has greater flexibility in how and where it deploys analytics. It can provide analytics to greater numbers of users, and for a wider range of applications. This is invaluable for services-based computing, since by definition the services will require great flexibility in how, where, and to whom they're deployed.

And at a still higher level, it represents a solid step toward the day when analytics will be integrated into the services and applications themselves—completely embedded, and working full time, in real-time, on behalf of the entire enterprise.

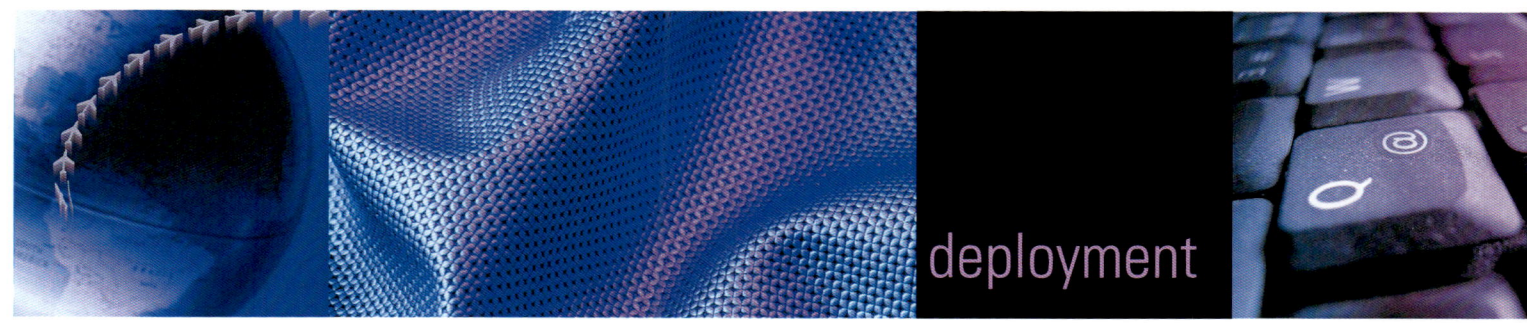

deployment

Enterprise Data Fabric: Weaving an Information-centric Grid Strategy

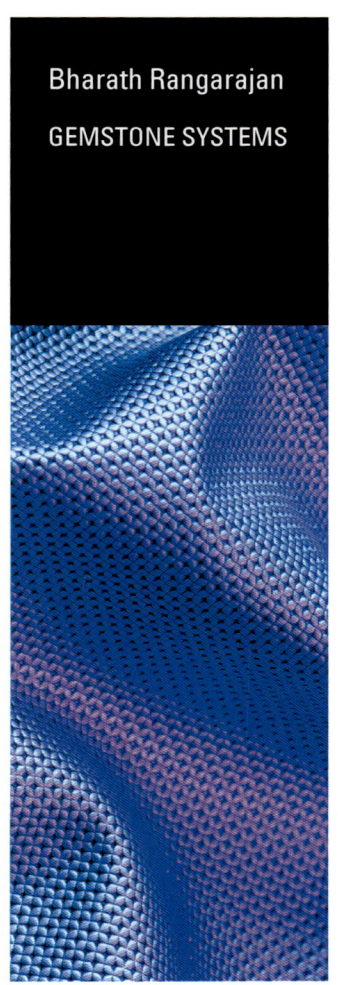

Bharath Rangarajan
GEMSTONE SYSTEMS

Industry pioneers and analysts alike are defining strategic initiatives such as 'on-demand computing,' 'the digital enterprise,' and 'cybersmart computing' to launch IT systems into a new era. An organization's allegiance to these metaphorical themes is driven by the need to revamp business processes and cope with the inherent changes in its ecosystem. To address these challenges, several progressive IT organizations are adopting Grid computing as one of the vehicles for transformation into a Service-Oriented IT (SO-IT) model. A key ingredient to make this transformation happen and turbocharge Grid computing environments is an Enterprise Data Fabric (EDF). An EDF symbolizes the ability to deliver complete, comprehensive, and consistent business information anytime, anywhere.

The World in Which We Live

To put emerging trends such as SO-IT and EDF in perspective, it is necessary to recognize three fundamental trends in today's business world. These trends can be summarized as the 'everything fast, everything online, and everything distributed' syndrome.

The First Trend—Everything Fast

This trend relates to the insatiable appetite for speed and performance across multiple industries. Be it electronic trading in capital markets, fraud detection in telecom, or RFID data management in the retail industry, operational efficiency and low-latency are becoming absolute necessities for a company's survival.

The Second Trend—Everything Online

We are constantly witnessing the proliferation of Web-based operations across an organization's functions like sales, marketing, support, and various information delivery modes. Companies, big and small, need to realign their business strategies to embrace an online world that services customers whom they do not know and may not even see.

The Third and the Last Trend—Everything Distributed

This phenomenon is a consequence of multiple factors, including:

a) Growing popularity of blade-like distributed hardware form factors.

b) Increasing rate of merger and acquisition that often necessitates management of disparate infrastructures.

c) Pervasive globalization, which demands a seamless process and information backbone.

This fast, online, and distributed world has resulted in a drastic upsurge in the user-loads and data volumes that flow through an organization. Further, IT budgets remain flat and technology teams strive to make the best use of existing hardware, software, and data assets. A Grid-based environment bolstered by an EDF helps put in place a method to all this madness. This approach enables optimal utilization and scheduling of resources. It also guarantees consistent availability and delivery of information across an enterprise application network.

Grid Evolution and Challenges

Grid computing, which until recently was primarily confined to the high performance computing community in research labs and academia, is now being considered as a possible solution for other IT applications. This planned mainstream adoption and growth of Grids is happening along two dimensions—scale and functionality. First, several organizations are interested in transforming their pilot Grid deployments (25–50 nodes) to more large-scale production Grids (100s to 1000s of nodes). Second, Grids are no longer restricted to just distributed numerical computations. Even stateful, transactional processing applications (for example, J2EE deployments) are candidates to run on a Grid. Consequently, Grids can now be deployed to meet a wide variety of applications such as risk analytics and portfolio management (capital markets), fraud detection (banking and telecom), and online customer service portals. However, an August 2005 report by The 451 Group revealed that many large enterprises have delayed broadening their Grid deployments because of the limitations in data management capabilities. This reality dose necessitates a more prosaic outlook toward Grid adoption to understand the main issues, which include:

- High data access latency.
- Lack of scalability with an increase in the number of compute nodes.
- Inability to share and distribute data across nodes.
- Inability to scale to large data volumes.
- Reliability and quality of service problems.

These challenges are a direct consequence of the absence of sophisticated data management functions in most Grid deployments, where the focus is primarily on optimizing compute resources. For Grids to scale and become more functional, a new look at data architecture is needed. Traditional RDBMS, file-systems, messaging, or simple caching do not provide necessary performance or enable data sharing among Grids. Fast and reliable data access/distribution is not feasible without a robust data infrastructure. This can relegate most compute Grids to fast running processes with no data to process—like a Ferrari with no fuel! It is in this context that an EDF becomes absolutely critical.

An EDF Pulls IT Together

An EDF is an operational data layer that provides instantaneous data access in multiple formats/APIs for distributed deployments such as Grids. It can be envisioned as a pervasive, distributed in-memory data network that spans hundreds or even thousands of nodes, and is characterized by extremely low latencies and high throughput.

Data Virtualization

An EDF offers location transparency, through which Grid applications are abstracted from the actual data locations, formats, and access protocols. Hence, large volumes of data from multiple backend sources can be provisioned via an EDF to deploy a data Grid (see Figure 1). It also guarantees high availability via multiple mechanisms, which ensures that even in the case of

> The IT landscape is constantly changing—more data, more users, more distributed applications, and more stringent requirements.

application failure there is no data loss. For Online Transactional Processing (OLTP) applications, an EDF offers a distributed transaction framework with support for querying and filtering of data.

Multi-format Data Storage Model

An EDF brings about a shift from a traditional centralized, single format storage model to a distributed, multi-format data storage model, wherein data can be managed in formats like objects (Java, C++), XML documents or database result sets. This way an application can enjoy data locality as well as have the data immediately available in a format it understands, avoiding any complex transforms. The net result is a significant improvement in performance and lower latencies. Case in point: performance and throughput of a large-scale risk computation Grid in a capital markets firm increased 100-fold with the introduction of an EDF.

From a business perspective, the operational efficiency improvements achieved through an EDF adoption can translate to higher profits, better customer services, or better risk management depending on the nature of the Grid application. Since data bottlenecks are avoided, hardware utilization is significantly improved. This translates to lower hardware procurement and maintenance costs and bodes well for IT environments that operate on tight budgets. A leading investment bank, for instance, adopted an EDF to revamp their post-trade risk analytics cluster that handles about two to three billion calculations. Their EDF implementation virtualized information from multiple sources like reference data, historical data, and market data, and provided a data backbone for their theoretical calculations as well as the actual fine-grained risk applications. Adopting an EDF enabled instant sharing of intermediate results across risk calculators

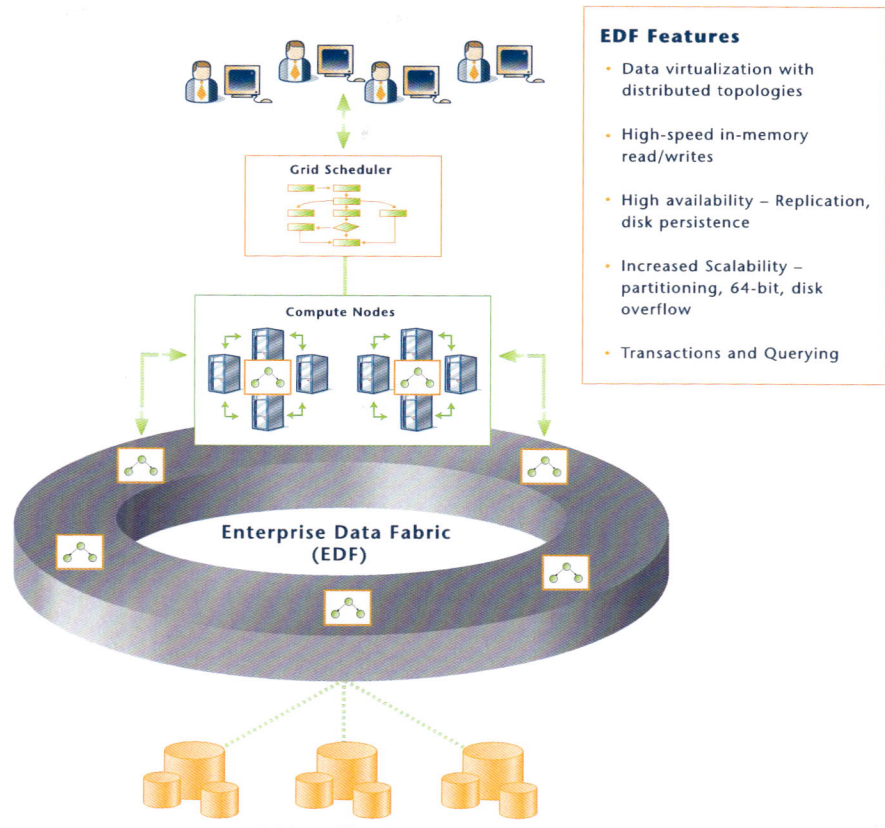

Figure 1: Enterprise Data Fabric Solutions to Data Management in a Grid Environment

and almost a 300% reduction in data access latency. Consequently, the overall process time was reduced from eight hours to two hours, which ensured that all computations were completed well before the markets opened the subsequent day. A shorter cycle time also enabled running these calculations more often during the day with the latest market data snapshots, thereby increasing the accuracy of the results, which in turn impacts profitable trading.

Table 1 summarizes how technology facets of an EDF address some of the key data management requirements in a Grid environment.

EDF Synergy: Compute Grids and Hardware

Though a compute Grid/Grid scheduler (like Data Synapse GridServer or Platform Symphony), an EDF, and the underlying hardware (processors and servers) have distinct roles and functions in the context of Grid, there are elements of synergy that these entities share. This synergy can be leveraged to further enhance Grid deployments.

EDF and Compute Grid Synergy

A compute Grid engine's primary function is to manage the workload on the Grid and provision necessary compute resources for a Grid task. With an EDF in place, a compute Grid can understand data placement on different nodes and facilitate data-aware routing. That is, if a particular data entity is available on a certain node, then tasks that require this data entity can be routed to that node. This intelligent routing can lower latency and avoid network congestion due to unnecessary node-to-node data transfers. An EDF can also be used by a compute Grid engine as data layer to share intermediate results among a sequence of tasks. Such data sharing is crucial for Grids to scale to thousands of nodes.

EDF and Hardware Synergy

Distributed hardware form-factors like blades can benefit from the data distribution and virtualization capabilities available through an EDF. Certain key CPU/chipset-level advancements also offer added ability for an EDF to decrease server I/O latency and increase scalability. The advent of 64-bit processors provides a much greater addressable memory space for an EDF to provision large data volumes on a Grid. Also, Direct Memory Access (DMA) capabilities available through server platforms like Intel® I/O Acceleration Technology, provide low-latency mechanisms for an EDF to distribute data across a network. By eliminating unnecessary hops in moving data from a network interface to an application, DMA saves CPU cycles and further enhances Grid efficiency.

This confluence of compute Grid, data, and processor technologies propels Grids as a solution approach for a wide variety of demanding IT environments.

Summary

The IT landscape is constantly changing—more data, more users, more distributed applications, and more stringent requirements. EDF forms an integral part of an information strategy aimed at countering these challenges. It complements and leverages innovations and breakthroughs in hardware, network, and application infrastructure technologies. As organizations march from vertical silos toward SO-IT with a Grid-based infrastructure, operational data management becomes a crucial requirement, which is successfully addressed through an EDF.

Data Management Requirements for a High-Performance Grid	EDF Solution Characteristics
1. Ultra-high performance, low-latency data distribution and high data throughput	■ In-memory data management with no disk latency ■ Highly parallel data distribution and optimized transportation layer
2. Caching and persistence models for extremely large volumes of data across distributed environments	■ Multiple, flexible data caching topologies (local, peer-to-peer, hierarchical, partitioned) ■ Distributed data partitioning and re-balancing schemes across servers for large data volumes
3. Data virtualization and location transparency	■ Pool distributed memory and disk ■ Access and synchronization of data from multiple data sources ■ Standards-based querying
4. Guaranteed quality of service for data access and high data availability for reliable operations	■ Advanced data placement strategies to co-locate data and avoid expensive transformations and network hops ■ Main-memory replication, or disk persistence to guarantee availability of data ■ Distributed transactions
5. Multiple data format and language support with true interoperability	■ Native support for multiple data formats—Java, XML, C/C++ ■ Automatic bindings for conversion for Java to XML and vice-versa
6. Seamless fit into existing enterprise architectures	■ Standards-based interfaces for easy insertion into distributed environments ■ Pre-configured interceptors/drivers for zero code integration with databases

Table 1: EDF Solutions to Data Management Requirements in a Grid Environment

serialization

RFID and SOA: A Marriage Made in Heaven

Dan Stimson

SAP

Some call it the "X-Internet." Others call it the "Internet of things." Most call it RFID (Radio Frequency Identification), and many view it as a critical component in—and a challenge to—the Service-Oriented Architecture, or SOA.

Think of it. Take one application, say, inventory control. Each unit of inventory contains a tag that uniquely identifies its host. This tag can transmit a wealth of information about its host to the inventory control application. It can also collect information (like location or physical condition) about itself and its host as it moves through packing and shipping. And it can be used later in the event of a product recall, return, or service order, simply by identifying itself to its original product development database.

Now look at all the possible uses for this technology, many of which are under active development today. There are literally hundreds of applications already identified in industries as diverse as healthcare, government, manufacturing, and finance. And that's only the proverbial tip of the iceberg, since experts acknowledge that the real potential for RFID technology is virtually unknown.

Then you've got to multiply each of these applications by the numbers of devices that will contain the tags. Take an automobile, for instance: five years from now, that auto—and just about every other part in the car—will likely have its own RFID sensor. That car, those parts, and other cars and parts, will be purchased by a few hundred thousand people worldwide. Finally, for each of the cars and parts, consider that every RFID device will be constantly collecting and disseminating information about itself, for the life of the part.

The potential for RFID, in terms of bringing new levels of visibility, efficiency, and competitiveness to the world's businesses and other organizations is clearly massive. Likewise, the impact of RFID on the design and operation of enterprise applications is destined to be substantial. Both of these—the ability to unlock new levels of enterprise performance and the potential for influencing enterprise application design point directly to the second part of the puzzle posed at the introduction—the symbiotic relationship that is developing between RFID and SOA.

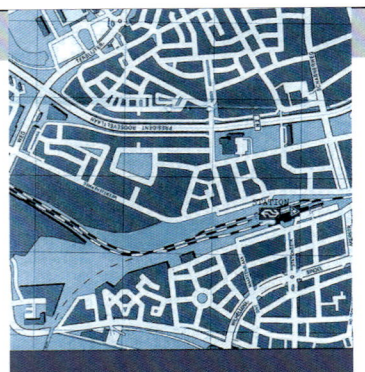

The potential for RFID, in terms of bringing new levels of visibility, efficiency, and competitiveness to the world's businesses and other organizations is clearly massive.

What it's All about—the Pilot and the Airplane

First, let's look at the fundamental goal of RFID. Take the aeronautical analogy. Today's airplanes are so smart, they fly themselves. The only thing they need the human, the pilot, for, is to handle the exceptions.

That is the basic goal of RFID, too: to make it possible for machines to communicate and work together on routine tasks without requiring human intervention. An RFID tag updates the inventory database; the inventory database updates the Enterprise Resource Planning (ERP) system; the ERP system responds with a "shipment received/date" message, which goes back into the RFID tag—all with no human involvement. And that's a simple ex-

---

Coming: More Sensors, Mass Serialization

In a sense, today's discussion of RFID presents only the tip of what will be a very large iceberg of data-generating and application-handling requirements in the future.

First, realize that RFID will be joined, supported, and complimented by varieties of other sensor technologies, from Global Positioning Systems (GPS) in the field to smart controllers on the factory floor.

Second, take a look at the explosion of data—and the application handling challenges—that will result from what industry experts are calling "mass serialization." Thanks to unique identification standards now in place such as the Electronic Product Code (EPC) and the U.S. Department of Defense's Unique Identification (UID) program, sensors will be able to identify themselves and their hosts right down to the individual unit, down to each pencil, for instance, or each semiconductor in a computer system.

These trends will have a major impact on business and government, because they will deliver unprecedented visibility into the product development process. This might mean, for instance, that a critical replacement part for an Apache helicopter would "know" that it should be used only in those helicopters manufactured before a certain date, before, say, the engine configuration was changed.

But they will also drive the need for ultra-fast and ultra-flexible Service-Oriented Architecture (SOAs). That way, the enterprise will be able to respond quickly to insights presented by sensors—to re-route a failing malfunctioning assembly process, for instance —by quickly modifying existing applications, or writing new service applications on-the-fly.

ample; much more is in store for RFID as it evolves over the coming years.

Now let's look at the goal of the Service-Oriented Architecture, the SOA. At a high level, it's about the same. The SOA is intended to serve as a framework for service-based applications that can do the bidding of their users and their organizations without requiring much, or even any, human intervention. You need an update on regulatory compliance projects in the past quarter, so you simply launch a Web service. The Web service goes out, looks through the appropriate information repositories, consults with your business intelligence system, and delivers your reports.

But the importance of the RFID/SOA connection goes deeper than the philosophical similarities; the relationship is critical to helping RFID achieve its full potential, and so it is critical to helping enterprises make the most of their RFID initiatives.

SOA: Platform-of-choice for RFID

Five years from now, there's no doubt that RFID-based applications will be running in, and as part of, service oriented architectures, such as SAP's business-driven SOA, Enterprise Service Architecture, or ESA.

RFID will be highly complimentary to Web services because of RFID's ability to collect and convey "end-to-end" information and intelligence about their hosts. Web services will be able to trace product sales and many other types of transactions right to the SKU or unit level, and this capability will be invaluable to helping SOA achieve its goal of complete machine-to-machine interaction.

At the same time, being able to operate from a true SOA platform will be essential to RFID's success. RFID (and other types of sensors) will contain varying degrees of local intelligence, so they will need "global" control systems—as the airplane needs the airport's flight controllers—to realize their full potential. A few of the most important reasons follow.

Support for RFID's Performance and Scalability Needs

No technology to date, except perhaps the Internet, has the potential to generate so much data as RFID. RFID applications will demand significant throughput from their IT architectures, because of the multi-dimensional nature of RFID scaling that will occur. Currently, many pilot deployments of RFID are underway; as organizations gain experience with the technology and see the value of RFID, these pilots will go national then global, and the technology will have to scale to meet the new requirements. In any case, the IT infrastructure will be called upon to scale quickly upward, and to handle exponentially greater data volumes on literally a moment's notice.

Scalability is especially important because the RFID application, like many other service-based applications, will need to encompass varieties of different applications, such as Supply Chain Management (SCM), Customer Relationship Management (CRM), and analytics, and talk to the applications of numerous trading partners of the enterprise. Not just scalability but security will be important, so the IT infrastructure will have to be easily updatable in order to keep from slowing down the progress of RFID initiatives.

Open-ended Configuration Flexibility

RFID will demand the open-endedness and flexibility of a robust SOA infrastructure, too, for a number of reasons. For one, no business or IT managers know the extent or benefit of RFID today, so the infrastructure will have to be open to many possible changes that come along. An example involves how mass serialization, made possible standards such as the Electronic Product Code (EPC), will add to RFID's potential for generating reams of data, and requiring high flexibility for modifying or building applications "on the fly" (see sidebar: Coming: More Sensors, Mass Serialization).

For the second reason, the ability to reuse and reconfigure elements of RFID and supporting applications—without having to redo the entire application—will also be critical, and this is one of the SOA's main benefits. That way, enterprises can get started quickly with RFID prototypes, without having to worry about wasting their designs in the event a new paradigm emerges.

A third reason is that the evolution of RFID is today on a kind of fast track,

> The basic goal of RFID is to make it possible for machines to communicate and work together on routine tasks without requiring human intervention.

thanks to mandates from industry and government agencies. While mandates are being launched in the retail supply chains, defense and aerospace, and pharmaceutical industries, compliance deadlines are being issued, as well, even while the technology is still emerging. This inherent conflict is driving up the intensity of new development in hardware and software, as well as in the new business processes that will use RFID. Because of this, it is important for suppliers to begin piloting SOA frameworks that can support fast ramp-up of RFID applications, and that will give them the flexibility to upgrade and expand their RFID applications over time.

Four Benefits of SOA-based RFID

Indeed, SOA-based RFID won't be the only choice open to enterprise executives and managers; packaged RFID applications will grow quickly, too. But executives should beware of "quick-fix" packaged applications—they may have to be discarded as their SOA-based competitors outgrow them.

In case anyone still needs convincing that RFID and SOA are perfectly suited to one another, consider these major benefits of basing RFID on and SOA infrastructure:

- *Keeping up with a world of change*—RFID applications will need a supporting platform that gives them high extensibility, so they can be quickly modified and deployed to take advantage of shifts in everything from market trends to world political situations.
- *Preserving IT investments*—An SOA infrastructure will make it easier to infuse the new RFID capabilities into existing enterprise applications such as order-to-cash and produce-to-pay, since the infrastructure will turn both the RFID application and the "consuming" application into services.
- *Stimulating partnerships*—Thanks to the vast potential of RFID, it's certain that no one company will capture the market for RFID applications. Instead, the most successful enterprises will be those that can build partnerships that result in new and better services, and this effort will be greatly enhanced by basing new developments on an SOA platform.
- *To RFID and beyond*—The final benefits reach beyond RFID itself to the broader world of sensor technologies in general—both those that exist today, such as Global Positioning Systems (GPS), and those that haven't been invented yet. Wherever the next sensor opportunity presents itself, the SOA-driven enterprise will be better able to respond than will the traditional, applications-based infrastructure.

Both Play a Role

The trip may still get a bit bumpy, but it's clear where the IT world is heading: toward a day when services will be at the beck and call of enterprise executives, managers, and knowledge workers, and where the underlying issues of "compatibility, scalability, performance," and so on will be nothing but quaint recollections to most of us. For this new direction, and for its incredible potential to lift productivity to vastly higher levels, we can thank, in large part, the abilities of RFID and the vision of the SOA.

> It's clear where the IT world is heading: toward a day when services will be at the beck and call of enterprise executives, managers, and knowledge workers.

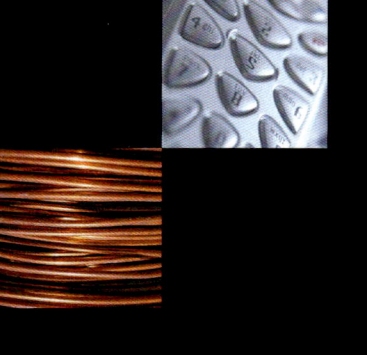

Contributors, Contacts, and Glossary

Contributors and Contacts

The book, "The Emergence of Grid and Service-Oriented IT: An Industry Vision for Business Success," was a true collaborative effort from the industry leaders listed below. Each of the organizations is available to provide additional information on successes, products, and future plans.

The 451 Group

CONTACT

Kim Kent
Manager, Client Relations and Marketing Communications
The 451 Group
52 Broad Street, Second Floor
Boston, MA 02109 USA
617.261.0566
kim.kent@the451group.com

AUTHORS AND ARTICLES

William Fellows, Principal Analyst, and Steve Wallage, Director of Research, The 451 Group
  Introductory articles for each chapter of this book

William Fellows, Principal Analyst, and Steve Wallage, Director of Research, The 451 Group
  Where is Enterprise Grid Computing Going, and How Do we Get There?

ABOUT THE 451 GROUP

The 451 Group is an independent technology industry analyst company focused on the business of enterprise IT innovation. The company's analysts provide critical and timely insight into the market and competitive dynamics of innovation in emerging technology segments. Clients of the company—at vendor, investor, service-provider and end-user organizations—rely on 451 insights to support both strategic and tactical decision-making for competitive advantage. The 451 Grid Adoption Research Service (GARS) is an investigation into user experiences and vendor strategies within the grid technology market. It analyzes the track record as commercial enterprise users introduce Grid technologies to their core IT operations, and it examines the effectiveness of the strategies of vendor companies whose technologies early adopters are deploying.

  http://www.the451group.com

  http://www.the451group.com/intake/tabor-Gridbook-Mar06

Aberdeen/Group/

CONTACT

William Mougayar
Vice President and Service Director for the Technology Research Practice
Aberdeen/Group/
6985 Coolihans Sideroad
Caledon, ON L7K 0P8 Canada
905.584.8686
wmougayar@gmail.com.

AUTHOR AND ARTICLE

William Mougayar, Vice President and Service Director, Information Technology Research Practice, Aberdeen/Group/
  How SOA is Changing IT

ABOUT ABERDEEN/GROUP/

Aberdeen/Group/, Inc. provides fact-based research and insights focused on the global, technology-driven value chain. Aberdeen's benchmarking, market and solution assessments, sales acceleration programs, and conferences support Global 5000 value chain and technology executives and the solution providers who serve them.

  http://www.aberdeen.com

BEA Systems, Inc.

CONTACT

800.817.4BEA (US toll free)
408.570.8000

AUTHOR AND ARTICLE

Annie Shum, Ph.D., Vice President, SOA Strategy, BEA Systems, Inc.
  Leveraging City Planning and other Social Metaphors to Guide SOA—Why Meta Matters

ABOUT BEA

BEA Systems, Inc. (NASDAQ: BEAS) is a world leader in enterprise infrastructure software, providing standards-based platforms to accelerate business liquidity by delivering the secure flow of information and services. BEA product lines—WebLogic®, Tuxedo®, JRockit®, and the new AquaLogic™ family of Service Infrastructure—help customers reduce IT complexity and successfully deploy Service-Oriented Architectures to improve business agility and efficiency.

  http://www.bea.com/

Capgemini

CONTACT

Jenny Clarke
Marketing Director
Capgemini
76 Wardour Street,
 London W1F 0UU
+44 (0)870 906 7352
jenny.clarke@capgemini.com

AUTHOR AND ARTICLES

Andy Mulholland, Global Chief Technology Officer, Capgemini
 From Big to Small: Moving from Monolithic Applications to Granular Services
Andy Mulholland, Global Chief Technology Officer, Capgemini
 Critical Technology Factors for the Successful Future of 'Services': How and Where to Create Business Benefit with the SOA Revolution

ABOUT CAPGEMINI

Capgemini, one of the world's foremost providers of consulting, technology, and outsourcing services, has a unique way of working with its clients, called the Collaborative Business Experience. Backed by more than three decades of industry and service experience, the Collaborative Business Experience helps our clients achieve better, faster, more sustainable results through seamless access to our network of world-leading technology partners and collaboration-focused methods and tools. Through commitment to mutual success and the achievement of tangible value, we help businesses implement growth strategies, leverage technology, and thrive through the power of collaboration. Capgemini employs approximately 61,000 people and reported 2005 revenues of 6,954 million euros.

 http://www.capgemini.com/

DataSynapse

CONTACT

Myra Aja
Director Field Marketing
632 Broadway, 5th Floor
New York, NY 10012 USA
212.842.8846
myra@datasynapse.com

AUTHOR AND ARTICLES

Kelly Vizzini, Chief Marketing Officer, DataSynapse
 Virtual Application Infrastructure (Grid) and the Migration to SOA
Kelly Vizzini, Chief Marketing Officer, DataSynapse
 Grid Computing Drives Business Agility: Enterprise Case Studies

ABOUT DATASYNAPSE

DataSynapse is a global provider of virtual application infrastructure software that virtualizes business-critical applications and adaptively provisions them across available system resources. The company's flagship products, GridServer and FabricServer, are integral components of an SOA strategy, helping clients improve business agility while reducing the cost and complexity of their IT infrastructure. Open and standards-based, DataSynapse's self-managed solutions eliminate performance barriers and improve productivity levels across the enterprise. DataSynapse works with market leaders in the financial services, government, telecommunications, energy, and industrial sectors. The company is headquartered in New York; see www.datasynapse.com.

 DataSynapse SOA Executive Portal: http://datasynapse.com/portal/soa/
 DataSynapse Webcast Replays: http://www.datasynapse.com/news/replays.asp

Dell Inc.

CONTACT

Jimmy Pike
Director/Distinguished Engineer
 and Enterprise Architect
Office of the CTO
Dell Inc.
One Dell Way, Mail Stop 8511
Round Rock, Texas 78682 USA
512.728.5801
jimmy_pike@dell.com

AUTHORS AND ARTICLES

Narayan Devireddy, Senior Development Manager, Dell Platform Embedded Software, and Michael Brundridge, Technology Strategist, Dell Inc.
 Implementing Computing Grids Using Blade Servers
Zafar Mahmood, Senior Consultant, and Anthony Fernandez, Senior Analyst, Dell Database and Application Solutions Group, Dell Inc.
 Building and Scaling Out a Database Grid Using Industry-Standard Grid Components
Jimmy Pike, Director/Distinguished Engineer and Enterprise Architect, Office of the CTO, and Tim Abels, Enterprise Architect, Dell Server Architecture and Technology, Dell Inc.
 The Scalable Enterprise Architecture: A Practical Underpinning for Grid Computing

ABOUT DELL INC.

Dell Inc. is a trusted and diversified information-technology supplier and partner, and sells a comprehensive portfolio of products and services directly to customers worldwide. Dell designs, builds, and delivers innovative, tailored systems that provide customers with exceptional value. Uniquely enabled by its direct business model, Dell sells more systems globally every day than any computer company, placing it No. 28 on the Fortune 500.

 http://www.dell.com/
 Dell news: http://www.dell.com/RSS

contributors and contacts

Economic Strategy Institute

CONTACT

Robert B. Cohen
President, Cohen Communications Group
Fellow, Economic Strategy Institute
30 East 40th Street, PHSW
New York, NY 10016 USA
212.986.7720
bcohen@bway.net

AUTHOR AND ARTICLE

Robert B. Cohen, Cohen Communications Group and the Economic Strategy Institute
The Evolution of IT Infrastructure into a Services Oriented Model: Grid Computing and a Moore's Law for Services

ABOUT ECONOMIC STRATEGY INSTITUTE

The Economic Strategy Institute is a 501(c)3 organization that has done extensive work on trade and technology policy issues. It has been the organization funded by a number of corporations to support two studies of Grid adoption in the U.S. and Japan. These studies had a wide base of industrial support, including funding from IBM, Intel, Juniper Networks, Cisco, AT&T, and MCI. The projects were the first to estimate how rapidly Grids would be adopted by specific industries, what the scale of the benefits would be over the 2003–2010 period, and how Grid adoption would impact the US and Japanese economies. The institute plans to follow these studies with similar analyses of Europe and China. Summaries of the completed studies are available on our Web site.

http://www.econstrat.org

http://www.Gridforum.org

GemStone Systems

CONTACT

Jason Quan
Director of Marketing
1260 NW Waterhouse Ave., Suite 200
Beaverton, Oregon 97006 USA
503.533.3212
jason.quan@gemstone.com

AUTHOR AND ARTICLE

Bharath Rangarajan, Director, Product Marketing, GemStone Systems
Enterprise Data Fabric: Weaving an Information-Centric Grid Strategy

ABOUT GEMSTONE SYSTEMS

GemStone Systems is a privately held infrastructure software company that provides data services solutions for enterprise business architects and data infrastructure managers that are building, enhancing, or simplifying access, distribution, integration, and management of information within and across the enterprise. Founded in 1982, and with over 200 installed customers, GemStone is recognized worldwide for its unique competency and patented technology in object management, virtual memory architectures, high-performance caching, and data distribution technologies. GemFire, the enterprise data fabric (EDF) from GemStone Systems, provides a scalable, distributed platform to manage increasing volumes of enterprise data and streaming events with almost zero latency. With advanced data virtualization, distributed caching, and complex event processing (CEP) capabilities, the GemFire EDF enables the delivery of actionable information to the right application at the right time.

http://www.gemstone.com/solutions/Gridcomputing.php

http://www.gemstone.com/solutions/soa.php

Global Grid Forum

CONTACT

Steve Crumb
Executive Director of GGF Inc.
Global Grid Forum
9700 S. Cass Avenue, Building 221-A142
Argonne, IL 60439 USA
630.252.4300
scrumb@ggf.org

AUTHOR AND ARTICLES

Mark Linesch, Chairman, Global Grid Forum and Vice President, HP
The Global Grid Forum: Leading the Journey to Pervasive Grid Adoption
Interview: Mark Linesch, Chairman, Global Grid Forum and Vice President, HP
Preparing Grid for the Mainstream: An Interview with HP's Mark Linesch

ABOUT GLOBAL GRID FORUM

The Global Grid Forum (GGF) is the community of users, developers, and vendors leading the global standardization effort for Grid computing. The GGF community consists of thousands of individuals in industry and research, representing more than 400 organizations in over 50 countries. The work of GGF is carried out though community-initiated working groups, which develop best practices and specifications in cooperation with other leading standards organizations, software vendors, and users. GGF is funded through its Sponsor Members, including technology producers and consumers as well as academic and government research institutions. GGF hosts events for the worldwide Grid community three times annually.

GGF: http://www.ggf.org

GGF Conferences: http://www.ggf.org/ggf_events_next.htm

HP

CONTACT

Kathleen Ackerman
Marketing Programs Manager
High Performance Computing Division
Hewlett-Packard Company
Cape Cod, MA
508.498.2853
kathleen.ackerman@hp.com

ARTICLES

Interview: Mark Linesch, Chairman, Global Grid Forum and Vice President, HP
Preparing Grid for the Mainstream: An Interview with HP's Mark Linesch
Contributed by HP
Stripped-down Grid: A Lightweight Grid for Developing Countries

ABOUT HP

HP is a technology solutions provider to consumers, businesses, and institutions globally. The company's offerings span IT infrastructure, global services, business and home computing, and imaging and printing. HP is a market share leader on many fronts, including high-performance computing, servers, Linux®, and high-end enterprise UNIX.

HP's Grid and HPC Solutions: http://www.hp.com/go/hptc

OurGrid: http://www.ourGrid.org.

IBM

CONTACT

http://www.ibm.com/Grid

AUTHORS AND ARTICLES

Sherry Brewer, Grid Solution Portfolio Manager, and Rob Vrablik, Grid Computing Strategy and Technology, IBM
Get Started with Grid for a Competitive Advantage
Patricia Chavez, Marketing Manager, IBM
Delivering Results with Grid: An Industry Perspective
Ellen J. Stokes, Senior Technical Staff Member, Grid Strategy, Technology and Standards, and Matthew P. Haynos, Program Director, Grid Strategy and Technology, IBM
Grid and SOA in Business Solutions

ABOUT IBM

IBM has a strong heritage in addressing both the technology and business issues that have led to the Grid computing evolution. Virtualization, the driving force behind IBM Grid computing, continues to lead IBM's history of IT innovation for business. Continuing to play a leading role in the Grid community, IBM offers a strong portfolio of products, solutions, and services that continue to evolve for those beginning with virtualization or for those ready for next steps. Further, by marrying IBM's expertise in virtualization and SOI with IBM's industry leading SOA processes, methodologies, and tools, IBM is the market leader in helping enterprises adapt and indeed capitalize on today's dynamic business environment to enable increased performance, productivity, and innovation.

http://www.ibm.com/Grid

http://www.ibm.com/software/info/openenvironment/soa/

IDC

CONTACT

Earl C. Joseph II
IDC Research Vice President
Executive Director,
    HPC User Forum
365 Summit Ave.
St. Paul, MN 55102 USA
612.812.5798
ejoseph@idc.com

AUTHOR AND ARTICLE

Dan Kusnetzky, Vice President, System Software, Enterprise Computing Group, IDC
Taking a Fresh Look at Grid Computing

ABOUT IDC

IDC is the premier global provider of market intelligence, advisory services, and events for the information technology, telecommunications, and consumer technology markets. IDC helps IT professionals, business executives, and the investment community make fact-based decisions on technology purchases and business strategy. More than 850 IDC analysts in 50 countries provide global, regional, and local expertise on technology and industry opportunities and trends. For more than 42 years, IDC has provided strategic insights to help our clients achieve their key business objectives. IDC is a subsidiary of IDG, the world's leading technology media, research, and events company.

http://www.idc.com

contributors and contacts

Intel Corporation

CONTACT

Robert Fogel
Worldwide Director of Grid and
    Service-Oriented IT
Intel Corporation
2200 Mission College Blvd.
Santa Clara, CA 95054-1549
408.765.6404
robert.fogel@intel.com

AUTHORS AND ARTICLES

Robert Fogel, Vice-Chairman, Global Grid Forum; Worldwide Director of Grid and Service-Oriented IT, Intel Corporation
The Innovator's Opportunity: Capitalizing on the Convergence of Business and IT

Tom Gibbs, Director, Worldwide Strategy and Planning, Customer Solutions Group, Intel Corporation
On the Edge of the Grid: Using the Grid to Digitally Enable the Point of Action

Parviz Peiravi, Senior Solutions Architect, Customer Solutions Group, Financial Services Industry, and Enrique Castro-Leon, Enterprise Architect and Technology Strategist, Intel Solution Services, Technology Office, Intel Corporation
Grid Solutions for the Enterprise

Ravi Subramaniam, Enterprise Architect, End User Platform Integration, Digital Enterprise Group, Intel Corporation
Standards Landscape in Service Oriented Grids

ABOUT INTEL CORPORATION

This is the year 100 million people around the world will discover digital for the first time, and 150 million more will become part of the wireless world. The year the living room will grow more interactive and the digital divide will shrink. The year more people will be using technology in more fascinating ways than ever imagined.

And behind all of this progress you'll find innovative Intel® technology.

More than 40 years ago, our co-founder Gordon Moore boldly predicted that the number of transistors on a computer chip would double every 24 months, dramatically increasing processor performance. Since then, we've made Moore's Law a reality-and its spirit of innovation continues to drive us.

Intel engineers are developing new multi-core microprocessor architectures that are 10 times more energy efficient than previous generations. They have already dramatically increased processor performance through the world's most advanced 65 nanometer manufacturing process. Intel continues to enable and accelerate the digital revolution, deliver market-driving technology, rally the industry, and drive new standards.

http://www.intel.com/

http://www.intel.com/go/grid

Microsoft

CONTACT

Randy Hinrichs
Microsoft Corporation
One Microsoft Way
Redmond, WA 98052 USA
425.703.5524
randyh@microsoft.com

ARTICLE

Interview: Tony Hey, Corporate Vice President Technical Computing, Advanced Strategies and Policy, Microsoft
Understanding the Impact of Grid and Service-Oriented IT: An Interview with Microsoft's Tony Hey

ABOUT MICROSOFT

Microsoft has signaled its intent to engage with the technical computing community. With its Web Services implementations in Windows Vista and the OpenXML format in Office, interoperability and open standards are now a key focus for Microsoft. The release of the Windows Compute Cluster Server software also shows that Microsoft is entering with the commodity high-performance computing market.

http://www.microsoft.com/

Penguin Computing

CONTACT

Pamela Sufi
Marketing Communications
    Manager
Penguin Computing
300 California Street, Suite 600
San Francisco, CA 94104 USA
415.954.2845
psufi@penguincomputing.com

AUTHOR AND ARTICLE

Donald Becker, Chief Technology Officer, Penguin Computing
The Future of HPC: Second-generation Clusters, Grid Management Software, and Greater Commercial Adoption

ABOUT PENGUIN COMPUTING

Penguin Computing is the leader in cluster virtualization, delivering virtualized cluster systems driven by Scyld Beowulf®, its unique Linux software, which makes large pools of Linux servers appear and act like a single virtual system. Through a single point of command/control, thousands of systems can be managed as if they were a single, consistent, virtual system, dramatically simplifying deployment and management and significantly improving server performance and data center resource utilization. Focused on the high-performance computing, enterprise consolidation and Web hosting markets, the company has an extensive customer base including Fortune 1000 companies, government agencies, and educational institutions. Founded in 1998, Penguin Computing is headquartered in San Francisco, California.

http://www.penguincomputing.com/

http://www.scyld.com

Platform Computing

CONTACT

Robert Shecterle
Vice President – Marketing
Platform Computing Inc.
3760 14th Avenue
Markham, Ontario, L3R 3T7
　Canada
905.948.4505
robert@platform.com

AUTHORS AND ARTICLES

Songnian Zhou, CEO and Co-Founder, Platform Computing
　Rewriting the Rules for Enterprise IT: Using Grid to Orchestrate Enterprise IT Resources
Robert Shecterle, Vice President, Marketing, Platform Computing
　Reconstructing the Big Bang! What the Business of Particle Physics Has in Common with Business IT

ABOUT PLATFORM COMPUTING

Platform Computing is the global leader for Grid computing solutions and a technology pioneer of the supercomputing world. The company's solutions for enterprise and high-performance computing help the world's largest organizations integrate and accelerate business processes, to increase competitive advantage and enjoy a higher return on investment from IT. With more than 1,700 customers, most in the global 2000, the company has achieved a clear leadership position in the market through a focus on technology innovation and execution. Founded in 1992, Platform Computing has strategic relationships with Apple, Dell, HP, IBM, Intel, SAS, Sun, and SGI, along with the industry's broadest support for third-party applications.

　http://www.platform.com

SAP

CONTACT

Georg Dittmar
Product Manager,
　Adaptive Computing
SAP AG
Dietmar-Hopp-Allee 16
D69190 Walldorf/Baden Germany
+49 6227/7-66466
georg.dittmar@sap.com

AUTHORS AND ARTICLES

Lothar Schubert, Director, Solution Marketing, SAP NetWeaver, SAP
　Accelerating Analytics in the SOA
Amit Sinha, Director, Solution Marketing, SAP NetWeaver, SAP
　Adaptive Computing: Thinking Beyond the Box
Dan Stimson, Marketing Director, RFID, SAP
　RFID and SOA: A Marriage Made in Heaven

ABOUT SAP

SAP is the world's leading provider of business software solutions. Today, more than 32,000 customers in over 120 countries run SAP® software—from distinct solutions addressing the needs of small and midsize enterprises to suite offerings for global organizations. Powered by the SAP NetWeaver® platform to drive innovation and enable business change, SAP business solutions help enterprises of all sizes around the world improve customer relationships, enhance partner collaboration, and create efficiencies across their supply chains and business operations. SAP industry solutions support the unique business processes of more than 25 industries, including high tech, healthcare, retail, public sector ,and financial services. With subsidiaries in more than 50 countries, the company is listed on several exchanges, including the Frankfurt stock exchange and NYSE under the symbol "SAP."

　SAP Developer Network : http://www.sdn.sap.com
　SAP Service Marketplace: http://service.sap.com/adaptive

Sun Microsystems, Inc.

CONTACT

Bjorn Andersson
umpk18-116
18 Network Circle
Menlo Park, CA 94025
650.786.6855
bjorn.andersson@sun.com
http://www.sun.com/secure/
　contact/

AUTHORS AND ARTICLES

Victoria Livschitz, Principal Architect, Sun Microsystems, Inc.
　A Broad New Role for Grid in Commercial Applications: A Financial Services Case Study
Heinz J. Schwarz, M.S., Director, Global Healthcare and Life Science Center of Excellence, Sun Microsystems, Inc.
　Service-Oriented Architectures and Grid Computing—A New Generation of Middleware for Grid-enabled Data Centers

ABOUT SUN MICROSYSTEMS, INC.

Sun Microsystems is a global supplier of network computing solutions. Sun's singular vision—"The Network Is The Computer"—guides it in the development of technologies that power the world's most important markets. Sun's hardware systems, software, and services represent one of the most complete and proven portfolios on the planet. And, with more than 37,000 employees worldwide and offices in over 100 countries, we are dedicated to one thing—making your business more successful.

　http://www.sun.com/
　http://sun.com/hpc

Glossary

This glossary of terms was contributed by the Open Grid Services Architecture (OGSA) working group of the Global Grid Forum. It provides information to the Grid community regarding the concepts and terms used by the OGSA and related documents. It does not define any standards or technical recommendations. The full copyright notice can be found at the end of this glossary. Grid Forum Document (GFD)-I.044

A

AAA Authentication, authorization and accounting.

Abstract name See name.

ACID Four properties that must generally apply to stateful resources used within the context of a transactional unit of work within a traditional, two-phase-commit-enabled transaction system. Briefly:
- Atomicity: Updates must be made in an all-or-nothing fashion.
- Consistency: Resources must be left in a consistent state, even in the event of failure.
- Isolation: Partial updates must not be visible outside of the transaction until the end of the transactional unit of work.
- Durability: The permanence of updates made under the transactional unit of work.

Source: http://en.wikipedia.org/wiki/ACID.

Address See name.

Agreement An agreement defines a dynamically-established and dynamically-managed relationship between parties. The object of the relationship is the delivery of a service by one of the parties within the context of the agreement. The management of this delivery is achieved by agreeing on the respective roles, rights and obligations of the parties. The agreement may specify not only functional properties for identification or creation of the service, but also non-functional properties of the service such as performance or availability.

Entities can dynamically establish and manage agreements via Web service interfaces.

See https://forge.gridforum.org/projects/graap-wg for information about work being carried out by the GGF's Grid Resource Allocation Agreement Protocol (GRAAP) working group.

Allocated See allocation.

Allocation The process of assigning a set of resources for use by a job.

B

BLAST Basic Local Alignment Search Tool—a commonly-used biotechnology tool for searching sequence databases.

See http://www.ncbi.nlm.nih.gov/BLAST/ for more information.

C

Candidate set generator In EMS, a service that determines the set of container resources on which a service or job may execute.

Capability In OGSA, a set of one or more services that together provide a function that is useful in a Grid context.

OGSA's Execution Management Services are an example of an OGSA capability.

Chargeback Within an organization, the practice of charging individual departments for the IT resources they consume.

Choreography, orchestration and workflow The following concepts are closely related:
- Choreography describes required patterns of interaction among services and templates for sequences (or more structures) of interactions.
- Orchestration describes the ways in which business processes are constructed from Web services and other business processes, and how these processes interact.
- Workflow is a pattern of business process interaction, not necessarily corresponding to a fixed set of business processes. All such interactions may be between services residing within a single data center or across a range of different platforms and implementations anywhere.

CIM Common Information Model: An object-oriented model for resource management, published by the Distributed Management Task Force (DMTF).

See http://www.dmtf.org/standards/cim/ for more information. Also see WBEM.

CMM GGF's Common Management Model working group (CMM-WG).

See https://forge.gridforum.org/projects/cmm-wg/ for more information.

Component A modular part of a system that encapsulates its contents and whose manifestation is replaceable within its environment. A component defines its behavior in terms of provided and required interfaces.

Container See hosting environment.

Context The conditions and circumstances under which an operation takes place.

For example:
- In programming languages a calling context is a set of bindings of values to variables.
- A VO is a possible context for a request to a service.
- A security context is a set of credentials under which execution can occur.

D

Data resource An entity that can act as a source or sink of data together with its associated framework.

Deployment The process of installing components and related contents (e.g. programs and data) on a set of resources to meet the requirements of the job to which they have been allocated.

Deployment may be followed by resource configuration.

Denial-of-service (DoS) attack A form of attack on a computer system that results in some part of the system being prevented from providing its normal level of service to its users.

DoS See denial of service attack.

EMS See Execution Management Services.

Endpoint A Web service endpoint to which a client may bind in order to consume a service.

Endpoint reference (EPR) A WS-Addressing construct that identifies a message destination. In WSRF an EPR conveys the information needed to identify or reference a stateful resource.
See http://www.w3.org/2002/ws/addr/ for information about WS-Addressing.

Entity Any nameable thing. For example, in OGSA an entity might be a resource or a service.

EPR See endpoint reference.

Event Anything that occurs in or to an IT system that is potentially interesting to a person, to some other part of the same system, or to an external system, may be considered to be an event.
Information about an event may be expressed as a log record and stored in a log service. It may also be communicated to other interested services through a notification message.

Event consumer A service that receives an event.

Event producer A service that emits an event.

Execution Management Services (OGSA-EMS) An OGSA capability that is concerned with the problems of instantiating and managing, to completion, units of work.

Failure A state in which a service or other entity is not correctly meeting its specified behavior.

Failure recovery Restoration of a service or other entity to its specified behavior.
Recovery might be effected either by correcting the failure condition or by routing subsequent requests to an alternate entity that is capable of providing the same service.

File path A string in some directory system that can be bound to some file (or pseudo-file)—for example, /home/mydir/data.
Usually a file path on one machine is invalid or resolves to a different file on other machines (in the absence of some sort of distributed file system).

Global Grid Forum (GGF) A community forum that promotes and supports the development, deployment, and implementation of Grid technologies.
See http://www.ggf.org for more information.

GGF See Global Grid Forum.

Grid A system that is concerned with the integration, virtualization, and management of services and resources in a distributed, heterogeneous environment that supports collections of users and resources (virtual organizations) across traditional administrative and organizational domains (real organizations).

Grid fabric The core set of service interfaces that must be implemented in order to realize an OGSA Grid. Also known as the OGSA infrastructure services.

Grid service 1. (deprecated) In OGSI, a Grid service is a service that implements the GridService portType. This use of the term is considered to be deprecated.
2. (informal) In its more general use, a Grid service is a Web service that is designed to operate in a Grid environment, and meets the requirements of the Grid(s) in which it participates.

Grid service handle (GSH) An abstract name for an OGSI-based Grid service. The term has no meaning in a Grid based on WSRF.

Grid service reference (GSR) A GSR contains sufficient information to communicate with an OGSI Grid service—i.e. it is an address. The term has no meaning in a Grid based on WSRF.

GSH See Grid Service Handle.

GSR See Grid Service Reference.

Hosting environment Any environment in which a task can execute—for example a Web services execution environment, an operating system, etc.
Also referred to as a service container, or simply container.

HTTP Hypertext Transfer Protocol—a text-based protocol that is commonly used for transferring information across the Internet.
See http://www.w3c.org/Protocols for more information.

HTTPS Hypertext Transfer Protocol (Secure)—HTTP encrypted using SSL.

Human-oriented name See name.

Identity An attribute, such as a name, that allows one entity to be distinguished from all others.

Interface In a service-oriented architecture, a specification of the operations that a service offers its clients.
In WSDL 2.0 an interface component describes sequences of messages that a service sends and/or receives. In WSDL 1.1 an interface is specified in a portType element.
For more information see http://www.w3.org/TR/wsdl20 and http://www.w3.org/TR/wsdl20-patterns.

Intermediary In OGSA information services, a service that decouples message (event) producers from message (event) consumers.

IPC Inter-process communication via message-passing, shared memory (including shared files), or TCP.

IT Information technology.

Job A user-defined task that is scheduled to be carried out by an execution subsystem.
In OGSA-EMS, a job is modeled as a manageable resource, has a resource handle, and is managed by a job manager.

glossary

Job manager In OGSA-EMS, a service that manages a set of one or more job instances, which may be structured (e.g. a workflow or dependence graph) or unstructured (e.g. an array of non-interacting jobs)

The job manager encapsulates all aspects of job execution, including interacting with execution planning services, the provisioning system, containers, and monitoring services. It may also deal with failures and restarts, it may schedule jobs to resources, and it may collect agreements, reservations and job service data.

Job Submission Description Language (JSDL) A language for describing job submissions, including details of their required execution environments.

See https://forge.gridforum.org/projects/jsdl-wg for more information.

JSDL See Job Submission Description Language.

Legacy program A pre-existing program such as BLAST, which must be Grid-enabled before it can be executed as a Grid resource.

Legacy file system An existing file system that is not Grid-enabled.

Log record An expression of an event for the purpose of persisting the event in a logging service.

Log service See logging service.

Logging service An intermediary that serves as a repository for log records.

Manage See management.

Manageability The ability to be managed.

Manageability interface The interface through which a resource is managed.

Manageable resource See resource.

Management The administrative process of deploying, configuring, monitoring, metering, tuning, and/or troubleshooting resources.

Managed See management.

Manager Software that manages manageable resources. A manager may or may not require a human operator.

Message A self-contained unit of data that is transferred between a message producer and one or more message consumers.

Message broker An intermediary in a messaging service.

Message consumer A service that receives a message.

Message producer A service that emits a message.

Messaging service An intermediary used for transmitting messages from message producers to message consumers.

Metadata Data that describes OGSA services or other data. Metadata may include references to schemas, provenance, and information quality.

MPI Message Passing Interface: a standard API for implementing message-passing libraries. MPI libraries are generally used to coordinate activity within parallel applications.

See http://www.mpi-forum.org for more information.

Name An attribute used to identify an entity.

In OGSA-naming, there are three types of names: human-oriented names, abstract names, and addresses.

- A human-oriented name is based on a naming scheme that is designed to be easily interpreted by humans (e.g. human-readable and human-parsable).
- An abstract name is a persistent name suitable for machine processing that does not necessarily contain location information. Abstract names are bound to addresses.
- An address specifies the location of an entity.

Notification A message communicating the details of an event to an interested party.

Notification message See notification.

Notify Send a notification message.

OGSA Open Grid Services Architecture.

OGSA-EMS See Execution Management Services.

OGSA-Naming An OGSA capability used to associate names with entities.

OGSA Information Services An OGSA capability that provides access to information about applications, resources and services.

OGSA Infrastructure Services See Grid fabric.

OGSI Open Grid Services Infrastructure. A GGF specification that defines the common interfaces and behaviors of a Grid service. OGSI is deprecated in favor of WSRF and WSN.

Orchestration See choreography, orchestration and workflow.

Policy Statements, rules or assertions that specify the correct or expected behavior of an entity.

For example, an authorization policy might specify the correct access control rules for a software component.

portType In WSDL 1.1, a named set of abstract operations and the abstract messages involved. In WSDL 2.0, portTypes are renamed as interfaces.

Provisioning The activity of specifying, reserving, allocating and deploying the set of resources required to accomplish a task.

Quality of service (QoS) A measure of the level of service attained, such as security, network bandwidth, average response time or service availability.

QoS See Quality of service.

R

Real organization The computers and resources that constitute a traditional administrative and organizational domain.

Registry An authoritative, centrally-controlled store of information.

Web services use registries to advertise their existence and to describe their interfaces and other attributes. Prospective clients query registries to locate required services and to discover their attributes.

Release The action of returning an allocated resource to the pool of available resources.

Reservation The process of reserving resources for future use by a planned task.

Resource Resources are entities that can be managed. However not all entities are resources.

Resources can be programmatically managed through a manageability interface, or through some other mechanism such as a policy file.

The term "resource" encompasses not only entities that are pooled (e.g. hosts, software licenses, IP addresses) or that provide a given capacity (e.g. disks, networks, memory), but also processes, print jobs and virtual organizations, which do not expose interfaces by themselves but may still be managed by some other means.

Resource allocation See allocation.

Resource configuration The process of adjusting the configurations of a set of resources to meet the requirements of the task to which they have been allocated.

For example, configuration may involve setting appropriate parameters and storing policies for middleware, O/S, firmware and hardware.

Resource configuration may be preceded by resource deployment.

Resource deployment See deployment.

Resource handle An abstract name for a resource and its associated state (if any).

Resource lifecycle management The process of managing resources allocated to a task, from the time of allocation until the time of release.

Resource management A generic term for several forms of management that may be applied to resources. These include (but are not limited to) typical IT systems management activities.

Resource manager A manager that implements one or more resource management functions.

Resource model An abstract representation of manageable resources that defines their schema (conceptual hierarchy and inter-relationships) and characteristics (attributes, management operations, etc.).

Resource provisioning See provisioning.

Resource release See release.

Resource reservation See reservation.

Resource virtualization See virtualization.

S

Schedule A mapping (relation) between services and resources, possibly with time constraints. A schedule can be extended with a list of alternative schedule deltas.

Schedule deltas A set of transformations that may be produced for use if some part of the current schedule becomes invalid.

For example, if a resource becomes unavailable, it may be possible to use a schedule delta rather than reschedule the job from scratch.

Scheduling The process of reserving resources for future use by a planned task.

Self-management A capability by which system components—including hardware components, such as computers, networks and storage devices, and software components such as operating systems and business applications—are self-configuring, self-healing and self-optimizing.

A self-managing IT infrastructure is less complex and more cost-effective to operate, and can react more quickly to component failures and to changing business needs than can a traditionally-managed environment.

Service A software component participating in a service-oriented architecture that provides functionality and/or participates in realizing one or more capabilities.

Service composition Aggregation of multiple small services into larger services.

See http://www.serviceoriented.org for more information.

Service container See hosting environment.

Service endpoint See endpoint.

Service level agreement (SLA) A contract between a provider and a user that specifies the level of service that is expected during the term of the contract.

SLAs are used by vendors and customers, as well as internally by IT shops and their end users. They might specify availability requirements, response times for routine and *ad hoc* queries, and response time for problem resolution (network down, machine failure, etc.).

Source: http://www.hostchart.com/webhostingterms.asp.

Service level attainment The act of meeting a pre-established service level objective.

Service level manager (SLM) A service level manager ensures that the service level objectives for a set of resources are met.

Service level management typically entails monitoring availability and performance, analyzing the results of the monitoring activity and projecting future requirements, determining what adjustments, if any, are needed to meet the objectives, and acting accordingly.

Service level objective (SLO) A target level of service for a resource or a set of resources.

A service level objective might be expressed in units such as average response time for a representative set of transaction types, or in terms of the monthly availability of a given service.

Service-oriented architecture (SOA) This term is increasingly used to refer to an architectural style of building reliable distributed systems that deliver functionality as services, with the additional emphasis on loose coupling between interacting services.

Note: An SOA can be based on Web services (which provide basic interoperability), but it may use other technologies instead.

See https://forge.gridforum.org/projects/ogsa-wg/document/Proposed_SOA_Definition/en/1 for additional considerations of service-oriented architecture.

SLA See service level agreement.

SLM See service level manager.

SLO See service level objective.

SOA See service-oriented architecture.

SOAP An XML-based protocol for exchanging structured information in a decentralized, distributed environment.
See http://www.w3.org/2000/xp/Group and http://www.w3.org/TR/soap12-part1/ for more information.
(Originally the acronym SOAP stood for "Simple Object Access Protocol," but that name is no longer considered by the W3C to be descriptive of its use, so "SOAP" is now considered to be a name rather than an abbreviation.)

SSL Secure Sockets Layer: a communication protocol whose primary goal is to provide private and reliable communication between two applications.

Task A task is a definable unit of work.

TCP Transmission Control Protocol. A packet-level protocol used to exchange data over the Internet.

Trust The willingness to take actions expecting beneficial outcomes, based on assertions by other parties.

Trust authority An entity that is trusted to make specified assertions.

Trust management Trust management defines trust authorities and specifies what they should be trusted to do.

Trust relationships Polices that govern how entities in differing domains honor each other's authorizations.
An authority may be completely trusted—for example, any statement from the authority will be accepted as a basis for action—or there may be limited trust, in which case only statements in a specific range are accepted.

UDDI Universal Description, Discovery and Integration: a specification that defines a way to publish and discover information about Web services.
See http://www.uddi.org for more information.

Unit of work A request, typically user-defined, to execute an OGSA application or a legacy program.
In OGSA-EMS, a unit of work has both a manageability aspect, represented by a job, and an execution aspect. Its execution aspect, e.g., a running application or service, is managed through the associated job.

UML Unified Modeling Language.
See http://www.uml.org/ for more information.

URI Uniform Resource Identifier: A string used for identifying an abstract or physical resource.

URL Uniform Resource Locator: the address of an Internet resource.

UUID Universally-unique identifier.

Virtualize Make a common set of abstract interfaces available for a set of similar resources, thereby hiding differences in their properties and operations, and allowing them to be viewed and/or manipulated in a common way.

Virtual organization A virtual organization (VO) comprises a set of individuals and/or institutions having direct access to computers, software, data, and other resources for collaborative problem-solving or other purposes.
VOs are a concept that supplies a context for operation of the Grid that can be used to associate users, their requests, and a set of resources. The sharing of resources in a VO is necessarily highly controlled, with resource providers and consumers defining clearly and carefully just what is shared, who is allowed to share, and the conditions under which sharing occurs.

VO See virtual organization.

WBEM Web Based Enterprise Management: a set of management technologies developed to unify the management of enterprise computing environments.
WBEM has three main components: the CIM resource model; a representation of CIM classes and instances in XML; and a mapping of CIM operations onto HTTP. A means of accessing CIM through Web services is currently under development.
See http://www.dmtf.org for more information.

Web service A software system designed to support interoperable machine- or application-oriented interaction over a network.
A Web service has an interface described in a machine-processable format (specifically WSDL). Other systems interact with the Web service in a manner prescribed by its description using SOAP messages, typically conveyed using HTTP with an XML serialization in conjunction with other Web-related standards.

Workflow See choreography, orchestration and workflow.

WSDL Web Services Description Language—an XML format for describing Web services.
See http://www.w3.org/TR/wsdl for more information.

WSDM Web Services Distributed Management: A Web services architecture for managing distributed resources.
See http://www.oasis-open.org/apps/org/workgroup/wsdm for more information.

WS-Notification A set of proposed specifications dealing with notification.
See http://www.oasis-open.org/apps/org/workgroup/wsn/ for more information.

WS-Resource Framework A set of proposed specifications dealing with the association of Web services with stateful resources.
See http://www.oasis-open.org/apps/org/workgroup/wsrf/ for more information.

WSN, WS-N See WS-Notification.

WSRF, WS-RF See WS-Resource Framework.

XML Extensible Markup Language—a flexible text format that is used for data exchange.
See http://www.w3.org/XML for information.

Grid Forum Document (GFD)-I.044

http://forge.gridforum.org/projects/ogsa-wg

ogsa-wg@ggf.org

Copyright © Global Grid Forum (2004, 2005). All Rights Reserved.

Additional GFDs can be found at http://www.ggf.org/documents.

This document and translations of it may be copied and furnished to others, and derivative works that comment on or otherwise explain or assist in its implementation may be prepared, copied, published, and distributed in whole or in part, without restriction of any kind, provided that the above copyright notice and this paragraph are included on all such copies and derivative works.

However, this document may not be modified in any way, such as by removing the copyright notice or references to the GGF or other organizations, except as needed for the purpose of developing Grid Recommendations in which case the procedures for copyrights defined in the GGF Document process must be followed, or as required to translate it into languages other than English.

The limited permissions granted above are perpetual and will not be revoked by the GGF or its successors of assigns.

This document and the information contained herein is provided on an "as is" basis and the Global Grid Forum disclaims all warranties, express or implied, including but not limited to any warranty that the use of the information herein will not infringe any rights or any implied warranties of merchantability or fitness for a particular purpose.

Additional Glossaries

CIO Magazine
http://www.cio.com/archive/051504/grid_sidebar_1.html

D-Grid
http://www.d-grid.de/index.php?id=57&L=1

National e-Science Centre: Glossary
http://www.nesc.ac.uk/global/glossary.html

OGSA-DAI terms
http://www.globus.org/toolkit/docs/development/3.9.5/techpreview/ogsadai/doc/reference/glossary.html

Open Science Grid: Grid Vocabulary
http://www.opensciencegrid.org/home/terminology.html

Oracle
http://www.oracle.com/technologies/grid/OracleGridGlossary.pdf

World Wide Web Consortium (W3C): Web Services Glossary, W3C Working Group Note 11
http://www.w3.org/TR/2004/NOTE-ws-gloss-20040211/

XVAND
http://www.xvand.com/glossary.asp